WITHDRAWN

Wilderness and the Quality of Life

CONTRIBUTORS

Phillip S. Berry
Stewart M. Brandborg
Noble E. Buell
Albert E. Burke
Edward P. Cliff
Robert H. Finch
Orville L. Freeman
Michael Frome
Rudolph W. Gilbert
James P. Gilligan
Cadet Hand
George B. Hartzog, Jr.
Lawrence G. Hines
R. H. Hultman
Charles B. Hunt
Estella B. Leopold
George E. Lindsay
Norman B. Livermore, Jr.
Daniel B. Luten
George Marshall
J. Michael McCloskey
Dean E. McHenry
Frank E. Moss
Roderick Nash
Kenneth S. Norris
Sigurd F. Olson
Dennis A. Rapp
Boyd L. Rasmussen
Robert Rienow
Raymond J. Sherwin
Anthony Wayne Smith
Walter P. Taylor
Adan Treganza
Peggy Wayburn
Caspar W. Weinberger
John A. Zivnuska

WILDERNESS
and the Quality of Life

 EDITED BY *Maxine E. McCloskey*
AND *James P. Gilligan*

Sierra Club · SAN FRANCISCO · NEW YORK

We are grateful to the following authors and publishers for quotations used within this book:

Armour, Richard. From *I Loved you, California,* Look Magazine, September 25, 1962. Reprinted by permission of Richard Armour.

Editorial of November 20, 1966. © 1966 by The New York Times Company. Reprinted by permission of The New York Times Co., New York, New York.

Frome, Michael. Speech printed in *Student Conservation Program Newsletter* for Spring–summer 1966. Reprinted by permission of The Student Conservation Association, Inc., Oyster Bay, New York.

Frome, Michael. From *Strangers in High Places,* Reprinted by permission of Doubleday and Co., Inc., New York, New York.

Peattie, Donald Culross. From *The Unleashing of Evolutionary Thought* by Oscar Riddle. Reprinted by permission of Vantage Press, Inc., New York, New York.

From "Helen's Exile" in *Lyrical and Critical Essays* by Albert Camus. Translated from the French by Ellen Conroy Kennedy. © copyright 1968 by Alfred A. Knopf, Inc. and 1967 by Hamish Hamilton, Inc. Reprinted by permission of Alfred A. Knopf, Inc., publisher.

EDITORS' PREFACE

The steady growth of the biennial wilderness conferences sponsored by the Sierra Club (and cosponsored in 1967 by the Sierra Club Foundation) reflects expanding national concern over the disappearance of wild places in our environment. The theme of this conference, "Wilderness and the Quality of Life," stresses the relevance of wilderness to modern man—beyond the usual perception of its being a remote place in which to fish, hunt, and hike. Urbanized America, as it pushes development into the hinterlands, now recognizes that surviving wilderness is a significant value in our culture.

The tenth conference held April 7–9, 1967 in San Francisco, upon which this book is based, brings together the Secretary of Agriculture, a United States Senator, the Lieutenant Governor of the State of California, leaders of federal land administering agencies and conservation groups, professors in the physical and social sciences, attorneys, wilderness travelers and writers, a minister, and a commercial outfitter and guide. They explore, each from his own viewpoint, the influence of wilderness on the quality of life. A consensus results among all thirty-six speakers that because wilderness reservations are irreplaceable assets, the 2 per cent of our nation's land still remaining as wilderness must be jealously guarded not only against an expanding number of development thrusts, but perhaps must be protected even from the wilderness user as his numbers increase.

The conference provided opportunity for a thorough review of progress made by affected federal agencies since the enactment of the Wilderness Act of 1964. To facilitate understanding of the action and problems of wilderness reclassification required by the act, the appendix contains a table showing reclassification progress for the first three-year review period ending September 3, 1967; wilderness management and usage criteria of the Forest Service, the National Park Service, and the Bureau of Sport Fisheries and Wildlife; and the complete text of the Wilderness Act of 1964. The editors hope these additions will aid students of wilderness and conservation, as well as broaden the public's understanding of wilderness.

A portion of the conference stressed, for the first time, the value and urgency of reserving representative segments of wilderness found in vast desert and semidesert regions of the Far West, and off-shore marine environments rapidly being overwhelmed by exploitation. Two maps display the extent and jurisdiction of western arid lands.

Color plates used in this volume mark their introduction to the series of books based on wilderness conferences. This representative collection of color reproductions of nineteenth-century American landscape painting documents Professor Roderick Nash's speech on the influence of wilderness on American cultural life.

This book is part of the continuing discussion of wilderness that Wilderness Conferences encourage. Aspects of the subject that may be of special interest to you may be found in the record of past conferences, or you may have to await the next conference, scheduled for March 14–16, 1969 in San Francisco. Earlier conferences are published in the following volumes: *Wilderness in a Changing World* (Ninth Conference); *Tomorrow's Wilderness* (Eighth Conference); *Wilderness: America's Living Heritage* (Seventh Conference); *Meaning of Wilderness to Science* (Sixth Conference); and *Wildlands in Our Civilization* (Fifth Conference).

The editors wish to express their appreciation to the Sierra Club Foundation for financial support for preparing this volume for publication. We thank executive director of the Sierra Club, David Brower, for his help in the preparation of the manuscript, and for his encouragement of the use of color plates. Our gratitude is also expressed to Alfred Frankenstein, art critic of the San Francisco *Chronicle*, for supplying seven original color slides from his personal library. Cartographer Adrienne E. Morgan prepared the maps, combining information from a wide assortment of sources.

The expense of putting on a conference of this magnitude is not met by registration fees. Numerous special donations from conference attendees and these major contributions are gratefully acknowledged:

Sierra Club
Sierra Club Foundation
Belvedere Scientific Fund
E. Morris Cox
Foundation for Environmental Design

Daniel B. Luten
Pacific Gas and Electric Company
Lurline B. Roth Charity Foundation
The S&H Foundation
Standard Oil Company of California

Members of the conference planning and arrangements committees are listed in Appendix F. Their countless hours of volunteer labor were indispensable to the success of the conference.

Maxine E. McCloskey and
James P. Gilligan

FOREWORD

Mankind has known since prehistory that his environment cannot accept unlimited exploitation. We have the ruins of several civilizations, and of countless wilderness areas, to remind us that limits exist. What we seldom have had is the intelligence to act on our knowledge. There is a certain irresistible expediency to the thought that probably we can get away with just a little more.

Unfortunately, the earth, unlike man, *is* an island, and unlike its human inhabitants, it has limited itself. It will not conveniently expand to accommodate us. And while we are bound to its limits, we also are bound to considering it as a whole, since our increase in population and technology now affects the balance of the entire world as an ecological unit. The cumulative effect of regional problems is global, and the global crisis affects all regions; our future depends on its resolution. We are limited to the earth in both directions.

Of course the same technology that now exploits the world could find ways to make that exploitation unnecessary, and the population explosion that makes exploitation inevitable could be stopped. But to do either will require a major, if not revolutionary, change in human attitudes. To put it more openly, we must come to love our island, and our own position, however unique, as part of its natural processes. As Albert Camus wrote twenty years ago: "We tense ourselves to achieve empires and the absolute, seek to transfigure the world before having exhausted it, to set it to rights before having understood it. Whatever we may say, we are turning our backs on this world. Ulysses, on Calypso's island, is given the choice between immortality and the land of his fathers. He chooses this earth, and death with it. Such simple greatness is foreign to our minds today. Others will say that we lack humility, but the word, all things considered, is ambiguous. Like Dostoevski's buffoons who boast of everything, rise up to the stars and end by flaunting their shame in the first public place, we simply lack the pride of the man who is faithful to his limitations —that is, the clairvoyant love of his human condition."

It may seem strange to link a love of the human condition with the wilderness experience, but the two are only different aspects of the same consciousness. The wilderness is a window on the natural order, of which man is—and must realize himself to be—a part. To accept it unaltered returns us to an acceptance and enjoyment of the earth, not as a defeat but as a freedom. The ability to accept freedom within the limits of the natural world requires the human pride of which Camus spoke, the pride which can comprehend limits that do not restrict, but simply define, our existence. In understanding those limits we define ourselves, and by that definition we can finally understand what our real possibilities are. We are set free to act in a truly human way by our comprehension of the whole within which we exist. Even in escaping from the earth we defined its limits. The circumference of our entire island can be contained in one photograph from space—but for the first time also we can see it as a whole.

If we love our island and our human existence on it, we will leave unaltered what we did not create, and alter instead what we have created badly. We can see our cities as islands, and we can understand that we don't escape from them by creating more suburbs—we only extend the problem. A city is our man-made environment, a communal work of art whose quality depends totally on our own decision to act. At the same time, we can realize that the quality of our natural environment depends on our decision to leave it alone, not to use it as an expedient for avoiding problems of our own creation. We've been doing our thing for too long; the time has come to begin doing it well.

David Brower
Executive Director, Sierra Club

Berkeley, California
April 3, 1969

CONTENTS

George Marshall

INTRODUCTION

This seems to be a year of anniversaries, for this tenth biennial Wilderness Conference comes on the seventy-fifth anniversary of the founding of the Sierra Club by John Muir and his associates. One hundred years ago John Muir left his Wisconsin home and started for California by a rather roundabout route. It included his thousand-mile walk to the Gulf of Mexico, his sailing to Cuba and New York, crossing the isthmus, and finally arriving in San Francisco on March 28, 1868. Well, not finally, for he left town for the Sierra the same day.

The first Wilderness Conference, in 1949, stressed techniques of wilderness use without destruction, and Norman B. Livermore, Jr. proposed, perhaps for the first time, that cans be carried out of the mountains instead of buried there. At the second Wilderness Conference, Howard Zahniser made his first formal suggestion for a wilderness bill. At the fifth conference, David Brower said: "The conservation force, I submit, is not a pressure group. It merely demonstrates the pressure of man's conscience, of his innate knowledge that there are certain things that he may not ethically do to the only world he will ever have, and to the strictly rationed resource of natural beauty which still exists in the world. The conservationist force does not need to be pressured into action. It needs only to be made to realize what is happening, and its voice of conscience speaks."

The last five conferences have explored such interrelated subjects as wildlands in our civilization, the meaning of wilderness to science, wilderness: America's living heritage, tomorrow's wilderness, and wilderness in a changing world. The topic this year is wilderness and the quality of American life. We look forward to hearing how the participants develop this theme.

Wilderness is not—and should not be—a past and vanishing force in American life. It is, as far as anyone can see into the future in our rapidly changing and uncertain world, an abiding value—a necessity not only for the good life, but for life itself. This was recognized by two of the best known Americans writing on wilderness. About the turn of the century John Muir, after knocking about the most rugged parts of the Sierra Nevada for some years and making significant geological, biological, and philosophical observations, announced with enthusiasm: "The tendency nowadays to wander in wilderness is delightful to see. Thousands of tired, nerve-shaken, overcivilized people are beginning to find out that . . . wilderness is a necessity." Some four decades earlier Thoreau, in his essay on walking, reached a similar conclusion, but in more universal and succinct terms. He wrote, "In wildness is the preservation of the world." Each man in his own way proclaimed that wildness, or wilderness, is essential for mankind's survival.

If wilderness is to have abiding value, it must be preserved in size and quality and as an ecological whole. Just prior to the last Wilderness Conference, a great step was taken with the passage of the Wilderness Act. In the meantime, this act has been implemented— recently at an extraordinary rate, with the land administering agencies proposing a new area for inclusion in the wilderness system about once every four days. This demands much of the agencies and the conservationists in study, participation in field hearings, and eventually in hearings before Congress. This month the first congressional hearings will be held on a wilderness classification under the act.

In addition to the areas specifically covered by the Wilderness Act, there are thousands of acres of unclassified *de facto* wilderness, especially in the West, in Alaska, and in Hawaii, and also elsewhere. If these areas are to have a chance of survival, it is essential that they be administered as wilderness until there is an opportunity for the public and the agencies to study them. Most should be classified and preserved as wilderness.

Wild and magnificent places like the Grand Canyon of the Colorado and the remaining unprotected great redwood forests on the California coast must be saved from dams and lumbering before it is too late. To accomplish this it will be necessary to include the entire Grand Canyon in Grand Canyon National Park, and to create a new, large Redwood National Park based in Redwood Creek.

At the same time that wilderness boundaries are being established and protected by acts of Congress, attention must be given to the quality of wilderness within these boundaries, or we may be preserving empty shells. Maintaining the quality of wilderness requires great understanding and restraint on the part of both administrators and the public. There are many dangers to the quality of wilderness, among them: (1) ignorance of how to behave in wilderness, (2) mechanical travel in wilderness and wild lands, (3) the use of mechanical equipment for administrative convenience, (4) the construction of trails with an 8 per cent grade and other overengineered trails, (5) a tendency to try to make wilderness safe for anyone who enters it, but dangerous for any insect that may attack a so-called commercial species, (6) the continuance of the superannuated Mining Law of 1872, (7) the destruction of the silence of wilderness by conventional and supersonic aircraft, (8) the attitude that most wildlife should be administered as a growing crop to be harvested for pleasure and that predators should be treated as pests, (9) the demagogic theory that there may be no limitation on the number of people entering a wilderness when limitation of visitors may be necessary for preservation.

There are also many dangers to wilderness from without. These include uncontrolled population growth and rampant technological development; pressures to degenerate life and the land to a single level of mediocrity; failure to solve the basic problems of humanity; insensitivity to aesthetic values and ignorance of the biological sciences; confusion of the need for wilderness with the need for recreation; political, corporate, and individual selfishness that ignores both the future and universal values; wholesale pollution; and atomic war. Most, if not all of these, and especially the last, will destroy not just wilderness—at least living wilderness—and the quality of life, but life itself.

We indeed face numerous difficult problems, and I can think of no more appropriate conclusion to the opening of these discussions than Howard Zahniser's statement of faith and vision to the fifth Wilderness Conference. He said: "Our wilderness preservation purposes include perpetuity. We are trying to keep unchanged by man, areas that have grown through the eternity of the past and, although we stand in awe at our presumption, we dare to plan that they may so persist through the eternity yet ahead."

Wilderness and the Quality of Life

James P. Gilligan

WELCOMING ADDRESS

I would like to examine with you a few reasons for holding this tenth biennial Wilderness Conference. The meetings reflect more than just a special interest in wilderness or in conflicts arising between wilderness and development proposals.

Certainly there is concern about the growing number of land-use controversies and the ensuing debates that center on local development and utilization versus concepts of the national interest. There is continuing alarm at the far-reaching impacts of growing population, air and water pollution, and vast development activities. Wilderness, with its pure air, clean water, natural beauty, and open space, offers strong contrast to the urban environments where most of us live or work.

Dr. Louis S. B. Leakey, the well-known British anthropologist, offered an indirect argument for reserving wilderness when he said: "But in one thing today man is very overspecialized, and that is his brain power. It has led him to create the means of his own destruction and has also made him create for himself such a highly specialized material culture that we are far more, not less, at the mercy of nature than man ever was before."

But when we search for justification for reserving sizable units of land in wilderness condition, in a country where development is equated with progress, the answers are basic to the way people feel about wilderness.

The idea of retaining specific undeveloped areas as wilderness reserves receives nationwide public support for a variety of reasons. A probing of them must ultimately recognize the major role that wilderness has played in shaping the American character and its distinct culture. To reserve some samples of this molding environment—either as a monument to our heritage or as an integral part of our culture—is a primary justification that not only supersedes the benefits of wilderness for recreational use, but possibly even supersedes its scientific value.

It is upon the premise that wilderness may be more important to the people of this country than is consciously recognized, that the planning committee of this conference adopted the theme "Wilderness and the Quality of American Life." We hope the conference will lend credence and understanding to this concept.

When the Outdoor Recreation Resources Review Commission's wilderness study was made (ORRRC Report No. 3), directed from the University of California School of Forestry, we were required to define a minimum size or acreage that would distinctly represent wilderness and that could be inventoried nationally. Although we concluded that the largest roadless areas of country best represented all the composite values that a wilderness could offer, we could include only those areas that were available, regardless of size. The difference is vast between a five-thousand-acre and a million-acre tract of land now held in a few wilderness reserves. Because the conference planning committee accepted this range of size, the focus of this conference is on large units of roadless and undeveloped land and water areas, now reserved or unreserved, either protected in parks and wilderness reserves or awaiting development. In total we will be talking about the last remaining fifty million acres of still undeveloped land, about 2 per cent of the national land area. Only one-fifth of this acreage is currently reserved under the Wilderness Act. At the same time we must note the special value of wild zones and small islands of nature existing near cities, and the importance of particular species of plant and animal life needing preservation.

In addition to providing an opportunity to examine how wilderness affects the quality of American life, the conference is planned as a forum for discussion of several urgent issues. Emphasis is placed on the current national review under the Wilderness Act of dozens of roadless areas, on the prospects and problems of establishing desert and marine wilderness units (mostly bypassed in earlier designations of areas), and on the mounting difficulties of maintaining wilderness conditions in the reserved areas.

We are fortunate to have a distinguished group of speakers. They are highly knowledgeable about wilderness and are variously experts in human perception, in administration, in technical aspects of wilderness preservation, and in social and political evaluation. They will bring views to the conference that bear directly on the future of wilderness.

 *Part One*

The Wilderness Act
in Practice

NATIONAL FORESTS
Edward P. Cliff

NATIONAL PARKS AND MONUMENTS
George B. Hartzog, Jr.

NATIONAL WILDLIFE REFUGES AND RANGES
Noble E. Buell

THE FIRST THREE YEARS
Stewart M. Brandborg

DISCUSSION
J. Michael McCloskey and Anthony Wayne Smith

SUMMARY
Dennis A. Rapp

Phillip S. Berry, Moderator

~§ *Under provisions of the Wilderness Act of 1964, three federal land administering agencies are required to study the location and boundaries of units recommended for inclusion in the
National Wilderness Preservation System. After public hearings,
agency recommendations are submitted for the President's approval and congressional action. To be completed by 1974, the
studies cover five and a half million acres in thirty-four national
forest primitive areas and nearly forty million acres in seventy
units of the national park and the national wildlife refuge systems.
The amount, kind, and quality of wilderness to be retained by
this nation will be determined by these crucial studies currently
under way. In public hearings to date, the conservation groups
and agencies have sometimes expressed widely differing views regarding both the size of wilderness units and underlying planning
concepts. This section reviews the current status of wilderness
studies and the methods by which the agencies determine the
size and location of wilderness units.*

Phillip S. Berry

INTRODUCTION

The focus of our first session is the Wilderness Act in practice. There is a brief discussion of the act in the program introduction, which makes clear that interpretations of this law differ. To underline the reasons for these differences, I would like to quote the definition of wilderness that is contained in the act:*

> A wilderness in contrast with those areas where man and his own works dominate the landscape, is hereby recognized as an area where the earth and its community of life are untrammeled by man, where man himself is a visitor who does not remain. An area of wilderness is further defined to mean in this Act an area of undeveloped Federal land retaining its primeval character and influence, without permanent improvements or human habitation, which is protected and managed so as to preserve its natural conditions and which (1) generally appears to have been affected primarily by the forces of nature, with the imprint of man's work substantially unnoticeable; (2) has outstanding opportunities for solitude or a primitive and unconfined type of recreation; (3) has at least five thousand acres of land or is of sufficient size as to make practicable its preservation and use in an unimpaired condition; and (4) may also contain ecological, geological, or other features of scientific, educational, scenic, or historical value.

Now, if there isn't something in that definition to please everyone, I would say Congress failed in its effort to pass the buck to others, who now must decide exactly what wilderness is under the law. This is one —just one—of the problems that will be considered in this section.

* See Appendix A for complete text of the Wilderness Act.

5

Edward P. Cliff

THE WILDERNESS ACT AND
THE NATIONAL FORESTS

Ten years ago Dr. Richard McArdle, then chief of the Forest Service, sketched the history of the Department of Agriculture's protection of wilderness to that date. In 1963 I described our classification actions and plans for management of wilderness. Two years ago I discussed with you what lay ahead in administering the Wilderness Act, and now I am glad to have this chance to report on our progress. These discussions are especially timely now as the tempo of studies, hearings, and recommendations steps up.

One of our first jobs, two years ago, was to circulate our proposed regulations and policy guidelines for public review. The response was amazing. We received more than three thousand comments and suggestions. It became quite obvious that wilderness means many different things to different people. The job of analyzing the comments was a big one. Most of the responses came from the heart, but many sincere people interested in the protection of wilderness resources differed vigorously with other equally sincere individuals on some points. We also received many constructive suggestions from people who were primarily interested in water, timber, wildlife, livestock, mining, and other uses of the land. Although it was not possible to satisfy everyone, the regulations approved by Secretary Freeman on June 3, 1966, have been generally accepted.*

* See Appendix B for text of Forest Service Regulations: "Administration and Use of National Forest Wilderness and National Forest Primitive Areas."

These and other basic policy and administrative guidelines have been published in the Forest Service Manual. They may be reviewed at the office of any district ranger or forest supervisor. We appreciate your interest and your help in getting that important step accomplished.

The most pressing job now facing the Forest Service under the Wilderness Act is the review of the primitive areas; as you know, we have to develop recommendations as to their suitability for addition to the Wilderness System. The act requires the Department of Agriculture to recommend to the President, and the President to forward recommendations to Congress, on one-third of our thirty-four primitive areas by September of this year. We expect to meet that deadline.

Perhaps it has seemed as if we were off to a slow start in getting these studies under way—but we have been filling the "pipeline." There is much work to be done before a specific recommendation can be prepared for the President's consideration. First, we have to make an intensive field study to evaluate the primitive areas and contiguous lands in light of the criteria set forth in the act. The sequence of studies must be geared to the work of the U.S. Geological Survey and the U.S. Bureau of Mines as they schedule the examinations of mineral resources called for by Congress. Formal notice has to be given to the governor of the state and to interested federal agencies. Arrangements have to be made for public hearings, and the hearing record must be held open for thirty days to receive additional written testimony before the analysis can begin. As you can see, it is a time-consuming process. Actually, this deliberate and thorough period of study and analysis required in each case is one of the strong features of the law. I am sure we agree that hasty or ill-conceived proposals have no place in this process.

In carrying on these primitive-area studies, we are guided by the Wilderness Act, which described what wilderness is and how it is to be managed. But we are also guided by the Multiple Use Act of 1960, which directs us to manage the resources of the national forests so that they are utilized in the combination that will best meet the needs of the American people. Thus, the decision to recommend a particular area for wilderness status is truly a very basic multiple-use decision. In this light, the study of wilderness suitability takes on a broader meaning. We must not only measure the suitability in terms of the land's qualification for wilderness; we must also measure it in terms of the public's need for wilderness as compared with its need for various other resources.

The hearings to date make it clear that not everyone agrees with our proposals. Some have felt that part or all of the land should be developed for resources other than wilderness. For example, in Utah we heard that the need for water development transcends the need for wilderness—to the extent that part of the proposed High Uintas Wilderness should be excluded—or at least that the decision should be postponed until all water development proposals could be fully evaluated. This viewpoint has very strong support in the state of Utah. Others felt that more land should be developed and made more accessible for general recreation. Still others told us we were much too conservative in our proposals; that our recommendations for wilderness should cover far larger areas. These kinds of differences are to be expected. They are indicative of ever-increasing competition for the full range of national forest resources.

Thus, our obligation in primitive-area review under the Wilderness Act is more than simply the study of boundary alternatives or an analysis of contiguous lands to see if they might be included in a wilderness proposal. We believe that Congress directed these reviews to make sure that all public values are considered. We believe that Congress intends that the quality and integrity of the entire system be maintained at the highest possible level. Therefore, every action recommended must be supported by analysis of all the present and potential public values involved.

We know that some lands in existing primitive areas do not meet wilderness qualifications. Some have roads and resorts and other developments; some other tracts may be more valuable and better suited for nonwilderness uses. On the other hand, lands adjacent to primitive areas not now set aside may qualify and prove to be best suited for wilderness. We have recommended additions as well as deletions, and no doubt will continue to do so. As you probably know, the acreage included in the eleven wilderness proposals that we have made to date increased the primitive-area acreage by 25 per cent. We have demonstrated our willingness to recommend additions where they appear to be fully justified.

There is a basic question that we all must answer: "What kind of land really qualifies as wilderness?" In the Wilderness Act, Congress gave us a definition of the kind of land intended for the National Wilderness Preservation System. By omission it also helped us understand what is expected. For example, it did not say that wilderness must contain outstanding scenery or even be attractive. It did not say that a wilderness, or an entire system, must include a complete range of vegetative types. It did put a limitation of five thousand acres as the lower standard in size. But it is interesting to note that the center of a tract of that size cannot be more than about one and one-half miles from its nearest perimeter.

The language of the law does specify that wilderness must be federal land; it must be an area where the earth and its community of life are untrammeled by man; it must be without permanent improvements or human habitation; it must generally appear to have been affected primarily by the forces of nature—with the imprint of man's work substantially unnoticeable; and it must have outstanding opportunities for solitude or primitive and unconfined types of recreation.

Obviously, we are not dealing with an exact science. Even though the criteria may never be precise, they will be made clearer by precedent as Congress acts on the series of recommendations. It is important for us to keep in mind that these criteria serve more than one purpose. They help us to decide what kinds of lands and resources should be added to the system, but they also guide us in understanding which lands should not be added to the system. Most of all, they set the quality level at which Congress intends the wilderness environment to be maintained.

Personally, I hope very much that we will not see a lowering of quality standards to make acceptable some manmade intrusions or defects of other kinds simply for the sake of adding acreage. If this is done, we will surely see an undermining of our defense against similar intrusions on lands already in the system. For example, it is difficult for us to argue against environmental damage from a proposed reservoir construction in one case if we have already recommended congressional approval for other areas containing water impoundments. Although there are historic or physical aspects involved that make each case unique, these distinctions must be very carefully drawn, or there is a real hazard in letting the bars down. Quality standards may be eroded and significantly lowered in the future unless we keep our sights high in these critical years of decision. I cannot emphasize these points too strongly. Right now we may seem to be preoccupied with wilderness classification, but we will be managing wilderness a long time after the classification job is done. The quality we insist on in classification will shape the character and quality of the environment that can be maintained in future management of the resources.

The proper location of boundaries is a live issue today. Forty-three years of experience in managing wilderness have taught us much about where boundaries can and should be located. The most desirable boundaries generally follow easily recognized topographic features. Ideally, the boundary should be on a ridge or other feature that itself helps to shield the wilderness environment from the impacts of civilization. Sharp ridges or rimrocks make the best boundaries. Stream bottoms are not so good, and surveyed or unsurveyed land lines or contour lines are usually even less satisfactory. Many existing primitive-area boundaries can be improved as our studies determine precisely the best locations to recommend.

Experience has shown clearly that a boundary placed along the edge of a reservoir, a road, or some other operating facility, leads to interminable problems. For example, the boundaries of both the Three Sisters Wilderness and the Mount Washington Wilderness in Oregon are sixty-six feet from the center line of the McKenzie Pass Highway. Even though the units have different names, in reality we have a wilderness with a highway through it. Not only is the quality of the adjacent wilderness resource reduced, but the operation of the facility is greatly complicated. Two years ago I told you that buffer strips of undeveloped wild lands will not be maintained outside wilderness boundaries. But neither will we recommend including substandard areas within wilderness boundaries in order to insulate the "real" wilderness inside.

Even when agreement is reached and a wilderness unit is established under the law, our job is just beginning. Each new addition, together with the original 9.1 million acres, must be managed most carefully. The Wilderness Act contains some paradoxes and contradictions. It says the wilderness character of the lands within the system will be preserved; but then it provides very specific exceptions to permit several uses that do not conform to its own definition of wilderness.

All the people who were concerned with enacting the legislation were aware of the basic philosophical conflicts built into the act. They recognized them, and accepted them as compromises that were necessary to accomplish the basic objective of establishing a National Wilderness Preservation System. In this case, too, I think we can look forward to getting more specific guidance from Congress as the legislative history is written concerning each specific new wilderness recommendation.

The administration of a wilderness entails some unusually thorny problems. For example, the law says there will be no use of motorized equipment; then it makes exceptions for its use as needed to meet administrative requirements. We are trying our best to minimize administrative use of such equipment. Yet, a great deal must be done to protect and administer wilderness. We must clean up after thoughtless visitors. We must manage game, pack animals, and domestic livestock where such use is permitted. We need to keep trails open and we need to build new trails. We need to prevent pollution, detect and fight forest fires, and perform other duties. And we are not the only ones with a job to do in the wilderness. For instance, the Geological Survey is expected to make periodic mineral examinations even after the wilderness preserve is created. State game and fish departments stock fish in some lakes and streams and sometimes they restock native mammals. The Soil Conservation Service and municipal water districts need to measure the snowpack. Scientific studies of wilderness are conducted by universities and others—and so it goes.

It seems clear that even moderate use of motorized equipment for essential administrative purposes could detract from the quality of the wilderness resource. We have, therefore, decided that only where absolutely necessary will the Forest Service or its cooperators make administrative use of equipment generally prohibited to the public by the Wilderness Act.

We are getting some cooperation in this approach. For example, the New Mexico Game and Fish Department transported ten mountain sheep into the heart of the Pecos Wilderness on horseback. The Geological Survey used horses to establish geodetic control in the Blue Range and Mount Baldy Primitive Areas—although helicopters are commonly used in this work outside wilderness. In some cases snowshoes or skis have replaced the helicopter in winter travel. Helicopters are still permitted where that use was well established prior to the passage of the act, and that is in accordance to the act—another paradox.

There is also strong resistance to our efforts to maintain the wilderness environment. Packers, who are essential to the use and enjoyment of the wilderness, want to use power saws to clear trails and cut firewood. Mining companies want to use helicopters extensively in the high country in mineral exploration where the field season is short. Other public agencies want to use equipment to do their work most efficiently—whether it is measuring snowpacks, making maps, making mineral examinations, or planting trout. All of them justify their activity as a reasonable exception to our basic policies. But we must conclude that Congress meant what it said in stating that certain uses were prohibited "except as specifically provided for in the act." When a nonconforming use is proposed, we test it against the special provisions of the act. Unless the specific situation is covered, we have no authority to grant permission. For example, even though an outfitter makes an important contribution to public enjoyment of the wilderness, he must use tents instead of cabins, and he must cut his firewood without the convenience of a power saw.

Many of us recognized that the wilderness law would be difficult to administer when it was passed, and these past two years have sharpened our awareness of the complexities and dilemmas inherent in its language. The examples that I have just mentioned are only a small part of the story. As you well know, we face a variety of other issues that relate to the language and intent of the act. For example, prospecting and mining activities, water development, livestock grazing, wildlife management, regulation of people—all of these and more are subjects which should be thoroughly explored.

Yes, there is much more that we need to talk about with regard to classifying and administering national forest wilderness resources. But I hope that my remarks here adequately convey our strong desire to help build a National Wilderness Preservation System that we can be proud to leave behind. I hope you agree with our conviction that each unit of the system and the management we bring to it should be of the highest possible calibre.

Although good progress is being made in implementation of the Wilderness Act, there is still a great deal to do. Working together, I am confident that the system we build will measure up to the high standards envisioned by those early pioneers of the wilderness concept. We should settle for nothing else.

George B. Hartzog, Jr.

THE WILDERNESS ACT AND THE NATIONAL PARKS AND MONUMENTS

The subject of this panel affords our first real opportunity to review to-gether the implementation of the Wilderness Act. During the past two years there has been much dialogue concerning the newly authorized Wilderness Preservation System and the national parks. It is impera-tive, if this is to become a constructive dialogue, that there be a clear understanding of the fundamental public land policies enunciated by Congress for national parks and for the Wilderness Preservation Sys-tem.

First, let us review the national parks and congressional policies laid down for their management and use.

In the landmark legislation of 1872 establishing Yellowstone Na-tional Park, Congress affirmed a federal responsibility and a new pub-lic land policy, first proclaimed in the Yosemite legislation of 1864, that some of our lands should be held in public ownership perpetually for other than material gain.

In the Yellowstone legislation, Congress laid down the criteria for se-lection of areas that should be set aside as national parks. As a general rule, it said, national parks should be broad and spacious lands. More-over, they should possess many special attributes. Nowhere are the special attributes of a national park summarized more clearly and con-cisely than by the young officer, Lt. Gustavus C. Doane, who com-manded the U.S. Army escort for the Yellowstone expedition. Lieutenant Doane wrote of the Yellowstone: "As a country for sightseers, it is without parallel; as a field for scientific research, it promises great results; in the branches of geology, mineralogy, botany, zoology, and ornithology, it is probably the greatest laboratory that nature furnishes on the surface of the globe."

It is clear that Congress intended that national parks should be for one purpose only: to bring man and his environment into closer harmony. From this one purpose many splendid values accrue to the society of mankind—scientific, cultural, aesthetic, educational, inspirational, recreational, and, yes, even economic.

From the Yellowstone legislation, we can also glean the broad foundations of policies for the management and use of national parks. Congress decreed that the Yellowstone country is "reserved and withdrawn . . . dedicated and set apart as a public park or pleasuring ground for the benefit and enjoyment of the people." It is to be managed "for . . . preservation from injury or spoliation . . . [and retained] in [its] natural condition." Leases for building purposes are to be granted "at such places . . . as shall require the erection of buildings for the accommodation of visitors." The construction of "roads and bridle paths therein" is also authorized.

By enunciating this new public land policy for the management and use of the national parks, Congress deliberately drew a sharp contrast with the baronial, feudal, aristocratic preserves of Europe, which the common man could enjoy only if he was willing to risk the punishment of the convicted trespasser.

The policy of Congress for the management and use of national parks is made abundantly clear, moreover, in the act of 1916 that authorized the establishment of the National Park Service, which declared: "The Service thus established shall promote and regulate the use of the Federal areas known as national parks, monuments, and reservations hereinafter specified by such means and measures as conform to the fundamental purpose of the said parks, monuments, and reservations, which purpose is to conserve the scenery and the natural and historic objects and wildlife therein and to provide for the enjoyment of the same in such manner and by such means as will leave them unimpaired for the enjoyment of future generations. . . . [The Secretary of the Interior] may also grant privileges, leases, and permits for the use of land for the accommodation of visitors in the various parks, monuments, or other reservations."

In establishing each new national park, Congress has reaffirmed the purpose of and the policies for their management and use that was first spelled out in the Yellowstone legislation of 1872. These pronouncements of public policy have resulted in three rather clearly defined land zones within national parks: (1) the enclaves of development "for the accommodation of visitors" connected with roads, bridle paths, and foot trails; (2) transition zones between these developed sites and the wilderness beyond; and (3) the untrammeled, primeval wilderness.

This spectrum of management and use, from the developed areas through the threshold or transition zones and beyond to the unsullied wilderness, provides a variety of personal outdoor experiences that has moved each generation of Americans for almost a century to strengthen and expand our national park system as the repository of the "crown jewels" of the nation's natural heritage.

Since enactment of the wilderness legislation of 1964, there appears to be a belief on the part of some that provision of facilities within national parks for the accommodation of visitors is now contrary to the purpose of national parks and congressional policies laid down for their management and use. The Wilderness Act provides no support for this view. On the contrary, section four of the Wilderness Act provides that "The purposes of this Act are hereby declared to be . . . *supplemental to the purposes for which . . . units of the national park system are established and administered. . . .*" (Emphasis supplied.)

Accordingly, in the wilderness legislation, Congress has not changed its long-established policies for the management and use of national parks.

Within the framework of existing congressional policy for park management and use, I am hopeful that we can join hands to solve some of the problems that command our most creative efforts. Briefly, I wish to share three of the more serious ones with you.

First, we must come to grips with the use of the automobile during the height of the visitor season. Shall we explore the possibilities of the monorail, the funicular, the shuttle bus, or other means of mechanical transport, in an effort to separate the visitor from his car while he enjoys his parks?

Of even more serious consequence is the continuing erosion of park values by the existence of private lands within our national parks. There are sixty-two natural areas (national parks and national monuments) within the national park system. Within these areas are approximately 293,000 acres of nonfederal—mostly privately owned—lands, many of which are being used in ways seriously adverse to park preservation. The rate of progress to date in acquiring these privately owned lands has been something less than spectacular: in the past ten years, only about 39,000 acres have been acquired. In the meantime, cost of the remaining lands has continued to accelerate. It is of the utmost importance, in my judgment, that the acquisition of lands in our older national parks be given equal priority with the acquisition of lands in the newly authorized areas. If we fail to do this, we run the risk of changing the very nature of our national parks by having full-blown subdivisions built in them that undermine our mutual objective of preserving the ecological integrity of our national parks.

The second point that I wish to examine with you is the Wilderness Act as it relates to the national parks. We in the National Park Service welcome the added strength in the provision of the Wilderness Act for the identification by legislation of specific lands within the national parks as units of the National Wilderness Preservation System. It is abundantly clear from the exhaustive legislative hearing records that you and we then agreed that legislatively identified wilderness areas in the national parks are desirable. It is equally clear, also, that we recognized then—and should acknowledge now—that from the time Yellowstone National Park was established in 1872, the idea of wilderness preservation has been part of the management of our national park system. The national park movement has been a focal point and a fountainhead for an evolving wilderness philosophy within our country for almost a century.

It is a fundamental tenet of national park management, moreover, that where other uses have impaired past wilderness values, the national parks are managed after acquisition to restore the wilderness character of these areas by the removal of adverse uses.

For example, seventy years ago the famous wilderness of Sequoia National Park was perilously close to permanent destruction. So thoroughly had sheep done their work that the once lush alpine meadows and grasslands were dusty flats. Eroded gullies were everywhere. Much of the climax vegetation was gone, and the High Sierra was virtually impassable to stock parties due to scarcity of feed. In 1893, the Acting Superintendent recommended that cavalry be replaced by infantry. No natural forage was available for horses!

Today, under National Park Service management policies, Sequoia National Park contains wilderness to compare with any other national park. And, in spite of increasing public use, these areas are in a less damaged condition today than they were seventy years ago. In an effort to continue to improve park management, a program of management-oriented research is under way at Sequoia National Park, including studies designed to help us understand and perpetuate the giant sequoia groves. Similar management-oriented research programs are under way in other national parks to insure the maintenance of natural ecological conditions.

It is essential to keep this background in mind as we now plan for specific areas within national parks that will henceforth be identified as units of the National Wilderness Preservation System. For to assume that the Wilderness Act establishes new standards and new criteria for national park wilderness, replacing the old and time-tested wilderness standards and criteria of the service, would jeopardize the whole national park concept. The Wilderness Act recognizes this all-important point when it provides specifically that "Nothing in this Act shall modify the statutory authority under which units of the national park system are created. Further, the designation of any area of any park . . . as a wilderness area pursuant to this act shall in no manner lower the standards evolved for the use and preservation of such park . . . in accordance with the Act of August 25, 1916, [and] the statutory authority under which the area was created. . . ."

It is obvious that Congress could only have intended that wilderness designation of national park system lands should, if anything, result in a higher, rather than a lower, standard of unimpaired preservation. This point is emphasized even further by recognition in the Wilderness Act of 1964 that all wilderness in the National Wilderness Preservation System is not to be managed alike.

The Wilderness Act recognizes the differences in the management practices of the various federal agencies charged with the administration of lands to be included in the National Wilderness Preservation System. For example, the Wilderness Act provides for certain multiple uses in wilderness areas other than national park wilderness, such as existing grazing; mineral prospecting and mining until 1984 (with authority to construct transmission lines, water lines, and telephone lines, and utilize timber for such activities); and water conservation and power projects as authorized by the President.

No such lowering of park values for areas designated by Congress as national park wilderness is contemplated by the Wilderness Act. Moreover, the Wilderness Act does not contemplate the lowering of park values on the remaining park lands not designated as wilderness. The status of all national parklands, including areas designated by Congress as national park wilderness, remains unique, for its management does not compete with any other resource use.

The third point I wish to examine with you involves our procedures for the implementation of the Wilderness Act, which requires that areas recommended for designation as wilderness be defined specifically. It attributes several characteristics to wilderness areas to be included in the National Wilderness Preservation System. Broadly speaking, these involve (1) man's sensitivities and reactions to wilderness and (2) the physical or ecological character of such wilderness areas.

With respect to man's sensitivities and reactions, it may be said that wilderness is where man finds solitude or where he may enjoy "a primitive and unconfined type of recreation" away from civilization and roads.

The physical or ecological characteristics of wilderness require that the area retain "its primeval character and influence," that it "have been affected primarily by the forces of nature," and be "at least five thousand acres of land or . . . of sufficient size as to make practicable its preservation and use in an unimpaired condition."

To comply with these requirements, wilderness recommendations can come only from a detailed knowledge of the land, its capabilities, the natural and cultural values found on it, and the regional factors that influence its management.

It has long been the practice of the National Park Service to prepare and to maintain a master plan to guide the use, development, interpretation, and preservation of each particular park. Graphics and narrative specify the objectives of management. These master plans are zoning plans; they not only define the areas for developments, they also define the areas in which no developments are to be permitted.

Nor are these master-plan studies limited to the specific park involved. The planning team first analyzes the entire region in which the park is located. Parks do not exist in a vacuum; it is important that our teams take into account the plans for and the availability of other park and recreation facilities within the region at the federal, state, and local levels, as well as those provided by the private sector.

The examination of these regional influences involves accommodations for visitors, access to the national parks, and provision of roads within them. Let me illustrate: In 1963 at Mount Rainier National Park and the adjoining national forests, we and the U.S. Forest Service began a joint effort to analyze the needs of visitors and develop cooperative plans for the accommodation of these requirements that would best insure the achievement of both missions. This program formalizes and broadens the informal efforts made for many years by some park superintendents and forest supervisors to coordinate visitor facilities and services. Such cooperative programs are authorized by section two of the act of August 25, 1916, establishing the National Park Service.

We and the Forest Service, likewise, are working cooperatively in planning for visitor accommodations at Yellowstone and Grand Teton National Parks and the adjoining national forests. Also, at Yellowstone and Grand Teton, we have involved the states of Montana, Wyoming, and Idaho, and the Bureau of Public Roads, in an examination of the roads into and through these parks. A primary consideration in solving the park traffic problems, particularly at Yellowstone, is the impact on travel through the park resulting from the designation of park roads as

U.S. highways by the states and the Bureau of Public Roads. We cannot solve these visitor traffic flows satisfactorily until we and the states, working hand in hand, develop some new approaches to the routing of traffic in and around Yellowstone National Park.

The administrative policy that guides us in planning roads within the parks was enunciated by our first director, Steve Mather, in 1924. "It is not the plan to have the parks gridironed by roads," he said, "but in each it is desired to make a good sensible road system so that visitors may have a good chance to enjoy them. At the same time, large sections of each park will be kept in a natural wilderness state without piercing feeder roads and will be accessible by trails to the horseback rider and hiker."

This is still our policy, fully buttressed by numerous legislative enactments of Congress. To ensure that these are low-standard park roads for visitor use, we are encouraging the routing of U.S. highways around the national parks.

All our master-plan studies are made by teams whose members have a different professional background, such as ecology, landscape architecture, architecture, natural history, park planning, resource management, engineering, archaeology, and history. The study teams include outstanding conservationists, scientists, and others who have special knowledge of individual parks. We expect, also, to consult frequently with persons outside the service during the master-plan study.

We use a land classification system similar to that proposed by the Outdoor Recreation Resources Review Commission and prescribed for application to federal lands by the Bureau of Outdoor Recreation. Under this system, lands may be segregated into any one of six classes: Class I—high-density recreational areas; Class II—general outdoor recreation areas; Class III—natural-environment areas; Class IV—outstanding natural areas; Class V—primitive areas, including, but not limited to, those recommended for designation under the Wilderness Act; and Class VI—historical and cultural areas. Consistent with the congressionally stated purpose of national parks, a park contains lands falling into three or more of these classes.

Master plans are reviewed by the park superintendent, the regional director, each assistant director of the service, and finally, by the director. The master plan for each national park is reviewed by the Secretary's Advisory Board on National Parks, Historic Sites, Buildings and Monuments. In addition to these reviews, public hearings are held on all our wilderness proposals. Notice of such public hearings is published in the *Federal Register* and newspapers having general circulation in the area of the park, at least sixty days prior to the hearings. During this sixty-day period, the master-plan documents are available for public review at the park, in the appropriate regional office, and in the Washington office. Moreover, public information packets explaining national park wilderness proposals are available for distribution on request.

Oral and written suggestions from the public concerning the appropriateness of the proposed wilderness areas are analyzed to form a basis for my recommendations to the Secretary of the Interior.

As I mentioned earlier, the Wilderness Act of 1964 supplements national park legislation—it does not replace it. Accordingly, a brief explanation is in order as to the management of lands within national parks.

If such lands are of historical significance (Class VI) or involve a unique feature, such as the Old Faithful Geyser (Class IV), they are accorded management befitting their special significance. Class V, of course, are the primitive lands from which park wilderness designations will be made by Congress. These are the lands that have remained pristine and undisturbed as a part of our natural inheritance. They also may include lands that, through National Park Service management, have been restored by the healing processes of nature to a primeval state. There are no mining, grazing, water impoundment, or other intrusions to mar their character and detract from the solitude of nature's quiet processes. Pure and undefiled, they represent the highest order of "preservation from injury or spoliation" of their natural condition.

I have attached to my remarks the "National Park Service Wilderness Management Criteria," * and I invite your careful review of these criteria. Consistent with congressional policy enunciated in the Wilderness Act, our management criteria contemplate a higher, rather than a lower, standard of unimpaired preservation of national park wilderness.

Class I and Class II identify the lands reserved for visitor accommodations (both existing and proposed), for administrative facilities, campgrounds, etc., of varying intensities. Facilities like these are needed so that the public may have adequate opportunity to enjoy and to use the parks that have been set aside for them. Moreover, such appropriate facilities, if wisely located, designed, and constructed, can serve to protect park values by directing the use of the parks. For example, a road, a trail, a formal campground, or needed concession facility, can serve to channel use in specific locations, thus preventing indiscriminate use of a larger area that could damage or destroy some of the very values for which the park was dedicated. Facilities can be

* See Appendix C for text of "National Park Service Wilderness Management Criteria."

compatible with the natural environment; facilities in discord with their surroundings can be avoided. It is our policy to relate all facilities to an overall architectural theme for each particular park—this being but another way of assuring full aesthetic consideration to the park environment.

Class I and Class II lands occupy relatively little space in any of the national parks. For example, we estimate that in Yellowstone National Park—an area larger than the states of Delaware and Rhode Island combined—Class I and Class II lands amount to something less than 3 per cent of the park acreage. The road system in Yellowstone National Park is mostly unchanged since 1908. Yet these limited lands absorb 95 per cent or more of the public use. In Sequoia National Park, the Class I and Class II lands amount to less than 2 per cent of the total acreage and, likewise, absorb 95 per cent or more of all public use.

Class III identifies the "natural environment" category of lands within the parks. Before saying what these lands are, let me say what they are not:

(1) They are not lands that meet our criteria for park wilderness. If we are to preserve the integrity of national park wilderness, we dare not lower its standard or compromise its integrity by the inclusion of areas that express in less than the highest terms the definition of national park wilderness.

(2) They are not lands intentionally reserved for future intensive developments of the Class I and Class II types. The lands we foresee a need to develop for these purposes are clearly marked on the general development plan accompanying our wilderness proposals. Even so, in my public statement of August 8, 1966, copies of which are available for distribution to you, I have made it abundantly clear that the National Park Service will give sixty days public notice of any future proposal for changing the designation of Class III lands—as well as Class I and Class II lands—from that existing at the time of the enactment of the wilderness legislation with respect to a particular park. The public will have the opportunity to be heard on the proposal. I believe that this procedure is fully in accord with the spirit of the Wilderness Act. Moreover, I believe it offers a creative new way in which we can give a continuing opportunity to the public to participate in the planning and the management of their national parklands.

If Class III lands are not wilderness, and they are not intentionally reserved for future intensive development—what are they? They are natural-environment areas, important to the proper preservation, interpretation, and management of the irreplaceable resources of the national park system identified in the Class IV, V, and VI categories. It is the existence of unique features (Class IV), or primitive lands, including wilderness (Class V), or historical or cultural lands (Class VI) in combination with a suitable environment (Class III) and with sufficient lands "for the accommodation of visitors" (Classes I and II) that distinguish natural and historical areas of the national park system from other public lands providing outdoor recreation.

In the natural areas (national parks and national monuments of scientific significance), Class III lands often provide the "transition" or "setting" or "environment" or "buffer" between intensively developed areas (Class I and Class II) *and* (a) the primitive or wilderness (Class V) areas; and (b) the unique natural features (Class IV) or areas of historic or cultural significance (Class VI) when these two categories exist outside of the Class V lands.

In the historical areas the environmental lands (Class III) provide the setting or atmosphere essential to preserving and presenting the national significance of historic properties included in the national park system.

Often, Class III and Class V lands both represent significant natural values. Generally, these values are different in type, quality, or degree. Accordingly, lands having natural values that do not meet service criteria for primitive or wilderness designation may be classified as Class III even when they do not involve the environment of either Class IV, Class V or Class VI lands. In natural areas, natural-environment lands are sometimes referred to additionally as "wilderness threshold" when they abut or surround wilderness.

The wilderness-threshold lands afford the newcomer an opportunity to explore the mood and the temper of the wild country before venturing into the wilderness beyond. Here in the wilderness threshold is an unequalled opportunity for interpretation of the meaning of wilderness.

The only facilities planned in these natural-environment lands are the minimum required for public enjoyment, health, safety, preservation, and protection of the features, such as one-way motor nature trails, small overlooks, informal picnic sites, short nature walks, and wilderness-type uses. Such limited facilities must be in complete harmony with the natural environment.

In addition to the research activities permitted in national park wilderness, Class III lands also serve important research needs of the service, independent researchers, and institutions of higher learning. Where, for example, in our country today is it possible to study the causes and effects of weather formation in a region free from the pollutants of our mechanized civilization? Such a place is Yellowstone National Park, which scientists have found has the purest air in the

United States. A skilled team of scientists from the State University of New York has been at work for the past several years in Yellowstone National Park, carrying out research that is expected to contribute new information on the science of weather.

In testifying on the wilderness bill, the late Howard Zahniser of the Wilderness Society said that in the establishment of a wilderness preservation system "we are facing a frontier," and indeed we are. Working together, each of us has learned a great deal in the last two years about the identification and classification of wilderness lands for congressional consideration. And if I am to judge by some of the comments the Sierra Club has made about some of my proposals, I am sure I have a great deal still to learn.

I believe the time is at hand for land managers and citizen organizations to join forces in a creative new program of wilderness appreciation and of wise use if we are to preserve the Wilderness System that Congress has chartered—I was pleased and delighted to hear your president refer to this in his welcoming remarks this morning. To this end, I have invited Ed Cliff of the Forest Service and several representatives of citizen organizations to join me in a meeting to discuss such a program.

With your help, I hope we can develop a continuing formal program for the refinement of wilderness-management techniques and leadership training for those who use and conduct trips into the wilderness.

As we proceed from this initial meeting, I am sure there will be a need to involve others of our youth and adult outdoor groups. Considering the vast need, this, indeed, is but a small effort. We hope it will supplement the fine programs of the Sierra Club, the Wilderness Society, and others. Working together, I believe that we can advance our common goals of not only identifying legislatively a National Wilderness Preservation System, but also achieving the preservation of the wilderness we all cherish.

In closing, let me share one more thing with you. Nearly one hundred years ago, the Department of the Interior was entrusted with its first national park. Fifty years ago the National Park Service was established in the department to administer the national park system. Our national parklands, after almost one hundred years, remain unimpaired for our continuing benefit and enjoyment. In them one may enjoy the finest wilderness in our nation—lands and waters that meet the highest standards yet devised for wilderness preservation. This is an achievement that speaks eloquently of the devotion to duty and the creative management of a long and distinguished line of National Park Service employees. They have been ably supported by growing numbers of citizens, such as you, concerned with the preservation of our natural and cultural heritage.

In the words of the Leopold Committee report, a national park should "represent a vignette of primitive America." Also, the wilderness areas in our national parks, freed as they are of the pressures of competing resource uses, represent the highest quality of wilderness in our land.

As we succeed in our mutual objective, all wilderness areas, but especially national park wilderness, will make an increasingly important contribution to the quality of American life. The body of law undergirding national park management, strengthened as it is by the Wilderness Act of 1964, ensures that national park wilderness will continue to offer a superlative and re-creative experience in God's great out-of-doors. To continue to preserve these values for our increasingly urban population is our challenge, our opportunity, and the management goal of the National Park Service.

Noble E. Buell

THE WILDERNESS ACT
AND THE NATIONAL WILDLIFE
REFUGES AND RANGES

We think the national wildlife refuge system will preserve more wilderness in a greater variety than any other category of public lands. We have selected ninety roadless areas and islands on seventy refuges for study. These total nearly 22.5 million acres. And there probably will be additions as our studies progress. These wilderness-study areas vary from one-acre islands to the nine-million-acre Arctic National Wildlife Range. They include forty-eight islands or island groups, and forty roadless tracts of five thousand acres or more.

We expect to complete the study of one-third of these areas this summer. This will involve twenty-one islands and island groups and portions of ten refuges. You may have noted that these thirty-one areas are some of the system's smaller, least complicated units, and that they are widely distributed. This is by design. We have had a time problem in meeting the act's requirements for the first three-year period, but most of all, we wanted an opportunity to appraise the initial public expression from the first hearings and the first considerations by Congress.

Many of you are intimately familiar with the long legislative history of the Wilderness Act. Like most controversial legislation, there was some compromise of ideas and ideals. From our viewpoint, some of the act's statements and implications appear to be inconsistent and on some matters the act seems strangely silent as to intent. We are not completely certain what Congress had in mind for wilderness as it relates to the national wildlife refuge system. One thing seems quite clear —that wilderness, like beauty, is often in the eye of the beholder. Which brings to mind the fact that yesterday I was in our Boston regional office, which handled the hearings on our wilderness proposal for the Great Swamp National Wildlife Refuge in New Jersey. This is only a two-thousand-acre unit, yet over six thousand letters had come in commenting on this proposal.

As a basis for discussion here, I would like to make three points. First, our wilderness study areas are in the national wildlife refuge system, that is, within units of land set aside primarily for wildlife purposes. We do not expect that either the philosophy or the regulations pertaining to wilderness status will be more liberal than those of the refuge, although they may be similar or more restrictive.

Second, our bureau has several authorities for land acquisition for wildlife purposes, but it has none for wilderness purposes. Any acquisitions for wilderness on refuge units must be specifically authorized by Congress.

Third, we regard the responsibility for preserving the character of a designated wilderness, based upon the language of the act— ". . . and shall so administer such area for such other purposes for which it may have been established as also to preserve its wilderness character"—as direction for selection and future administration of refuge wildernesses. We regard the purposes of the Wilderness Act as supplemental to wildlife refuge purposes. But the character of such refuge wildernesses as may be established will not be impaired by future administration as refuges. The act, we think, implies a higher, rather than a lower, standard of unimpaired preservation. Any special administrative needs will be recognized when a refuge wilderness is established.

In the minds of many people, the word "wilderness" conjures a vision of primeval, stately forests where there is no evidence of civilization—not even a jet trail. But this condition is hard to come by on the national wildlife refuge system. We feel the more liberal definitions in the act are appropriate for this jet age. Exceptions in the act, by implication, set modern standards for wilderness that accept something less than pure primitive conditions, but still offer substantial wilderness values in the system.

Therefore, we find no incongruity in continuing on refuge wildernesses those management activities that do not alter the land surface. For example, we do not believe that seasonal aerial counts of waterfowl on Malheur Lake in Oregon, or boat patrols to protect alligators from poachers in Okefenokee Swamp in Georgia, will preclude those areas' becoming wilderness. Nor do we necessarily foreclose minimum facilities for safety and sanitation.

We regard the phrase "with the imprint of man's work substantially unnoticable" as a workable criterion for refuge wilderness. We have potential areas that show the scars of pipelines below ground, but with time and care, these marks will be substantially unnoticeable. My point is that refuges have been managed as refuges, and for other purposes before they became refuges; thus, some imprints of development are there and will be for some time.

In those areas established as wilderness, there will be time and opportunity for a creative wilderness philosophy to be implemented. However, where future physical development is required to fulfill refuge purposes in areas that now meet wilderness study criteria, we will propose to the Secretary of the Interior that such areas not be recommended for wilderness status.

The refuge system offers an almost limitless variety of topography, climate, and life complexes. This situation is reflected in wilderness study areas as swamps, forests, tundra, deserts, lakes, barrier islands, bogs, dunes, cliffs, and grasslands, to name some. In some potential areas there are small native villages, and in others public ownership is incomplete because of substantial private inholdings, some of them life tenures.

Some islands are extremely small, many only a few acres, and many of these are not and cannot be isolated from the sight and sounds of civilization. Other islands are so isolated and of such configuration that human visitation is very difficult.

Certain refuge areas also exist in an undeveloped condition where refuge management has no foreseeable requirement for physical disturbance. We think these should be preserved in a pristine condition as part of our natural heritage, and we believe this philosophy is implicit in the Wilderness Act.

We are most interested, of course, to find out how the public will react to this variety of wilderness possibilities. The response from hearings, and from meetings like this, will be helpful in planning our refuge future.

We have not yet developed special regulations for the management of wilderness areas, because we first need to get at least a preliminary reading on public response to our proposals. We see no great problem, however, for we believe our wilderness regulations will basically be refinements of present refuge regulations contained in Part 28 of Title

50—Code of Federal Regulations.* This part covers access, use, and recreation, and provides for specific area regulations, such as those governing access and travel within a refuge wilderness area.

The act is almost completely silent on the subject of refuge wilderness management, although there are perhaps some clues in the sections establishing national forest wilderness. Three aspects seem to evoke the most interest to date: hunting and fishing; visitation regulations; and commercial uses, such as mining, mineral leasing, and grazing.

Hunting and fishing on refuge wildernesses will be determined by refuge management considerations. I do not expect that wilderness status of an area within a refuge will in itself have much bearing on hunting or fishing within it. It will have a bearing on the means of doing so and the means of access.

We intend that wilderness on refuge areas will accommodate only such visitors as "will leave them unimpaired for future use and enjoyment as wilderness" and will also be consistent with refuge wildlife requirements. This probably will mean no visitors at all on some areas, such as bird rocks, and probably will mean seasonal closures of certain waterfowl and eagle nesting areas. Some areas may be used only for scientific or educational purposes, and retained as wilderness areas with visitor use restricted or not permitted at all.

It is important to remember that all lands of the refuge system are subject to the mineral leasing laws, although some are closed to non-competitive oil and gas leasing by secretarial order. The current group of study areas now include "desk" studies of the minerals subject to leasing. We will make specific recommendations to the Secretary on each study area following our review of the public hearing and other response. In some cases we expect to recommend that wilderness legislation include the withdrawal of the proposed area from application of the mineral leasing laws.

Classes of minerals subject to location under the mining laws will be studied only in connection with the unwithdrawn portion of the Cabeza Prieta Game Range and the Kofa Game Range in Arizona; the Charles M. Russell National Wildlife Range in Montana; the Charles Sheldon Antelope Range and the Desert National Wildlife Range in Nevada; and the Clarence Rhode National Wildlife Range in Alaska. I do not know what our recommendations will be; however, we believe that an established wilderness area should be withdrawn from the mining laws either simultaneously with its establishment or as soon thereafter as possible.

* See Appendix D for text of regulations for public use of federal wildlife refuge and range areas.

I have frequently heard people express the view that congressional designation of a wilderness "locks up" that area forever. I doubt this finality—laws are enacted, but they are also repealed or modified by future legislation as national needs change. My point is that wilderness designation on refuges is not necessarily for eternity; but it *is* the strongest possible insurance that any future demand to use a wilderness area for some other purpose will get public attention and will require a national review through congressional consideration.

Back to some particulars. Grazing, as a wildlife management tool, now exists on some study areas. While we do not expect to consider new grazing use of an established wilderness, neither do we expect to recommend abrupt termination of existing grazing. Rather, we expect to phase out existing grazing as it can be done without serious economic impact.

We have concluded there will be few "typical" wilderness areas among our refuge system contributions, and we think that there will be special considerations for many of the areas. All refuge areas recommended by the Secretary of the Interior will require individual legislative consideration, so everyone will have a chance to understand the intentions for future management if Congress designates them as wilderness. We believe that the Sierra Club's interest in the establishment of such areas on refuges will continue through these congressional deliberations and we hope it does.

The crowded schedule of this initial period on refuge wilderness, with nineteen public hearings between January and May—held from Anchorage, Alaska, to St. Petersburg, Florida—meant considerable inconvenience to many of you. But our schedule for studies during the remaining seven years will be more evenly spaced, and will provide more advance notice on each proposal. We hope you will forgive the moment's rush.

We are convinced of the immediate need to preserve a part of our heritage for scientific, educational, and aesthetic purposes, and you may be sure we are taking advantage of this opportunity to make a really significant wilderness contribution within the national wildlife refuge system.

Recreational uses of refuge areas, of which wilderness experience is one, are based on the simple idea that people come to a wildlife refuge to see and enjoy wildlife in the wild and that they should expect to see and enjoy wildlife in its natural setting. Refuges are as different as fingerprints, and the opportunity for wilderness experience is dictated by the capability of these refuge areas to provide high-quality recreational experiences, not the capability to accommodate quantity. On refuge wilderness areas, special attention will be given to opportunities for solitude, recognizing that this is a value that not only has changed and will continue to change, but also becomes more unique and difficult to find.

Thank you for the invitation to discuss some of our views and plans at this stage of our wilderness studies. We want your advice and support in developing these plans and making them realities.

Stewart M. Brandborg

THE WILDERNESS ACT:
THE FIRST THREE YEARS

Two-and-a-half years have passed since the culmination of the eight-year effort to gain passage of the Wilderness Act. On September 3, 1967, conservationists will have seen this landmark measure through its third year, for by that anniversary the President is required to present his recommendations to Congress for the first review period.* It is time for a critical assessment of how it is working.

The act itself established only a skeletal wilderness system, consisting of the fifty-four national forest units that had already been administratively designated as wilderness, wild, or canoe areas. These units, totaling 9.1 million acres, represent only about 20 per cent of the wilderness lands within the jurisdictions of the three administering agencies. Congressional sponsors originally hoped that passage of the bill would place all those wilderness lands in the wilderness system. Opponents of the bill, who were in a position to block its passage, demanded that national forest primitive areas—which had not undergone administrative reclassification—and wilderness lands of the national parks and monuments, the wildlife refuges and game ranges, be added to the wilderness system only upon the authorization of Congress.

The law is explicit in its requirement that no areas can be placed in the National Wilderness Preservation System without public hearings

* See Appendix E for complete table of wilderness hearings held during the first three-year review period.

and the other specified review procedures. When the reviews of over 150 agency proposals are completed in 1974, and assuming all the areas are recommended for wilderness classification, the wilderness system will represent no more than 2 to 3 per cent of the nation's land area. Except for a few important state-administered tracts such as New York's Forest Preserve, Michigan's Porcupine Mountains State Park, and the Baxter State Park in Maine, this will be nearly all the wilderness land we can expect to see preserved for the future. Additions of any remaining unprotected federal wild lands will depend on the increasingly improbable escape of *de facto* wilderness from development. It is also possible that some of the federally held wild lands within the jurisdiction of the Bureau of Land Management may ultimately be designated and protected as wilderness.

As we near the close of the first three-year review period, we can report that the wilderness staff specialists of the Forest Service, the National Park Service, and the Bureau of Sport Fisheries and Wildlife have worked diligently under severe pressures created by a shortage of time to develop their wilderness area proposals. Most of the proposals have been framed by field and regional office personnel of the three agencies who see the Wilderness Act as an instrument for reinforcing their own mandates for the management and protection of lands in their charge. In an encouraging number of instances, there has been a willingness on the part of the agency planners to discuss master plans and wilderness proposals with conservationists before these become final on the administrative or cabinet level.

The goal of conservation leaders has been to become useful allies of agency administrators by offering responsible, constructive criticism. With few exceptions, agency specialists have inspired confidence by their sincerity and competence, although in some cases limited personnel and time have produced dissatisfaction within both citizen groups and the agencies themselves. For the most part, these wilderness agencies are struggling to find an acceptable posture that combines their sincere appreciation of the values of wilderness with the administrative and political pressures that crop up at the local level.

About half the forty-five agency proposals already made for wilderness areas have been in essential agreement with the recommendations prepared by local wilderness committees working in cooperation with national organizations. These include, among others, proposals for the San Gabriel Primitive Area in California, Pine Mountain Primitive Area in Arizona, Craters of the Moon National Monument in Idaho, and wildlife refuge lake and island units in Florida, Massachusetts, Michigan, Wisconsin, Oregon, Washington, and Alaska. In one instance, Bear River National Migratory Bird Refuge in Utah, the citizen groups agreed with the agency that there was no qualified wilderness present.

Perhaps the most important contribution by local wilderness committees has been their on-the-ground field study to determine the adequacy of agency proposals. These study teams have included well-qualified local leaders—persons whose experience in conservation matters or special training in biological, archaeological, and other related professional fields, permits them to offer valid recommendations. There also have been strong representations from scientific and professional groups in support of wilderness proposals. The Ecological Society of America, for example, provided important information on the probable ecological impact of the National Park Service's wilderness and transmountain road proposals in Great Smoky Mountains National Park. Recommendations of the National Speleological Society for the protection of cave wilderness within Mammoth Cave National Park in Kentucky resulted in restudy and revision of master plans for this unit. The time invested by these local study groups in the development of their proposals has sometimes exceeded that spent by short-handed agencies.

The citizen committees have proposed boundaries for wilderness areas that would embrace fairly complete representations of native plant and animal communities and also outstanding scenic and wilderness features. Citizen groups have recommended larger wilderness areas than the agencies in many of the units on which hearings will have been held by September, 1967.*

Although testimony at the hearings generally has strongly supported agency proposals for wilderness designations, an impressive demonstration of public opposition developed at the two hearings for the Great Smoky Mountains National Park. Over three hundred witnesses presented oral statements. These ran three to one in opposition to the Park Service's inadequate wilderness proposal (247,000 acres from a potential 350,000 acres of wilderness) and in opposition to a proposed new transmountain highway in the western section that would bisect some of the park's finest wilderness. Six thousand letters and statements from people all over the country were received for the official hearing record. They ran more than ten to one in opposition to the proposed highway. At a February hearing in New Jersey, 115 witnesses testified orally or in writing in support of the establishment of a wilderness area in the Great Swamp National Wildlife Refuge in New Jersey. They asked that an additional one thousand acres be added to the agency's preliminary proposal for a 2,400-acre wilderness area. At last

* The table in Appendix E lists the discrepancies in all proposals made during the first review period.

count, over six thousand letters and statements from at least thirty-eight states and eight foreign countries had been submitted for the official hearing record.

With few exceptions, the public's showing at these hearings consists of presentations by a few dozen well-informed persons speaking for themselves or as representatives of conservation groups. They either strongly endorse the agency's proposal, or offer recommendations for rounding it out.

National conservation organizations generally have followed recommendations offered by informed local wilderness study committees who have consistently based their recommendations on careful field studies including unique scenic, ecological, geological, or other wilderness features worthy of preservation. In cases where agency recommendations have differed sharply with those of citizen groups, efforts have been made—sometimes cooperatively between agency people and citizen leaders—to restudy the recommendations. Where possible, the areas in question are revisited to check out the conflicting recommendations on the ground.

Representatives of commodity interests have spoken against establishment of only a few proposed wilderness areas. Ranchers have supported an encouraging number of recommendations by conservation groups and local wilderness committees. In the case of the Spanish Peaks Wilderness Area in Montana, they advocated additions to the unit beyond those recommended by conservation groups. In several instances, lumber industry spokesmen have endorsed wilderness area recommendations of the Forest Service, although not supporting larger areas proposed by local wilderness committees.

Some friends of wilderness express concern from time to time about the "purity" of the wilderness areas that citizen groups have recommended, and they speak of their fear that the wilderness law permits too much in the way of nonconforming uses. These reservations have some basis, but they overlook the recuperative power of the land under wilderness management and the fact that at best we may expect to preserve no more than 2 to 3 per cent of our total land resource as wilderness. Very few areas would pass the test of absolute purity.

Opponents who blocked congressional approval of the wilderness bill until it was amended to require congressional authorization for addition of new areas into the system, may find that they have made a great contribution to the wilderness cause by stimulating widespread involvement of interested citizens. Few conservation laws require the degree of citizen initiative and involvement to make them work that the Wilderness Act does.

While the boundary work has its relationship to our overall natural resource picture, we find in this struggle for preservation of wilderness another order of values: the reminders of our past history as a people and as a species that survive in wilderness, plus the faith in a future for the human race that will survive today's terrible pressures and emerge with this link with its past intact. Consciousness of these cultural values has contributed directly to the high quality of wilderness advocacy expressed by the public.

The review requirements of the wilderness law for the parks, forests, and refuges have set in motion a series of far-reaching, if not fully refined, planning activities. The ten-year review deadline in the act has forced both the agencies and citizen conservationists to take a closer look at the wilderness character of the public lands. Some of these studies have revealed major breakdowns in long-range planning to protect wild land areas such as the National Park Service's advocacy of a new transmountain road across Great Smoky Mountains National Park containing the largest mountain wilderness remaining east of the Great Plains. In scattered instances, Forest Service administrators have in effect prevented the enlargement of existing wilderness units by authorizing the construction of roads up to their present boundaries or by encouraging commercial timber cutting and other destructive practices on wild lands immediately adjacent to existing primitive areas. Drift in wildlife refuge and game range management policy has permitted extractive and recreational uses in refuges that sacrifice wildlife and its living areas.

The job of establishing boundaries for wilderness lands has made us aware that there are many different kinds of wild country. We have observed a tendency on the part of both agency people and citizen conservationists to favor certain types of wilderness over others. The principle characteristic of wilderness is its wild quality; to be wilderness, landscapes need not necessarily be scenically attractive or conform to the individual's personal concept of the ideal. How do we reconcile our concept of the ideal wilderness with the variety of nonconforming uses and evidences of past disturbances that have been found in proposed and established wilderness areas? It should be remembered that the Wilderness Act's criteria do not insist that wilderness be pristine, only that it appear to be affected primarily by the forces of nature with the imprint of man's work substantially unnoticeable. In both citizen groups and agency recommendations on areas that contain still-noticeable signs or remnants of man's work, an effort has been made to get assurances that such traces will be permitted to be obliterated by the natural processes of weathering and vegetative recovery. There have been a few cases in which the outstanding value of

the wilderness—its rarity as an ecological unit—has made conservationists unwilling to exclude it because of an existing nonconforming
use, and they have urged that the nonconforming use be discontinued
either before or after admission into the system. Acceptance of an existing noncompatible situation in the expectation that it will be eventually obliterated, to heal the wilderness, is not a precedent for permit-
ting a new invasion that would wound the wilderness.

There have been some highly significant and encouraging responses
from the agencies to the growing interest of people in the public lands.
One outstanding example is the August 8, 1966, statement called "National Park Wilderness Planning Procedures" by Director George B.
Hartzog, Jr., in which he welcomed the added protection that section
4(a)(3) of the Wilderness Act will provide the national park system.
He further defined the National Park Service wilderness policy as
emphasizing the need for zoning the parks to identify and protect their
wilderness areas and for channeling intensive public use to avoid overuse of the parks' back country.

The National Park Service, by opening to public study its master
plans for each unit in advance of scheduled wilderness proposal hearings, has made park planning—at least to some extent—a two-way
street. The suggestions of conservationists are being given serious consideration by some park planners at each step in the wilderness review
process. Conservationists applaud and encourage this new avenue of
communication with the National Park Service. Its efforts have contributed to awareness of the need for comprehensive regional planning
to protect parklands through diversion of nonwilderness uses to developed lands outside the parks and monuments. There, appropriate provision for motorist recreation can be made without sacrifice of wilderness and park values.

The Park Service has provided opportunity—after sixty days' public
notice—for public expression of views on any proposed changes in its
master-plan zoning of Classes I, II, and III lands within the parks and
monuments. These land classifications were proposed by the Outdoor
Recreation Resources Review Commission. This would apply to those
classifications that are in effect at the time Congress enacts legislation
to designate wilderness areas within any given unit of the national park
system.

In its outline of planning procedures, the National Park Service em-
phasizes the role of Class III (natural environment or threshold areas)
as transition zones between areas of development (Classes I and II)
and wilderness boundaries. In some of its early wilderness proposals,
such as that for Lassen Volcanic National Park in California, it recom-

mended exclusion of large acreages within the park from wilderness area designations for this threshold or buffer purpose. Conservation groups have rejected these large Class III exclusions because, in most cases, they embrace wild lands that, although peripheral to larger tracts of wilderness or in closer proximity to roads or other developments, are essentially wild in character and qualify as wilderness under the Wilderness Act's definition. They question the agency's insistence on broad, in-depth exclusions from proposed wilderness areas, since the agency declares that there are no plans to convert such Class III zones to Class II or I for development of intensive-use facilities. There continues to be an underlying, basic question of whether any lands in the national parks should be designated for high density, mass recreation uses.

In its August 8 planning statement, the Park Service has attempted to allay these fears. It has gone so far as to invite public expression— and it is to be hoped that this will permit public hearings where justified—before such Class III threshold lands are reclassified to Class I (high density) and Class II (general outdoor recreation) categories. This step is a highly significant and encouraging departure from earlier procedures of the Park Service and the Forest Service that discouraged the public's participation in basic decision-making and planning procedures. It will be conducive to increased public involvement that will not impede careful master planning, but will assist it. We should proceed with completion of the wilderness system unhindered by any policy requiring exclusion of unique features and extensive buffer or threshold areas.

This does not mean that conservationists will be unmindful of the need to provide basic interpretive and access facilities—in keeping with natural settings—when these cannot be provided outside the parks or in already-established development areas. Conservationists can be expected to continue to resist large exclusions of threshold areas around each wilderness area. This question should be resolved by reducing the threshold (Class III) zones to small transition areas of no more than a few hundred feet separating roads and areas of development from core wilderness areas.

The ORRRC classification system has created confusion by its implication that unique topography, scenery, and natural phenomena of all types (Class IV) and historical lands of significance (Class VI) are to be excluded from National Park Service wilderness area designations. The trial application of this classification system by the Park Service and the Forest Service to proposals for the North Cascades National Park in Washington demonstrates the extent of confusion that can result from its use. Lack of uniformity in the delineation of Class III (threshold), Class IV (unique features), and Class V (wilderness) categories has resulted.

The Bureau of Sport Fisheries and Wildlife has offered some excellent proposals, particularly in the case of Okefenokee Refuge in Georgia. However, it has confused its friends by focusing its wilderness field studies and its public hearing announcements on selected "wilderness study areas" only, rather than on entire refuges. This has resulted in the premature exclusion of major portions of some refuges and game ranges from the wilderness review process.

Early in 1966 the bureau announced that of the 852,000 acres in twenty-eight wildlife refuges then slated for review by September, 1967, only 506,000 acres in thirty-one selected "candidate areas" were to be given intensive study. Thus, without hearings, some 346,000 acres of refuge land were to be excluded from consideration. On October 11, 1966, the bureau published in the *Federal Register* its list of all refuge areas and islands that qualify for wilderness study, totalling 20,400,000 acres. There are 28,300,000 acres in the national wildlife refuge system, eight million acres of which had been excluded, at this point, from the wilderness review process. Obviously, many intensively managed waterfowl refuges do not meet the Wilderness Act's definition of wilderness, but conservationists will want to take a good look at those refuge lands that the bureau does not plan to review. Their potential as wilderness must not be disregarded.

It is understandable how the bureau found itself in this situation. A literal interpretation of sections 2(c)(3) and 3(c) of the Wilderness Act requires the bureau to make an inventory of all the roadless areas of five thousand acres or more as well as the roadless islands in its refuge system. In following this interpretation, the bureau may have overlooked some smaller wilderness acreages that can legally be placed in the wilderness system. While the act focuses on the inventory of islands and other lands of over five thousand acres, neither section precludes wilderness designation of units that are smaller than five thousand acres. The last clause of section 2(c)(3) allows inclusion of smaller units that are of sufficient size to make their preservation practicable.

An incomplete bureau wilderness proposal was recently released for the 241,000-acre Hart Mountain National Antelope Refuge in south central Oregon. A casual glance at the map provided by the bureau in its attractive brochure gave the impression that the bureau is proposing that practically all the refuge be included in the wilderness system. A closer look, however, reveals that the map shows only the 24,900-acre Fort Warner Study Area and the 17,130-acre Poker Jim Ridge Study

Area. The character and use of the land on the other 200,000 acres of the refuge is not described by the bureau. This acreage should be examined to determine whether it contains other potential wilderness system units, or whether some acreage can be added to the two proposed units.

Another potential problem is seen in the half million acres of the Kenai National Moose Range of Alaska that are outside the bureau's wilderness study areas. Some 300,000 acres of the Kofa Game Range in Arizona have been excluded from the intensive wilderness review process, as have almost 900,000 acres of the Charles M. Russell National Wildlife Range in Montana and almost 400,000 acres of the Charles Sheldon Antelope Range in Nevada. While existing developments and long-established nonwilderness uses may explain some of these exclusions, they must receive public consideration and study in the context of the bureau's wilderness proposals in order to avoid a serious procedural breakdown.

The priority given this planning and boundary work must not overshadow our concern for the proper management of wilderness. We should assure ourselves that the uses of each wilderness area are carried on without any sacrifice of its natural features and values. Under the firm legal foundation of the Wilderness Act, the agencies are in a much stronger position to protect wilderness. They now have, for the first time, a full opportunity to develop long-range programs that will assure adequate protection of the wilderness resource, including planning for uses that do not impair the natural environment or wild character of the wilderness lands involved.

We have hardly begun the important work of dispersing and channeling visitor use, providing much-needed interpretive programs and wilderness-edge facilities, and mapping and building appropriately designed wilderness trail systems. This work, and the critically important task of acquiring inholdings within national park and national forest wilderness, can be carried forward by wilderness agencies only with the support of congressional appropriations that will permit the agencies to do these jobs. Equally important is the need for wilderness research to guide the agencies in their wilderness management and protective programs.

The wilderness law has been useful already in the protection of two of the fifty-four wilderness areas initially placed in the National Wilderness Preservation System. These two units—the San Gorgonio Wilderness Area in California and the Bob Marshall Wilderness Area in Montana—continue to be the targets of development proposals promoted by powerful groups.

Bills to open a portion of the San Gorgonio Wilderness Area to commercial ski development may continue as a threat, but the bills introduced in the last Congress died without committee action following a field hearing. Proposals by the Bureau of Reclamation for flood control and irrigation dams on the Sun River within the Bob Marshall Wilderness Area have been unsuccessful despite the bureau's concerted campaign for early authorization of these projects. In both instances, militant leadership and effective educational campaigns by local conservationists were responsible for widespread national interest and public reaction against these threats.

A current threat to the wilderness system involves the Gila Wilderness Area and the Gila Primitive Area in New Mexico. There the Hooker Dam project on the Gila River is being proposed as part of the Central Arizona Project and the Lower Colorado River development program. While this dam would be constructed below the boundaries of both the primitive area and the wilderness area, its reservoir would extend from three-and-a-half to six-and-a-half miles, depending on the height of the dam, up the Gila River Canyon into the wilderness and primitive areas. As in the case of the proposed water impoundments in the Bob Marshall Wilderness Area and the proposed wilderness-destroying dams in the Grand Canyon, conservationists are advocating alternatives to the Hooker project—in this case a dam at one of several downstream locations.

Less dramatic than the threat of intrusions by big dams are more subtle violations of wilderness that come from those who ignore the wilderness law and agency regulations and who propose use of motorized vehicles, helicopters, and other equipment in wilderness areas. Some of these threats, such as a recently attempted jeep invasion of the Gila Primitive Area, have been resolved successfully. Recent court cases have resulted in the conviction of persons who have taken power-driven trail vehicles into national forest wilderness units.

There are persistent demands that helicopters, snow vehicles, and other mechanized equipment be used extensively in national forest wilderness for mineralogical studies by private mining companies, the Bureau of Mines, and the Geological Survey. Agencies and private groups concerned with water yield and snow measurements in high, back-country areas also have asked for exceptions to the law. These must be strongly resisted by the administering agencies and by the public. Both the Forest Service and the Park Service have shown aggressive leadership in meeting these threats, and the Forest Service is setting a good example by avoiding use of such equipment in its maintenance and everyday work in dedicated wilderness lands.

Another major threat to the National Wilderness Preservation System is posed by the Kennecott Copper Company's plans to develop an extensive open-pit copper mine on Miner's Ridge within the scenic heartland of the Glacier Peak Wilderness Area in Washington. This operation, on lands patented before passage of the Wilderness Act, would result in construction of fifteen miles of road and a processing mill within the wilderness area's boundaries. The mill's operation would cause serious pollution of Miner's Creek, Canyon Creek, and the Suiattle River, causing loss of the native trout fishery and other stream values.

This problem stems from the unsuccessful fight by congressional sponsors of the wilderness bill to eliminate all mining activity from national forest wilderness. Section 4(d)(2) permits prospecting, mining, and oil and gas development for nineteen years (through December 31, 1983) in the wilderness lands of the national forests. During this period, these lands remain open to the intrusions of mining development, and thereafter on valid mining claims and patented lands where rights are established before January 1, 1984. Prospecting and mining are subject to regulations of the Department of Agriculture that implement the act's requirement that mining operations be conducted in a manner consistent with the protection of the wilderness character of the land.

These regulations should be tightened to prevent damage to already-designated wilderness areas and to the primitive areas which are undergoing review. The Department of Agriculture has made significant strides in this direction through stipulations designed to control both mining and prospecting in the national forest wilderness. The efforts of the department and the Forest Service to prevent damage to the Glacier Peak Wilderness Area from the Kennecott Copper Company's proposed operations will serve as a revealing test of the operation of the wilderness law and the departmental regulations. If these efforts to protect the wilderness fail, there will remain but one recourse for conservationists and congressional sponsors of the Wilderness Act: to work for the amendment of the wilderness law by deletion of its section-four provisions that permit mineral prospecting and mineral development on lands of the National Wilderness Preservation System.

The act is explicit, through its references to national forest wilderness areas and national forest lands, in providing authorization of such mineral exploration activities *only* upon the wilderness of national forests. There is no provision in the act for such activity within the national park or wildlife refuge systems.

This requirement, as it has been applied to the primitive areas of the national forests, has resulted in major complications in the scheduling of reviews and public hearings. The Forest Service has requested completion of survey reports on each primitive area by the Bureau of

Mines and the Geological Survey in time for the agency's public hearings on the proposals to add these areas to the National Wilderness System. These reports are to be submitted to Congress by the President together with his recommendations and the complete public hearing record. The possibility exists that some of the national forest primitive areas will be found to contain mineral deposits that could profitably be developed. The Forest Service must be given strong support in its efforts to control these activities and to restrict survey teams to the use of equipment and techniques that are in keeping with the requirements of the law.

Although the mineral survey and mining provisions of the act clearly indicate that mineral surveys were to be confined to national forest wilderness lands, the Secretary of the Interior issued an order (No. 2893) on February 17, 1966, specifying that mineral study data, as developed by the Geological Survey and the Bureau of Mines, relative to minerals locatable under the mining laws, shall be taken into account in National Park Service reviews of four major wilderness units: Mt. McKinley National Park, Death Valley National Monument, Glacier Bay National Monument, and Organ Pipe Cactus National Monument.

The secretarial order also requires the Geological Survey and the Bureau of Mines to provide mineral study data on classes of minerals subject to location under the mining laws in connection with reviews of the Cabeza Prieta Game Range in Arizona (unwithdrawn portion), the Charles M. Russell National Wildlife Range in Montana, the Charles Sheldon Antelope Range in Nevada (unwithdrawn portion), and the Kofa Game Range in Arizona; and on classes of minerals subject to leasing under the mineral leasing laws in connection with reviews of areas in *all wildlife refuges and game ranges.*

The effect of the secretarial order is to open wildlife refuge and park system areas to mineralogical surveys. This was not contemplated in the act. Unless this order is rescinded or greatly modified, the Wilderness Act will become the vehicle for mineralogical studies and will threaten the integrity of both the national park system and the national wildlife refuges and game ranges. The intent of the act will have been perverted.

The fact that continued mineral exploitation in some park or refuge areas was permitted at the time these areas were established does not mean that the government must undertake the burden of aiding the miners to make discoveries. Public policy has already established that these areas are predominantly valuable for other purposes.

Publicly owned wilderness lands must be regarded as the very last resort for mineral exploitation—and then only in time of a national emergency. There is provision in the act for such a declaration of emergency. These areas are not to serve merely as a reserve for instant accommodation of a short-term need for adjustment of our import–export balance. They are far too valuable as wilderness to be bartered in such a manner.

The first proposal to reach Congress to add a new unit to the Wilderness System is the San Rafael Wilderness Area in California. The bill recommended by the President to be the instrument for accomplishment of this is a simple authorization for placement of the area into the system. Behind this proposal is the strongly supportive record of the November 8, 1965, hearing in Santa Barbara, California, which the law requires to be submitted to Congress. President Johnson, the Department of Agriculture, and the Forest Service have shown commendable leadership in advancing the San Rafael proposal so quickly.

The theme of this conference, "Wilderness and the Quality of American Life," reflects our concern that wilderness be recognized for the important contribution it makes to our society. We are increasingly encouraged by signs that people appreciate variety and quality in their recreational opportunities, and that they will abide a certain amount of regulation for the sake of protecting fragile wilderness lands, even from themselves. Through our programs we can inform more people and encourage their participation in wilderness studies and hearings. We are confident that the people want firmly protected wilderness.

This is the great and present challenge of our work. The world of the distant future will not know our names. But if we can preserve substantial stretches of the land as it was given to us, they will know we did it for them—not primarily for a pleasuring ground, and not certainly for subsistence, but for the special quality it can contribute to living.

It is the legacy we can leave to the future. The preservation of some land unchanged, alongside the miracles of technology, is a clear token of our faith in the future, and of our conviction that the wilderness will be prized more highly with each passing decade.

FROM THE FRIDAY MORNING DISCUSSION

Moderator Phillip S. Berry: Mr. Brandborg touched upon one worry we have because the Wilderness Act provides for a nineteen-year period during which mining claims can still be patented in primitive areas, that period ending on the stroke of midnight, December 31, 1983. Having had revealed to me by George Orwell's famous book, *1984*, the horrors that will descend upon us the next year, I took heart when I first read the act that at least mining explorations in our wilderness areas will have ceased by the time Big Brother starts watching us in 1984. The act can and should be amended to cut shorter the nineteen-year period during which explorations can continue.

J. Michael McCloskey: All the speakers today have said things we can applaud. Chief Cliff gave us reason for hope when he announced that, to date, the Forest Service's reclassification proposals provide a 25 per cent aggregate increase in the size of primitive areas. Also heartening to hear are his comments about the strictness with which the service plans to administer wilderness areas so as to exclude motorized equipment.

In turn, we can look forward to the cooperative training program for wilderness use in the national parks that George Hartzog proposes. And I think we are all grateful now for the opportunity to participate more actively in the planning process for national parks.

Noble Buell, too, said something very important when he mentioned that the Bureau of Sport Fisheries and Wildlife hopes to withdraw portions of refuges that are zoned for wilderness from entry under the mining laws.

With all the things that we can applaud in these presentations, however, some basic differences in perspective have emerged. In two of the presentations particularly, a perspective was evident that contrasts sharply with that of the other. Two of the speakers expressed special concern over lowering standards for what is put into the wilderness system. These speakers were the Chief of the United States Forest Service and the Director of the National Park Service.

From the point of view of the Sierra Club, we should certainly characterize the problem differently. It has appeared to us that some of the proposals from these two agencies have failed to extend wilderness protection to areas that are qualified. Depending on your point of view, then, standards are either being lowered or an agency is failing to pursue the opportunities that the act presents. I think this difference in perspective may stem from two basic differences in premise.

First, wilderness conservationists look at the fact that only 2 per cent of the country still retains its character as wilderness—actually, even less. In passing the Wilderness Act, Congress established a wilderness system, as the opening section states, "In order to assure that an increasing population, accompanied by expanding settlement and growing mechanization, does not occupy and modify all areas within the United States and its possessions, leaving no lands designated for preservation and protection in their natural condition."

The legislative history clearly shows that there was immense national concern about the shrinkage of unroaded land units to a mere 2 per cent of the country's surface. Basically the reviews were designed to allow the three agencies to sort out the spots that were already developed, with the goal of trying to protect as much as possible of the remaining wilderness. In other words, conservationists believe Congress intended to preserve most of the residuum of wilderness and that the reviews were to be merely technical surveys to identify precisely which areas are still free of development. The reviewing agencies, however, seem to still feel that the burden of their task is to find which limited parts of the 2 per cent residue have their highest public value as wilderness. The agencies, thus, foresee that much less than 2 per cent will be saved as wilderness.

A second difference exists over the question of what kind of a legislative tool the Wilderness Act is. Conservationists believe passage of the act marks a transition from a stage in which wilderness was essentially a very subjective idea, a stage in which the sense of wilderness was purely a matter of individual taste and—everyone could put forth his own definition. Now wilderness must be viewed in an institutional sense. As an expression of governmental policy, the statute sets the guidelines—the parameters for what will be done. We have to look to the act itself, eliminating, as much as possible, subjective variations in judgment on what a wilderness experience is for one man in contrast to another man. The agencies' task, we believe, is to look at certain specified categories of their holdings and the yardsticks the act sets forth, and to measure their holdings against what the act says. Admittedly it is a complex and, in some respects, an ambiguous legislative vehicle. Basically, though it is a statutory zoning device. Recognizing the complexity of its varying provisions, we must view the act as a whole as it applies to the total pattern of agency holdings. By such examination, we can easily conclude that there is no stereotype of the kind of lands eligible for the system. They are not limited to alpine scenery or to forest scenery. In a given unit of a national park, the wilderness does not stop where the glaciated bowl ends; it does not stop where the forest ends. The act speaks of undeveloped lands, of roadless lands. The character of wilderness itself is the main criterion (but it, too, is subject to certain modification).

The criterion of size has also been changed by the act. We used to think of wilderness in very expansive terms, as consisting of tremendous areas that would take many days to walk across. But with the concept of institutional wilderness, we now find wilderness proposals in the refuge system for units as small as one-acre islands. In these tiny tracts, we are looking just at the degree of wildness of the area in question. It seems a great anomaly to be urging protection of wilderness on one-acre islands in the refuge system when some wild units of thousands of acres in the national parks or national forests are not regarded as candidate areas at all. They are roadless; they are undeveloped. What sense does it make to exclude such units from the wilderness system when they involve park or forest lands, but to include them when refuge lands are involved?

When we come to the present condition of candidate areas, we also face a varied pattern. Certainly we have some nearly unimpaired areas, but others have histories of extensive alteration. When we look at sections of the act that spell out the qualifications, the specific language speaks in terms of an area as a whole appearing to be generally unmodified, with the marks of man being substantially unnoticeable. The act admits that there can have been some disturbances in the past. I think Noble Buell was very clear in recognizing these facts.

In the administrative sections of the act a great variation exists, too, in the amount of protection provided. Mining is allowed for nineteen more years; the President can admit water projects to the areas; grazing can continue. The ban on motorized equipment and on construction of structures and installations is subject to certain exceptions for administrative use.

A very mixed pattern emerges. Looking at all these things together, it seems to us that the era has passed when it should be a matter of somebody's subjective judgment to say this area is now pure enough to be admitted to the wilderness system. We think we have to take an objective look at the act. It must be construed specifically as a legal document; what does it allow in terms of the qualifying section? It does allow certain disturbances, including a past history of disturbance. All it requires is that an area should currently appear to be substantially unmodified. Does the area pass that test? Once a unit is in the system, with whatever limitations it possesses, the task of administrators is to give it the best protection the law allows. With this approach we can come close to protecting most of the 2 per cent of this country that Congress felt might qualify as wilderness.

As these hearings progress and as opportunities for discussion occur, I hope that we can reach agreement with the agencies over these questions of fundamental premise. The public support expressed at the hearings shows how deeply people feel about the problems implicit in these premises. The six thousand letters supporting wilderness status for New Jersey's Great Swamp are clear evidence of their feeling. This outpouring was for an area of two thousand acres—smaller than the five-thousand-acre minimum suggested in the act. The thousands of letters in support of wilderness in Great Smoky Mountains National Park also show how people feel. The attention people are giving to one-acre and twenty-acre units show this, too. The Wilderness Act, rather than being regarded as an indictment of past management, should be looked upon as an opportunity to provide the American people with the kind of system they contemplated the Wilderness Act would give them.

In conclusion, I should like to say we appreciate the outstanding leadership that Stewart Brandborg has been giving us as Executive Director of the Wilderness Society. The pace of wilderness hearings has been extremely demanding—twelve hearings are taking place in this month alone. This may be the most demanding month we will face. The society has kept us abreast of the schedule for these hearings. The agencies, too, have been issuing very helpful brochures. But it is Stewart and his staff who have been keeping the entire picture before us. If we get through all this successfully, it will be largely because of his leadership. I hope that we can cooperate with increasing effectiveness.

Anthony Wayne Smith: It is a great privilege to take part in these very important sessions. These Wilderness Conferences have become a vital and well-established institution in American life.

The National Parks Association is concerned primarily with the protection of the great primeval parks of America; hence it is first of all a wilderness protection organization.

Wilderness protection is a pro-people policy. People need wilderness experience for complete growth as mature persons; they also need the continuing awareness of wilderness as background of civilized life.

We hear the expression that parks are for people. Nobody argues that they are not for people; people need very greatly, very deeply, the kind of thing that wilderness in the parks, in the forests, in the wildlife refuges and outside them, can provide. It is unfortunate to approach the problem with the implication of people *vs.* parks. I think it is highly desirable to drop this kind of language. It would also be desirable to drop references to the European baronial society. We have not had anything of this kind in America at any time, and there is always the suggestion carried in such references that when use by heavy crowds is to be restricted perhaps somehow this is a baronial policy. We have to be very careful not to make that suggestion.

As the destructive impact upon the environment of urbanization and so-called development is felt more keenly, as population and mobility grow, the preservation of wilderness—whether mountain, forest, stream, valley, desert, subterranean cave, estuarial, littoral, or maritime —grows greatly in importance.

Wilderness is both symbol and experience of liberty. The concern Americans feel for it reaches back through our family memories to the frontier; it was the open frontier, and beyond it the wilderness, that gave birth to our free institutions. A nation professing democratic principles must preserve its wilderness for the experience of liberty and freedom it affords.

Wilderness in the great national parks, national forests, and wildlife refuges provides a refuge for people from the traffic, the streets, and the sprawling subdivisions. It also provides refuge for the world's endangered and vanishing wildlife.

With reference to the national park system, the National Park Service Act of 1916 specifies a priority in favor of the protection of the parks in natural condition; use and visitation are to be compatible with protection. The National Park Service Act is not a dual purpose act with protection and visitation on an equal footing; the act is primarily protective, and provides only secondarily for visitation, for otherwise visitation would be self-defeating.

And yet our public land management policies must of necessity provide not only for protection, but also for the enjoyment of the vast regions of open country available for that purpose.

There is no incompatibility here if planning is done in a big way. If we try to plan small, crowding both protection and visitation into the relatively small areas of our national parks, we are lost. There need be no difficulty if we plan big, putting emphasis on protection in the parks and on the dispersion of crowds into the much larger areas of our national forests, the public lands, the recreation areas, the reservoir areas, the soil-conservation regions, the state and local forests and parks, and into the privately owned land on the periphery of the public holdings.

The machinery for this comprehensive regional planning already exists. The Bureau of Outdoor Recreation has a statutory mandate to develop a national recreation plan, hence of necessity component regional plans; it has authority to recommend plans to the various bureaus; it has authority to require good planning by the states and localities receiving funds from the federal government.

The President's Council on Recreation and Natural Beauty has authority by Executive order to draw up standards for such planning; the Bureau of Outdoor Recreation is attached to the President's Council by Executive order; hence, the BOR is in a position to further a regional planning and crowd-dispersion program. The President's Council has adopted a practice of setting standards and making them binding on the various departments by signed agreements; this procedure should be utilized in regional planning.

I am a little surprised that the Director of the Bureau of Outdoor Recreation is not on this platform today,* because his bureau and the President's Council on Recreation and Natural Beauty hold the key to the kind of regional planning we must have if the wilderness in national parks, national forests, and wildlife refuges is to be protected. Only by comprehensive planning can we disperse the crowds that are otherwise going to destroy the very reasons for which they come.

This approach to the protection of wilderness in the parks has the merit of great simplicity. It has widespread support among the conservation organizations; it seems to have no opposition. It has had considerable lip service from public officials; but unfortunately they have taken no noticeable action.

I am sorry to be the Cassandra at this meeting, but all is not well in planning for the protection of wilderness in the national parks. I have reported to the 35,000 members of the National Parks Association that we seem to be headed for the greatest disaster in conservation history; the disaster is imminent, a matter of a few weeks or months at best; it will occur with the final formulation of park wilderness hearings.

Practically all the official proposals for park wilderness protection have recommended relatively small wilderness areas and have pro-

* The Director of the Bureau of Outdoor Recreation was invited to make a presentation at the conference, but he declined because of other commitments.— *The Editors.*

vided for visitor areas, euphemistically known as threshold areas, within which increasing crowds can be accommodated in years ahead. It makes no difference at all to say that these Class III areas will not be used for development of facilities. If they are not to be used for that purpose, then let them be protected as wilderness. Leading conservation organizations propose instead that wilderness units in the parks comprise essentially all present roadless areas and that buffer zones and facility areas, including heavy-use campgrounds, be placed outside the parks.

The National Parks Association has submitted detailed plans in hearings on the following units of the national park system: Great Smokies, Isle Royale, Pinnacles, Sequoia–Kings Canyon, Lassen Volcanic, Craters of the Moon, and Lava Beds, and without reference to hearings, Yellowstone. We have prepared maps showing the large surrounding regions into which crowds could be dispersed, and we have suggested efficient ways of doing so. We have also shown that well-planned, privately operated vacation businesses could be encouraged in specified commmunities in the vicinity; such resorts would be encouraged by assurances from the government against overdevelopment in the parks.

We have suggested referral stations on incoming highways to help people with advice and reservations for campgrounds in the national forests or on private land instead of in the crowded hearts of parks.

We have suggested the use of public conveyances for transporting visitors into the parks from outside resorts, thus replacing the private car. Small walk-in minibuses in central areas in parks like Giant Forest in Sequoia–Kings Canyon or the Geyser area of Yellowstone would also protect people from traffic.

The disaster consists in the fact that the parks are about to be subdivided into small wilderness areas and large facility areas. Such subdivision would, in our judgment, violate the policies of the National Park Service Act. If the subdivision is to be done on a theory of justification by that act, it would constitute, in effect, an administrative amendment of the act, and would be an administrative revision of a century of public policy governing national parks. The Wilderness Act of 1964 will have been used as the instrument of such amendment and revision; this was most certainly not the intention of the authors of the Wilderness Act.

What is needed is a modicum of courage and strength in the executive branch of the federal government. The solutions for the problem of protection on the one hand and visitation and enjoyment on the other hand are available; they are uncomplicated; they are self-explanatory. A strange paralysis hangs over the agencies responsible for the protection of the trail and campfire country that more and more Americans value more and more highly.

It ought not to be necessary for the President of the United States to take a hand in getting the proper executive policies applied; but the present hesitation and irresolution mean a drift toward catastrophe. The President may well have to step in personally to get things moving vigorously in the right direction.

George B. Hartzog, Jr.: There is really not a great deal of difference among the concepts we all espouse. There is, however, a great deal of conversation about our approach to their implementation. Let me say at the outset that the National Park Service subscribes to joint planning. As a matter of fact, we have been in regional planning for quite a long time. Many of the distinguished people that I see in the audience are retired park superintendents, like Eivind Scoyen, and retired forest supervisors, who have worked hand in hand over many years on joint planning. I have already mentioned the joint effort of the Forest Service and Sequoia–Kings Canyon National Park that restored the park to a wilderness condition.

Secretary Udall announced my appointment as Director of the National Park Service at Yosemite National Park in the fall of 1963. My first official act was to call Ed Cliff, who has been a long-time personal friend since before either of us became an agency head, and asked for a meeting of regional directors and regional foresters to discuss a program that would utilize the potential for recreation in the great national forests surrounding so many of our national parks. That meeting took place in 1964, and ever since we have formalized the informal efforts of our superintendents and our supervisors on planning region-wide needs.

To say this, however, is not to say that planning for uses of the national parks excludes people, because people are a part of the park environment. The problem at the very heart of conservation today is that for too long we have looked at conservation issues as separate and apart from man. It is only when you put man in the scene, in my judgment, that you achieve the objectives of conservation. When we talk in terms of "parks for people," we specifically say that parks cannot be all things to all people for all time everywhere. And it is for this reason that Ed Cliff and I started the joint programs at Mount Rainier, Yellowstone, and Grand Teton National Parks.

I agree that the national parks should not be filled with subdivisions. But let me share one thing with you: Yosemite and Sequoia are becoming subdivisions, and Olympic and all other parks containing privately owned land are going to become subdivisions. This will happen so long as the directive from the Appropriations Committees of Congress continues to exist saying priorities shall be given to the purchase of lands in newly established areas, meaning—in terms of time—those authorized since 1961.

Now, in my judgment, one of the most serious issues facing park preservation today is not people, is not traffic, but is private holdings within national parks. I have in my notebook details of an issue involving an area of some 850 acres, of which the government owns about 450, and of which 450 people own the remaining 350 acres. Now that is a subdivision, and it has all the inherent problems of subdivisions: garbage disposal, sewage, and everything else. So the emphasis in terms of priority is first to get our parklands allocated to public park purposes. If, when we finish wilderness classification, we still have subdivisions in parks, we defeat the very purpose for which the national parks were established.

Let me express one more strongly held opinion. The national park concept is the antithesis of the historic European concept of parks. It is absolutely essential to understand this in order to understand our national parks. To say otherwise is to ignore history. The national park concept, as expressed in the Yellowstone act, is the natural expression of free men in a democratic society reserving for all people—not just the few—these great natural preserves. Most of the people who came to this country came in large part because there was no possible opportunity for them to break out of the rigid class system of Europe and to own land.

The great westward-expansion epic in history—that molded and poured the foundation for the traditions that we call "the American way of life" today—was an extension of this restless search for land and a better life. And when the railroads began to crisscross the Great Plains, the railroad stations of Europe were plastered with posters advertising cheap land in America. Despite the lust for land—also called manifest destiny—men chose not to carve up all these superlative lands, but to preserve some as parklands from exploitation. If this is not to draw a sharp distinction between the baronial, feudal, aristocratic concepts of Europe and the concepts of free men in a free land, I don't know how else to explain it.

Dennis A. Rapp

SUMMARY

Much has been said about accomplishments to date and problems associated with the designation of candidate areas for addition to the National Wilderness Preservation System under procedures and guidelines set forth in the act. There appears to be tacit agreement that progress in the examination of these areas is satisfactory, measured in numbers of areas covered. The first years have been slow, but the normal delay associated with the get-ready, staff-up, and get-the-techniques-refined period in any new program accounts for most of this lag. Continued attention will apparently have to be given to obtaining adequate funds and personnel authorizations if the rates of examination specified by the act are to be realized. Considering some of the problems that have arisen so far, one might conclude that more staffing is necessary for the complex and intensive field work involved in boundary determination and area evaluation. Boundary setting, and criteria for boundary setting, seem to be the most prominent issues throughout the discussions.

Less has been said this morning about the programs and policies established for administration and regulation of the areas already in the system. All the panelists and discussants touched on some of the issues that have arisen or are likely to arise in the future. There is, of course, virtually unresolvable conflict built into the Wilderness Act itself. Those measures of the law designed to protect, preserve, and enhance the quality of wilderness, on the one hand, are intrinsically incompatible with those measures provided to guarantee the use of wilderness

53

areas for nonconforming purposes, most notably mining. Institutional arrangements short of changes in the law can perhaps be developed to minimize or eliminate the adverse effect of this conflict. Outright public purchase of valid mineral rights and properties within the system has been suggested as one solution. The people-management problem is, no doubt, the most difficult, and will probably become the most critical one as population pressures increase and a greater portion of the population seeks the attractive values wilderness offers. The National Park Service faces people-management problems in crisis proportions in many localities now. The developed areas within parks are becoming less attractive because of overcrowding, and the wilderness areas are, ironically, now facing the threat of overuse, and may, therefore, be the first to require a system of regulation or rationing.

To contemplate a change in the law that would remove its imperfections raises the prospect not only of years of effort and expense with slight hope of success, but also invites the risk of losing some ground already gained. To contemplate acceptable accommodations of existing and/or prospective nonconforming intrusion is, on the face of it, a bitter pill to swallow. The need for innovation in on-the-ground management practice and in developing institutional devices aimed at perpetuating a high-quality wilderness system is among the greatest challenges we face.

Whether the Secretary of the Interior has acted within the intent of the Wilderness Act by extending the mineral survey provisions of section 4(d)(2) to selected units of the national park system and to wildlife refuges and game ranges appears to be a legitimate legal question. It must be pointed out, however, that the act does not prohibit mineral surveys on these classes of federal lands. It was apparently the intent of Congress to review each proposed addition to the system on all its merits. One might ask, then, whether the best interests of expanding the system are served by recommending *any* new candidate area without first completing mineral surveys for each one.

The discussions of regional planning identify the complexities and difficulties involved in the planning process, and in producing a meaningful and comprehensive plan. The time frame is extensive. Once developed, such a plan is never current. And no workable, acceptable plan for such large areas can be formulated unilaterally; it must be developed through political interaction if it is to be even partially workable. Yet it seems wholly unsound to proceed with additions to the wilderness system without some consideration of the regional needs for land and resources and without some determination of the probable local–regional effect of the reservation of new areas. To create strong intergovernmental regional-planning arrangements directed at the development and maintenance of comprehensive land-use plans for both public and private land, supported by zoning, is a necessary and desirable goal. There seems to be agreement, however, that implementation of all provisions of the Wilderness Act cannot await either the launching or the completion of comprehensive planning. This fact adds emphasis to the need for more thorough study of new candidate areas, especially with regard to external effects on the region as a whole. Such study is insurance that the wilderness area, once established by law, can endure in the face of regional growth and change.

There is every likelihood that serious problems will continue to arise in the examination, selection, and setting of boundaries for new additions to the system under the ten-year schedule established by the act. As a result of this morning's discussions, I believe we have a better basis for understanding some of the major causes of these problems and the reasons disagreements arise. They start with the Wilderness Act. It imposes a new objective and a new public policy standard on different classes of federal lands already institutionalized and administered to serve other purposes. The concept and definition of wilderness set down in the act may not in theory be inconsistent with all the purposes for which these federal lands, or parts of them, have been administered. Sharp conflict occurs in many instances, however, when the concept is translated into operational procedures and when criteria for selecting wilderness candidates and drawing boundary lines around them are applied to specific landscape, relief, and ecology.

The law itself relates its wilderness purposes quite directly to existing policies and programs covering those classes of federal lands to which the Wilderness Act will be applied. In fact, it preserves the total integrity of other legal authorities applicable to the same lands. So there is a firm legal foundation for giving primacy to existing law and existing program objectives.

The reasons disagreements and difficulties arise in the selection and delimiting of new wilderness candidate areas in the national forest, national park, and refuge and game range systems are more apparent when these features of the law are kept in mind.

Take the question of whether unique features should be included or excluded for wilderness areas. It would seem unwise, indeed, if *all* those unique characteristics that qualify areas as national parks in the first place were to be included in new additions to the wilderness system. Then the works of men that were built to make these features accessible to people would have to be removed to conform to the wilderness standard. The probability is remote that the American public would tolerate the tearing up of the access roads to Old Faithful and the Paint Pots in Yellowstone National Park or the removal of the roadside vistas of Saint Mary's Peak and the Garden Wall in Glacier National Park. However, it has been persuasively argued that certain unique features in many of the parks, because of their fragile qualities, are best protected and appreciated in pristine and undisturbed surroundings and should, therefore, be included in units of the wilderness system.

This dilemma is as old as the national park system. It has plagued every Park Service director faced with the necessity of making the parks available to increasing numbers of people while sustaining park quality indefinitely. A requirement to furnish access so that the unique features of the parks would be available to the majority of Americans has been the dominant interpretation of the policy mandate contained in the act of 1916. Although it seems improbable that actions taken under this long-standing interpretation of policy will be reversed, the Wilderness Act presents a management mandate that could well be applied to new and to selected existing parks.

Although uniqueness is not a requisite to wilderness as it is defined by the Wilderness Act, this does not mean there is no place for it in the system. Certainly the primitive areas of the national forests, as well as the wild and wilderness areas already in the system, contain many unique geologic, scenic, biologic, and even historic features. These are equal in kind and quality to those found in many of our national parks. The policy choice must still be made in each case, however, as far as existing parks, new park candidates, and even new wilderness candidates are concerned. That choice is between the inclusion of unique features in the wilderness preservation system, with consequent restrictions on access to the majority of Americans in the future, or the omission of unique features from the wilderness system, thereby assuring greater opportunity of access to larger numbers of people. This is one of the major issues at the heart of the North Cascades controversy. Recent submission to Congress of a bill containing provision for a national park that would embrace some of the more striking scenic features of this area has the announced joint support of the Secretaries of Agriculture and the Interior. Should the bill become law in this form, it will be interesting to observe the degree of development introduced by the National Park Service.

The threshold classification employed by the Park Service in zoning a buffer to protect wilderness areas from the movements of large numbers of people in its Classes I and II areas appears to be a useful tool if each park is to be managed for both volume use and wilderness. An alternative might be to designate certain parks as wilderness parks in their entirety, while managing others for maximum user dispersion throughout the park regardless of the presence of potential wilderness. One thing is certain: bold new innovations in land-management techniques for various kinds of outdoor recreation are essential if our national parks are to endure as the showcases of our natural wonders.

I have every confidence that the American people will gladly accept strict rationing of use if they are faced with the unacceptable alternative of permanent deterioration of the parks and the unique experiences they can offer. The need for that rationing is here, now.

The institutional objectives of the Forest Service and the laws under which it works present quite a different problem in the setting of boundaries and inclusion of unique areas. The problems are virtually opposite those posed by the national parks in application of the Wilderness Act. By law the national forests are subject to a variety of uses, both economic and noneconomic. In order to plan for and allocate the resources of national forest lands among all possible purposes, a standard of uniqueness occurring in combination with pristine conditions would appear to offer the best guide to wilderness-area selection. In this respect we might even view the national parks and national forests as complementary to each other because they offer unique areas under two quite different sets of circumstances. Parks could provide convenient access to many special scenic features, and the national forests could encompass many such features within wilderness areas, accessible only by trail.

If the selection of wilderness areas within the national forests is made relatively easy by making uniqueness a condition, the problem in boundary setting is rendered much more difficult by the legal mandate for multiple use of these lands and by the absence of workable guidelines for consistent application of this concept on the ground. Many potential natural resource uses are incompatible with classic wilderness, such as timber harvesting, mining, and even various forms of outdoor recreation. In contrast to national park system areas in which many such uses are prohibited by law, the national forests are, by law, intended for and must be administered for these uses. Under this mandate, an area does not necessarily qualify for wilderness just because it is still wild.

There is much wild or near-wild land still in the national forest system that presents some alternative opportunity for both economic and noneconomic use. Development of these resources for regional economic growth and for meeting the rising national need for industrial raw materials is a long-standing and still legitimate goal of national forest administration.

Translated into new wilderness-candidate-selection and boundary-setting terms, these multiple goals pose hard choices, such as whether to remove large volumes of commercial-grade timber from the allowable cut base; whether to prohibit prospecting for and development of mineral resources; or whether to prohibit access roads, thus denying to larger numbers of people the opportunity to use areas for different forms of outdoor recreation.

The big challenge we face in the national forests is to prescribe the most efficient method for allocation of their resource base to different combinations of uses. The corollary challenge is to determine what combination of national forest uses best serves society's needs. The dimensions of these challenges are very difficult to define—and they pose innumerable abstract and difficult sets of subquestions. The answers lie not just in the landscape, but in the whole of society. Part of the answer is to be found in the market place, but part of it is also to be found in the ill-defined and changing fabric of our social culture. Still another part lies in the selection of the option available in order to structure arrangements for social and economic action through the political process. And yet another part depends on our knowing how to manipulate the land in order to obtain all we want from it. The need is urgent to achieve maximum efficiency in arranging patterns of land use that will yield the combination of economic and social products that serve society best at any one point in time, and over time.

It is clear that much of the boundary-setting dispute over the designation of wilderness areas in the national forest system arises from disagreement about best patterns of resource allocation and use. These disagreements are likely to continue. Settlements will continue to be less than satisfactory until more precise standards and vigorous processes are established and consistently applied. Standards must include methods for deciding between market and nonmarket uses of large areas of landscape. Processes must specify techniques for measuring and weighing opportunities suggested by the landscape in relation to the social and economic requirements to be satisfied by that landscape. This implies an extremely broad spectrum of considerations. It is obvious that the immediate landscape and the needs of the nearby population, as well as the interests of the distant population, must be part of the evaluation process in determining the management of our national forests.

The buffer or threshold zoning technique instituted by the National Park Service appears to offer useful applications in national forest management in general, and to wilderness-area designation within the national forests in particular. Because of the difficulty involved in wilderness boundary-setting posed by multiple-use options and requirements, boundaries should perhaps be established as broad zones rather than definite lines. Both economic and nonmarket activity occurring in these zones could be permitted under carefully controlled conditions aimed at minimizing environmental disturbances rather than eliminating them altogether.

If making parks available to people and if using national forests for economic as well as nonmarket purposes conflict with the purposes of the Wilderness Act, the primary purposes and management of our national wildlife refuge system probably offers the least conflict. Indeed, as Mr. Buell has suggested, certain of the refuges may even exceed the expectations of the wilderness lover. Some areas designated as wilderness within the refuge system may be inaccessible for even temporary visitation by man because of the overriding need to protect their wildlife inhabitants, particularly those species threatened with extinction by man's intrusion.

Nonconforming uses such as logging and livestock grazing are, nevertheless, permitted in many units of the refuge system when such uses are not inconsistent with the primary purposes of the refuge. Here, too, as in the case of the national forests, we face the need for a more precise criterion in deciding the most efficient allocation of resources to meet a variety of social and economic needs.

Perhaps the most subtle dilemma of the wilderness concept will become apparent first in those areas within the refuges that are brought into the wilderness system. If the ecology of a refuge is to be maintained in a state suitable for sustaining its wildlife populations, that ecosystem must be actively managed or its character will be changed by natural forces. When this occurs, the values of the area to wildlife will be diminished, and the natural environment itself will have been modified. How much acceptable natural modification of the environment can be tolerated in wilderness areas?

In summary, it is clear that imposition of the Wilderness Act standards on national parks, national forests, and refuge system lands that have been administered and managed under laws designed to meet other public objectives has raised different kinds of problems peculiar to each of these classes of federal lands. While the Wilderness Act sets new standards, the obligation to adhere to the policy mandates of pre-existing management laws still exists. Persistent conflict will ultimately be eliminated by adjustment of administration and development of better management techniques, or by changing the laws.

Whether, in fact, the accumulation of nearly two hundred years of public land policy reflects the needs and values of our modern society as it anticipates the twenty-first century is the question the Public Land Law Review Commission is asking as it proceeds with its charter. That charter is to review the laws, rules, regulations, and practices that govern the administration of the public lands, and to recommend to the President and Congress such modifications or changes in them as will assure that the public lands are retained, managed, or disposed of, in a manner that will achieve the maximum benefit for the general public. The commission is temporary; it is bipartisan and has membership from both the Congress and appointments by the President; it was created by law in 1964 and is due to report at the end of 1968.*

The commission has begun its work by undertaking a series of thirty-four specified contract and staff studies using techniques that will, collectively, produce a sweeping, in-depth description and analysis of (1) the statutes; (2) the legislative background and administrative promulgation of the law; (3) the quantity and quality of the public land resources; and (4) the specific features of the economic, social, and political structures of today as they compare with those reflected in the current law and its administration.

The questions of law and of conflicts between laws that have been raised here this morning will be part of these studies and the deliberations to follow.

Relationships between market and nonmarket uses of the land and the dynamics of their changing importance to our economic and social requirements are an integral part of the studies. The specific methods now employed to allocate individual goods and services of the land to private and public groups will be explored in detail. Criteria and procedures to be followed are of special concern in determining the quality and quantity of different goods and services to be produced from each tract and all tracts of land. Study titles like Regional and Local Land Use Planning, Economic Impacts, Environmental Quality and Ecological Factors, Payments in Lieu of Taxes and Revenue Sharing, and Land Grants to States, describe still other major areas of comprehensive policy analysis being undertaken by the commission.

It remains to be seen whether the commission can, in this relatively short period, produce a definitive report that will come to grips with the hundreds of procedural and substantive minutiae, and with the scores of broad philosophical subjects that constitute the tangled maze of public land policy. The vast array of economic, political, and social issues that the subject encompasses is overwhelming to contemplate.

The larger question is whether an affluent society, concerned with contemporary urban and international problems, is ready to face this emotionally charged subject with level-headed reasoning and to agree on a sorely needed foundation for a new public land policy.

It is significant and timely that this morning's discussion has been concerned with a law that ushered in a whole new era in natural resources policy and helped to write the prologue to an overhaul of our public land laws.

* The life of the Public Land Law Review Commission was extended by the 90th Cong., 1st Sess. (1967), to June 30, 1970.

While the United States declared its political independence in 1776, it was not until the 1830's that American art freed itself from the domination of English and European tastes and standards. The change was signalized by the Catskill paintings of Thomas Cole and extended by him, Albert Bierstadt, Frederic E. Church, Thomas Moran and others. They turned from traditional old world subjects and painted the rough beauty and uniqueness of the wilderness for their concern was the splendor of the American Earth. Americans should be grateful, Thomas Cole stated, that God, not man, had marked their landscape, making it ideal for "the contemplation of eternal things."

Landscape with Dead Trees by Thomas Cole.
Museum of Art, Rhode Island School of Design.

" . . . the raw, unkempt power of wilderness
with symbols such as ·
the shattered tree trunks
and surging storm clouds."

Course of Empire I: Savage State by Thomas Cole.
Courtesy of The New York Historical Society.

"The Savage State, the first of
a series of five canvases
which gave a dramatic explication
of the meaning of wilderness
for American civilization."

Landscape, Mount Katahdin by Frederic E. Church.
Addison Gallery of American Art, Phillips Academy, Andover, Massachusetts;
Gift of Mr. Winslow Ames in memory of Edward W. Ames.

"The crucial experience in
Church's development as an artist
was an 1856 camping trip of eight days
into the Mt. Katahdin region
of northern Maine."

A *Wilderness Lake* by Albert Bierstadt.
Smith College Museum of Art. Given by Mrs. John Stewart Dalrymple.

"Within a few years of his first visit
to the Rocky Mountains in 1858,
Albert Bierstadt was busy depicting
their peaks, canyons, and lakes
on gigantic canvases measuring up to
eighty-four square feet."

The Yosemite Valley by Albert Bierstadt.
Courtesy of Wadsworth Atheneum, Hartford, Connecticut.

"While Cole and Church painted
wildernesses of the East,
subsequent American landscape artists
took their palettes and their
national pride across the Mississippi.
In the American West
they found ideal subjects for both."

Lake Tahoe, California by Albert Bierstadt.
Courtesy of Museum of Fine Arts, Boston. M. and M. Karolik Collection.

"Bierstadt's exaggerated, dramatic style . . .
represented a sincere attempt to
express his awe and delight
in the American wilderness."

Grand Canyon, 1912 by Thomas Moran.

" . . . Moran accepted the challenge
of capturing the size and color
of the Grand Canyon of the Colorado."

 *Part Two*

The Contribution
of Wilderness to
American Life

THE CULTURAL SIGNIFICANCE OF
THE AMERICAN WILDERNESS
Roderick Nash

WILDERNESS: ECONOMIC CHOICE, VALUES,
AND THE ANDROSCOGGIN
Lawrence G. Hines

NOTES FROM A WILDERNESS LAYMAN
Rudolph W. Gilbert

DISCUSSION
Sigurd F. Olson and Adan Treganza

Peggy Wayburn, Moderator

The primary justification for the withdrawal of about 2 per cent of the nation's land area in wilderness reserves—without roads and commercial development—lies in the cultural, scientific, and recreational values these areas hold for Americans. In this session, important social, historical, and economic implications of wilderness in this country will be discussed.

Peggy Wayburn

INTRODUCTION

"The Contribution of Wilderness to American Life" is, on the face of it, a very big subject, but it has even more profound meaning than appears at first glance. At an earlier conference, Dr. John B. deC. M. Saunders said, "The nature of the land has always been a dominating force on its people." Certainly nowhere has this been more true than in America. The nature of the American land was wilderness, perhaps the richest wilderness of all time. And this wilderness provided not only the raw material for extraordinary economic development, but from the beginning it was the dominating force that shaped our political, social, and cultural life, and our very character.

The settlers who came to the New World brought with them a culture that was centuries old. While some of them were renegades, some seeking escape from the old ways or seeking new freedom, few of them expected or wanted to make drastic changes in their traditional way of life. Once they were in the wilderness environment, however, what the historian Oscar Handlin calls the "alchemy of wilderness" started to work on them.

On the frontier, independent men—beholden to none but one another—gradually evolved laws on their own authority to fit their needs. Handlin says our democratic government was literally shaped in the wilderness.

The wilderness soon made obsolete and alien the old ideas of rank, caste, and inherited aristocracy. These meant little in a frontier world where a man was what he was. He had a chance to prove himself.

63

Common man could be uncommon man. The idea of men's equality—long an ideal—became valid and practical. Along with it was joined the principle of freedom, proved in our wilderness as it had not been for centuries on the civilized continent of Europe. And so the concepts of grass roots democracy, of equality, and of freedom were incorporated into our Constitution.

Wilderness also shaped the American character, the cultural and social ideal that came about early in our history and still persists today. To survive and succeed in the wilderness, men had to be rugged individualists. They had to be tough, strong, and self-sufficient, courageous and resourceful—sometimes ruthless and too often destructive. Frederick Jackson Turner wrote: "The American character did not spring full-blown from the *Mayflower*. It came out of the forests and gained new strength each time it touched a new frontier."

Harold Gilliam, the San Francisco writer, puts it this way: "The wilderness presented a continuous series of new challenges, stimulating new responses, and it was there that Americans honed to a keen edge the frontier qualities of ingenuity, pragmatic imagination, and indomitable resourcefulness."

Of course these qualities were employed largely in exploring and exploiting the fabulous resources of the American wilderness. In the beginning, the pioneers were humble before the great forests, mountains, and plains. The limitless reaches of land were nearly overwhelming; there were so few men, scattered and vulnerable. But the roles were soon reversed. The men found they could tame the wilderness and tame it they did, with a speed and alacrity unmatched in all history. Today, scarcely two centuries later, only a scrap of our wilderness is left, and that is at our mercy.

It was the bounty of wilderness that made us the wealthiest people on earth, and its seeming boundlessness that helped make us the most profligate. Along with wealth and a disregard of waste, the great wilderness also fixed a kind of national optimism in the American character—there always seemed to be a new chance to strike it rich, a new opportunity waiting over the hill, a happy ending if you just kept looking. In using our wilderness resources, we have developed another unique facet of our American way of life—a dynamic society of change. We are always on the move, constantly altering our environment. We have gone from frontier to frontier, from idea to idea, from dream to success. We call this progress, and our wilderness has made it possible.

From the beginning there have been some Americans who valued the wilderness for its beauty alone. But to most, the dollar signs were bigger than the beauty. Not until the late nineteenth century—with

Thoreau, Muir, and later Teddy Roosevelt, raising their voices—did the appreciation of wilderness as a scenic resource gain impetus. More recently, the conservation of man's environment along with the conservation of his natural resources has become a recognized concept and ideal. Congress finally accorded wilderness a formal importance by passing the Wilderness Act of 1964, setting aside some 2 per cent of the land in protected wilderness status.

Wilderness, then, has made an almost immeasurable contribution to our American life. Various important aspects of that contribution will be discussed by our distinguished speakers this afternoon, who promise to bring you some highly interesting and valuable points of view.

Roderick Nash

THE CULTURAL SIGNIFICANCE
OF THE AMERICAN WILDERNESS*

Contrary to what professors of American history teach in their class-
rooms, victory over the British at Yorktown in 1781 and the subsequent signing of the Treaty of Paris did not really establish American
independence. Politically, the United States might be a nation, but
most of its citizens realized that true nationhood entailed more than
mere separation. The new republic had to demonstrate its capacity for
defense, government, and economic self-sufficiency. In addition there
was a cultural or intellectual requirement for independence. Eighteenth century philosophers of romantic nationalism made it clear that
every bona fide nation had a unique *Geist*, or spirit, manifested in its
art, literature, and the character of its people. This distinctiveness
formed the basis of national pride. If the upstart United States could
not demonstrate such cultural uniqueness, its claim to nationhood was
open to question, as was the validity of the American Revolution.

Almost desperately, as a consequence, Americans sought sustenance
for their national ego. They needed something valuable and distinctive
that could transform embarrassed provincials into proud and confident
citizens. But difficulties appeared at once. Our short history, shallow
traditions, and minor cultural accomplishments seemed paltry, espe-

* Dr. Nash's speech was illustrated with color slides of the paintings he discussed.
The section of color plates, following page 60, contains most of these paintings.—
The Editors.

66

cially in comparison to Europe's. For decades after the Revolution this realization frustrated American art and letters, branding it with imitation and self-pity. But gradually cultural nationalists began to sense that in one respect their country *was* different: nature in the New World had no counterpart in the Old. Specifically, it was *wilder*. Seizing on this distinction and adding to it newly minted assumptions about the aesthetic, religious, and romantic significance of wilderness, eager American patriots argued that far from being a liability to culture, as was traditionally assumed, wilderness was actually a cultural asset. To be sure, most Americans of the early national period continued to relish the destruction of wilderness, but recognition of its cultural significance had a major role in changing their attitude to appreciation of it.

As Americans explored the meaning of wilderness as a cultural resource, several reasons for pride came to light. Some argued that proximity to the wild sublimity of the American landscape would inspire artists and poets to great achievements. Wilderness, moreover, would furnish the subject matter for American art and letters: European models could be thrust aside and native creativity released. Others contended that if pure nature was the medium through which God spoke most clearly, then America with its abundance of wilderness had a distinct moral advantage over the Old World where centuries of civilization had deposited layers of artificiality on God's works. Another line of argument held that a wilderness environment produced a distinctive and desirable national character. The American, it was widely thought or, at least, hoped, combined the best of savagery and civilization into a kind of superman superior to both the Indian, on the one hand, and the European on the other.

With these ideas providing the intellectual foundation, Americans, in the anxious early years of their republic, turned repeatedly to wilderness as a source of pride. A number of illustrated "scenery" albums, for instance, made clear the link between nationalism and nature. As early as 1820, plans were made for a volume entitled *Picturesque Views of the American Scene* that would show "our lofty mountains . . . the unexampled magnitude of our cataracts, the wild grandeur of our western forests . . . unsurpassed by any of the boasted scenery of other countries." As romantic interest in nature increased in the following decades, there were numerous similar ventures.

Nathaniel P. Willis' text for *American Scenery* of 1840 was typical with its assertion that "Nature has wrought with a bolder hand in America." According to Willis, the native wilderness presented "a lavish and large-featured sublimity . . . quite dissimilar to the picturesque of all other countries." In 1852 came Elias L. Magoon's *The*

Home Book of the Picturesque, with an expression of gratitude to God "that there are yet wild spots and wildernesses left . . . whence thought may take the wildest range." Such places, Magoon believed, "have ever developed the strongest patriotism, intensest energy, and most valuable letters of the world."

Most of these albums followed a predictable format, beginning with an introductory essay defending the American landscape as being "as wild, romantic, and lovely as can be seen in any other part of the world." "And, certainly, our forests," this nationalist continued, "fresh, as it were, from the hands of the Creator, are, beyond dispute, incomparable." In 1872, William Cullen Bryant emphasized the same theme when he declared in *Picturesque America* that "we have some of the wildest and most beautiful scenery in the world." Why travel to the Alps, Bryant wondered, when there was an abundance of spectacular, wild mountains in the American West. In this idea the "see America first" concept had its birth, and it was the American wilderness that was to be seen.

Sometimes the American defense of the glories of the native landscape became impassioned. Tired of hearing Europe's claim to scenic beauty extolled, one patriot cried in 1847: "A fig for your Italian scenery! This is the country where nature reigns in her virgin beauty . . . this is the land to . . . feel your soul expand under the mighty influences of nature in her primitive beauty and strength!" Again wilderness was the nationalists' trump.

Horace Greeley, the long-time editor of the New York *Tribune*, was one of the earliest of a succession of American travelers whose European tours made them aware of their country's good fortune in having wilderness. Approaching London in 1851, Greeley contrasted the treeless English countryside with "the glorious magnificence and beauty of [our] . . . still unscathed forests . . . which I had long ago rejoiced in, but which I never before prized so highly." Greeley went from this sentiment to one of the first calls for preservation of the American wilderness. "Friends at home!" the 1851 *Glances at Europe* continued, "I charge you to spare, preserve and cherish some portion of our primitive forests; for when these are cut away I apprehend they will not easily be replaced."

Although actual cultural achievement fell short of what the nationalists hoped, it is still true that much of what was distinctively American in our early arts and letters utilized wilderness. James Kirke Paulding's 1818 novel, *The Backwoodsman,* alerted American writers to the literary potential of wild country. Looking west, rather than to Europe, Paulding declared, would be "the means of attaining to novelty of subject." It is well known how James Fenimore Cooper at first disregarded this advice and failed miserably with his first novel, *Precaution*, an English imitation. But in 1823 he turned to the wilderness in *The Pioneers* and became a national literary hero.

The history of American painting provides an excellent example of the way wilderness figured in the development of American cultural nationalism. Prior to the 1820's, our artists were virtually enslaved by European styles and subjects. When they did attempt a landscape, it was usually in the English pastoral tradition with purling brooks, placid cows, and, perhaps, a rustic swain or two. No one ever thought of painting a landscape divorced from human significance. There was always some sign of man or his works in evidence. Nature was background and setting, never important for its own sake. But in 1823 a young English immigrant, who had seen the beauty of the upper Ohio Valley, resolved to abandon portrait painting and devote his considerable talents to depicting, as he put it, "the wild and great features of nature: mountainous forests that know not man." With this statement Thomas Cole made a sort of declaration of independence for American painting. In the next few years he ranged, sketchbook in hand, through the wilder parts of northern New York and New England. The result was a series of wilderness landscapes, such as his study of the Catskill Mountains, that won Cole artistic fame and launched the Hudson River School of American painting. Excluding man and civilization from many of his canvases, Cole delighted in depicting the raw, unkempt power of wilderness with symbols such as the shattered tree trunks and surging storm clouds that appear in *Landscape with Tree Trunks*. The contrast of such paintings with the ordered, pastoral landscapes inspired by Europe was sharp.

In 1829 Thomas Cole sailed to Europe for a period of study. His admirers feared that exposure to the Old World might lure him away from the American wilderness as a subject for art. William Cullen Bryant, in fact, wrote a special poem pleading with Cole to "keep that earlier, wilder image bright." Yet in spite of Bryant's charge Cole was moved by what he saw in Europe. The way the face of the land, with its ruins and castles, reflected a long and rich history especially impressed him. Back in New York in 1835, Cole had an opportunity to summarize his reactions in an address before the National Academy of Design. Europe received its due: "Time and genius," Cole declared, "have suspended an imperishable halo" over the Old World landscape that rendered it "glorious." But, he quickly added, Americans need not feel inferior. While lacking a storied past, "American scenery . . . has features . . . unknown to Europe. The most distinctive, and perhaps the most impressive, characteristic of American scenery," he explained, "is its wildness." Americans should be grateful, Cole concluded, that

God, not man, had marked their landscape, making it ideal for "the contemplation of eternal things."

In 1836 Cole completed a series of five canvases entitled "The Course of Empire," in which the meaning of wilderness for American civilization received dramatic explication. In the first painting, *The Savage State*, Cole showed a wilderness inhabited by a hunter race. Time passed, and when Cole depicted the scene again it was the home of a people living in the arcadian or pastoral stage. Wilderness had partially given way to a rural landscape, but in the right corner the artist retained an untamed mountain peak. Man continued to alter the face of the earth, and in the third painting, *The Consummation of Empire*, we see a flourishing civilization. Wilderness had been reduced to that single peak in the right corner but in so doing, Cole implied that the society had cut itself off from the source of its physical and spiritual vitality. While outwardly luxurious, this civilization was actually moribund and in the next scene we see the inevitable result: barbarians from wilder environments swept down and reduced the great city to ruin. In the final picture all is desolation. But the symbolic peak still looms in the corner and its influence is beginning to spread as wild vines and grasses cover the scars of battle. We are left to believe that in time wilderness conditions will be restored and, perhaps, the cycle repeated.

The relevance of "The Course of Empire" to the United States in the 1830's was clear: Europe, having lost its strength-giving wild roots, was declining. America, because of its proximity to wilderness both chronologically and geographically, was on the rise—the new race of conquerors. Yet this very growth and prosperity was reason for concern. Might not the nation commit the error of Cole's civilization, or of Greece and Rome, and, by severing itself from the influence of wild nature, become prey for a wilder race? From Cole and Henry David Thoreau to Theodore Roosevelt, this question haunted many Americans. It also created a frame of mind favorable to the idea of preserving wilderness. Cole's empire had permitted its original wilderness to be reduced to a single peak, forgotten amid the pomp and splendor below. America's parks and reserves, it was hoped, would be reservoirs of wildness in the midst of civilization and halt Cole's cyclical progression at the mid-point of perpetual greatness. Wilderness, moreover, could serve the nation as a kind of historical document reminding Americans of the frontier heritage that many believed was responsible for giving the national character a unique and desirable shape.

Thomas Cole died prematurely in 1848, but his pupil, Frederic E. Church, carried on the tradition of American wilderness painting. The crucial experience in Church's development as an artist was an

1856 camping trip of eight days into the Mt. Katahdin region of northern Maine. Greatly inspired, the artist returned to his studio and painted a Maine lake and surrounding mountains at sunset. A crude road and a few sheep in the foreground are the only reminders of civilization. Four years later Church painted the little-known but magnificent *Twilight in the Wilderness*. Again the setting was northern Maine, but this time all traces of the pastoral had vanished. In the brilliant sunset and brooding Katahdin-like mountains there is a suggestion of the apocalyptic expectations of the virgin continent.

While Cole and Church painted wildernesses of the East, subsequent American landscape artists took their palettes and their national pride across the Mississippi. In the American West they found ideal subjects for both. Within a few years of his first visit to the Rocky Mountains in 1858, Albert Bierstadt was busy depicting their peaks, canyons, and lakes on gigantic canvases measuring up to eighty-four square feet. Turning to the Sierra in the 1870's and 1880's, he painted Mt. Whitney and Mirror Lake in Yosemite Valley. He also was one of the first to paint the Hetch Hetchy Valley, later the object of a classic battle in the early history of wilderness preservation. Bierstadt's exaggerated, dramatic style provoked criticism, but represented a sincere attempt to express his awe and delight in the American wilderness.

Many of the early western landscapists were necessarily explorers as well. Thomas Moran participated in the famous 1871 Ferdinand V. Hayden expedition into the Yellowstone country, and his drawings of its wonders assisted in the successful campaign for the national park the following year. Subsequently Moran painted throughout the West. He especially loved the Teton Range, one of whose peaks bears his name. Working in watercolor, Moran depicted California's Sierra. He also accepted the challenge of capturing the size and color of the Grand Canyon of the Colorado. When Congress in 1874 appropriated $10,000 for one of Moran's studies of the Canyon to hang in the Senate lobby, wilderness received official endorsement as a mainspring of American nationalism.

William H. Jackson, a pioneer landscape photographer, accompanied Moran and Hayden on the 1871 Yellowstone expedition. Jackson's artistic medium soon became a potent new force in directing American attention to wilderness as a source of pride. Following him have come Cedric Wright, Ansel Adams, Eliot Porter, and Philip Hyde, artists who have used cameras to expand the potential of landscape art. Indeed, at the 1961 meeting of this conference, Adams expressed his faith in photography as the medium most suitable for catching the elusive qualities that draw men to wilderness. Certainly the prints in the Sierra Club's Exhibit Format Series have gone far in this direction, and to an historian of ideas these books stand squarely in the tradition of nine-teenth century scenery albums in their attempt to use wilderness as an ingredient of American culture. It is highly appropriate that the Ex-hibit Format Series should have received international publishing awards since for over a century Americans have been calling the world's attention to their wilderness as something unique and precious.

If wilderness had been the only basis of American pride, the history of our attitude toward it would be much simpler. I mean that not just possessing wild country but also transforming it into civilization has been and remains a source of satisfaction for Americans. Our national ego is fed by both preserving and conquering wilderness. As a conse-quence, we tend as individuals to be ambivalent toward it. Ancient as-sumptions rooted in primitive man's perilous situation compel us to fear and fight wilderness. Appreciation has only recently challenged this unfavorable bias, and the change in attitude is incomplete. We are not quite sure which is progress, a national park or a hydropower dam, nature wild or nature ordered in man's interests. In the light of this un-certainty, we often affirm both at once: with Katherine Lee Bates we sing anthems to purple mountain majesties (wilderness) above the fruited plain (civilization). Or we join Emerson and Thoreau in cham-pioning the man who maintains contact with both wildness and civi-lized refinement. Similarly, the leaders of the wilderness preservation movement over the past quarter century, men like Benton MacKaye, Howard Zahniser, David Brower, and Sigurd Olson, have said time and again that their love of wilderness does not eclipse but may even heighten their appreciation of civilization and their recognition of its claim on natural resources. On the other hand, turn to any collection of recent statements opposed to preservation and count the number that begin, "Now I appreciate wilderness as much as the rest of you . . ." Then, to be sure, comes the "but in this case" and the defense of devel-opment. Yet the ambivalence, I think, is genuine.

In the heat of battle over a wilderness area or wilderness policy, it is easy to forget this ambivalence. Sometimes it seems that entire philoso-phies of the good life, if not the very definition of good itself, are at stake. Darkness and light appear locked in combat. In this atmosphere rational solution of problems is difficult. But from a more detached viewpoint, the conflict over wilderness involves values, not individuals or groups. That is, the real clash is between the claims of wilderness and the claims of civilization in the mind of each person. Remembering this, we can help create the common ground on which intelligent plan-ning for the future of the American wilderness must take place. If we do not remember the double-mindedness most of us share, our discus-sion of wilderness will continue to be a series of confrontations and showdowns between people who think they are unalterably opposed. It will help us remember if we recall that wilderness has been vitally important in American history in two ways: to the economy as a natural resource, and, as a cultural resource, to the national ego.

Lawrence G. Hines

WILDERNESS: ECONOMIC CHOICE, VALUES, AND THE ANDROSCOGGIN

Many assume that wilderness areas have no economic value because their worth is not recorded in dollar units in the market place. The standard textbook tells us that if a resource has the capacity to satisfy a want and is scarce, it possesses economic value. Because wilderness does satisfy a want and is scarce, it does have economic value. Indeed, in the matter of scarcity, we might wish it otherwise.

It is not the absence of economic value that distinguishes between wilderness and other resources; it is the measurability of that economic value. Because the value of wilderness is not easily expressed in dollar units, its economic value is intangible in contrast with the economic values of most resources, which are expressed in dollar units. Therefore, it is frequently erroneously assumed that because of the absence of a market economic value, wilderness has no economic value.

Economic value can be conferred by several methods in addition to appraisal in the market. But the main advantages of market data are that they are measurable and comparable. This does not mean that what can be measured is more important than what cannot be measured, nor that the standards used for measurement are socially justified. The yellow Rolls Royce hardly benefits society more than an unpolluted atmosphere. Moreover, reliance on the dollar-recorded values of the market place as a guide to public policy is subject to serious question.

74

People enter the market place to accommodate their self-interest rather than the community's welfare; and their ability to affect the market varies directly with their purchasing power. The decisions of this commercial arena have no more ethical validity than the underlying distribution of income that provides the basis for individual decisions. We can assume that a more nearly equitable distribution of income will yield a pattern of resource use that more closely approaches ethical validity. But even here, additional reservations have to be acknowledged in the operation of the American economic system. Moreover, if we add to our earlier assumption that an equitable distribution of income provides a basis for ethical decisions, there will still be impediments to the translation of these ethical expressions into economic reality. Barriers to free flow of resources and information occur in the limitation of output imposed by producers, by trade union restrictions surrounding the use of labor, by advertising influence upon consumer decisions, and from the general lack of knowledge by consumers and producers of the social effects of their decisions.

For the variety of above reasons, it can only be concluded that the decisions of the market place are inadequate indicators of the contribution of wilderness to American life. Aside from the failure to reflect the full range of social and ethical considerations, the market economy provides no way for society or the individual to express interest in preserving wilderness or promoting public projects. This deficiency of the private market is, of course, not limited to wilderness preservation, but extends to the more familiar public goods, such as schools and highways. In these cases, however, a systematic extra-market procedure has been developed to evaluate the need and plan for such public goods.

The private market is ill designed to cope with the increasingly large number of opportunities of choice resulting from the expansion of the twentieth century American economy. In an earlier and less affluent era, when economic resources were of necessity concentrated on the rudiments of life—food, shelter, and clothing—the range of choice of economic output was essentially limited and largely self-evident. But from its beginning in the industrial revolution and continuing with increasing technological pace to the present day, our economic choice has expanded at least as rapidly as our increase in economic productivity.

Higher national income has brought not only more goods and services, it has also brought more decisions about how to allocate our increasing productive capacity: for automobiles or schools, for superhighways or forest preserves, for housing or Mediterranean cruises. Increasingly, the public sector attracts more of our attention and more of our resources. As dams and highways reach farther into previously untouched areas, government decisions more frequently impair than protect wilderness and scenic areas. As the government agency extends its activities, it threatens hitherto safe regions. This inevitable conflict between agency interest and public interest has been somewhat concealed by the recent preoccupation with benefit-cost analysis as a means of assisting public investment decision making.

The purpose of benefit-cost analysis is to provide assistance in making two kinds of decisions: (1) whether resources during a period of full employment should be shifted from the private to the public sector of the economy, and (2) the relative importance (rank order) of different government projects. So far, benefit-cost analysis has been used mainly by the federal government in capital investment in water resource projects, such as flood control and reclamation installations. If benefits are greater than costs, that is if the benefit-cost (b/c) ratio is greater than one, the shift of resources from the private sector of the economy to the public sector is held to be economically justified. If the b/c ratio is less than one, however, the return from resource use in the private sector of the economy is presumably greater than the return from the public sector. More than economic considerations are relevant in public policy decisions, however, and it is to be expected that some projects with high b/c ratios will not be undertaken just as some with less than unity ratios will be justified on other than economic grounds. Given the desirability of shifting resources from private to public use, a higher benefit-cost ratio is cause for priority in congressional authorization. If benefit-cost analysis is a valid measure of the economic and social worth of a government project, a greater-than-one ratio will automatically insure that society will be better off with the project than without. But even if we assume that a benefit has never been overstated or a cost understated, the nature of the analysis largely stands in the way of according wilderness and scenic areas the economic and social importance that they actually hold for American society.

The answer that benefit-cost analysis gives in deciding resource use is too much that of the private market: the standards of value are confined to the same limited horizon; the ratio appraisal strains out all elements that cannot be expressed in units of the dollar. If it is so similar to the private market, and so deficient in measuring intangible resource worth, why has benefit-cost analysis received increasing attention as a device for decision making? Primarily, for two reasons: because it provides a handy indicator in the form of a ratio that is immediately comparable, and—most importantly—because benefit-cost analysis is frequently a means of presenting the government project in an artificially favorable light. This is not just because the benefit-cost approach is largely confined to market factors. It is because those agencies making greatest use of this technique have built into it automatic inflation of benefits and deflation of costs.

More often than not, for example, the reason for the multipurpose feature of a government project is not to accommodate carefully integrated functions, but simply to add to the benefit column. As such, a multipurpose project is likely to be a collection of individually unjustified undertakings: a little bit of flood control (or reclamation) at an exaggerated risk appraisal, a large amount of hydroelectric power, and a scattering of recreational opportunities that may or may not be superior to those destroyed. The benefits of these activities will be fully recorded and loudly proclaimed.

In the matter of costs, however, the researches of the federal agencies have been distinguished by remarkably less ingenuity. Indeed, the agency enthusiasm for the market measure of value seems abruptly to vanish when the critically important questions of the level of the interest rate and the period of time for capital repayment are considered. The market interest rate is inevitably found to be too high and the amortization period too short. A halving of the market interest rate is sometimes considered appropriate, and an increase of the amortization period to one hundred years are illustrations of agency double standard.

In addition to the built-in bias in the application of the benefit-cost analysis, the use of this technique confers upon the agency report a false aura of scientific impartiality. Quite the opposite should be the case. The agency personnel responsible for the planning and construction of dams, bridges, highways, and port-authority buildings should be automatically suspect. They are dedicated specialists, totally committed to the expansion of their activity, and are under no circumstances to be trusted with the decision of where to build dams, where to put highways, how tall to construct buildings, and the like. A New York *Times* editorial of November 20, 1966, expresses this inherent conflict between the public interest and the bureaucratic specialist:

> Once upon a time, a road was a friend to man. It enabled the farmer to get his produce more easily to city markets, and it enabled the city man to escape the crowded streets for the quiet, green countryside. Most adults can remember when "a drive in the country" was a pleasant way to spend a Sunday.
>
> At some time in the past thirty years, automobiles and trucks and the roads on which they move ceased to be man's servants and became his masters. The point in time is imperceptible, but probably it can be dated from 1956 when Congress authorized and President Eisenhower approved—with relatively little controversy—the 41,000-mile Interstate Highway System.

It is not commonly realized that this is the most enormous public works project in the history of the world. In cost, it is likely to exceed $60 billion by the time it is completed in 1972. In size and complexity, it dwarfs all of mankind's previous engineering works such as the Pyramids, the Great Wall of China, the Panama Canal, or Grand Coulee Dam.

The vast program has developed a life of its own, an inherent bureaucratic momentum that seems almost unstoppable. Every major city from Boston to Los Angeles is festooned, draped—or is it strangled?—with ribbons of concrete. The countryside is leveled and rolled and graded. The road-builders march—imperially, relentlessly, inexorably—across stream, meadow and woodland, through parks and nature preserves, through private homes, businesses, and historic sites. As neighborhoods are sliced in two and cemeteries are relocated, neither the quick nor the dead are safe. . . .

The truth is that most federal and state highway officials are alike in their basic indifference to community values, natural resources or esthetics. Their principal interest is moving people and vehicles in the shortest, cheapest way between two points. They regard concern for a historic neighborhood, an ecologically important watershed, an unspoiled valley, a grove of handsome trees or a rare stretch of wilderness as sentimental or irrelevant.

The point is that the agencies planning highways or dams are compelled to adopt a single-purpose approach, generally ignoring other considerations except when they are forced upon them by an aroused public. For the agency to do otherwise—for example, to admit the economic and aesthetic loss that results from the destruction of wilderness—is to weaken the case for the agency's projects, to reduce the number of projects that can be undertaken by the agency. As our nation becomes more crowded with highways, people, dams, automobiles, and buildings, it becomes increasingly difficult to find a place where one of these can be put without encroaching upon the other. The remnants of wilderness are, of course, subject to mounting pressures to accommodate capital installations at the same time that the sponsoring agency must resist admitting the growing economic and aesthetic worth of the regions invaded in order to maintain the façade of project feasibility.

It is a historic weakness of the American system that private interests have at times subverted the public interest; it is a more modern and bizarre development that the very agencies of the government designed to protect and promote the public interest are sometimes responsible for its degeneration. Such a perversion of governmental function is planned for northern New Hampshire by the Army Corps of Engineers' Pontook Dam project. This project will destroy the part of the Androscoggin River that is wild and clean and replace it with a fluctuating pond and miles of muddy runoff. The Androscoggin River in its northern reaches is as yet undeveloped and unpolluted; it carries no paper mill wastes, and the technology of the truck has relieved it of its former burden of logs. The Androscoggin rises in northern Maine and flows swift and clear through upper New Hampshire and eventually again into Maine and out to sea, accumulating a heavier and heavier charge of industrial wastes in its journey. But before it encounters the New England mills and towns, the Androscoggin is a challenge to the salmon and trout fisherman and the white-water canoeist. That this short but unspoiled stretch of eastern fast water was not even noted for "preliminary consideration" by the federal Wild River Study Team does not speak well for this group—or indicates that one federal agency is inclined to keep hands off when another is staking out its bureaucratic claim.

But if overlooked by the federal Wild River Study Group, the Androscoggin has not gone unnoticed by the Corps of Engineers. The corps has announced plans to construct a dam at the Pontook site, to be built at an estimated expenditure of $75 million, which is almost precisely three-fifths of the 1966 New Hampshire state budget. This comparison is important because it is sometimes hard for a smaller, less wealthy state to resist an appropriation that would bring only indifference in a more affluent state. In any case, there is evidence here of what may be called the axiom of fiscal seduction: ease of attaining the agency goal is directly proportional to the size of the federal expenditure and inversely proportional to the income of the region in which the expenditure is to take place. The corps is well aware of the encouragement to consensus that is produced by a massive expenditure, and for northern New Hampshire an expenditure of this magnitude may be irresistible. But the corps' Pontook project is a flagrant case of benefit–cost camouflage. It purports to have a benefit–cost ratio of 1.8/1, but the Public Service Company of New Hampshire in its engineering study of the identical site and only slightly smaller installation finds the investment unjustified. The Pontook project is planned to produce peak-load hydroelectric power, which will be marketed largely in southern New England (Connecticut and Massachusetts) for which at present there is no demand; but when demand appears, there will be high transmission costs, and consequent scarring of the countryside.

The Pontook Dam on the Androscoggin is justified, according to the Corps of Engineers, on the basis of 88 per cent hydroelectric benefits, 7 per cent recreational benefits—which is a cruel irony—and 5 per cent flood control benefits. Obviously, the corps is in the flood control business just enough to provide it the opportunity to build dams for hydroelectric purposes. Continuing improvement of nuclear power production is reducing the need for hydro and steam generation, but at least for peak power in New England hydro still plays a role. In the case of the Pontook project, however, the planned installation is an outrageous example of disregard of the economic principles of resource allocation. In a modern equivalent of carrying coals to Newcastle, the corps plans to ship high-cost hydro power into a market area where there are lower-cost opportunities for pumped hydro or steam generation of power. Specifically, engineering studies by the New Hampshire Public Service Company show an investment ratio of $225.68/kw for Pontook hydro as contrasted with one of one-third this magnitude, $75.00/kw, for either pumped hydro or gas-turbine power generation. When fuel costs and operation and maintenance are added, annual total costs for pumped hydro and gas turbine are respectively 50 per cent and 61 per cent of the Pontook cost.*

The corps thus proposed to provide peaking power at costs that are either double or more than a third higher, not including transmission costs, than can be achieved by production in the market area of need. To accomplish this gross misallocation of resources, one of the superlative stretches of an eastern wild river will be obliterated. More than this, the consequences of impoundment for hydroelectric power production go beyond creating a mud lake and runoff silted to the point that it will be unfit for industrial and recreational use; the artificial lake may turn portions of the nearby area into swampland, and the cold of winter may ice-pack the re-regulating area below the main dam to the point that power generation may be curtailed during the season of greatest need.

But we are a wealthy nation. We have survived economic absurdities before, and we will undoubtedly encounter them again. It is not the reduction in our income that is important, although it is senseless. It is the destruction of irreplaceable resources that is critical. We can pay more for our electricity, but there is no payment that we can make in the future that will raise the Androscoggin from the silt of a Pontook lake.†

* *Report on the Pontook Study* (Manchester, N.H.: Public Service Company of New Hampshire, 1967), Appendix G, p. 3. The above investment ratios are for installations of 262,500 kws and do not include the cost of transmission, which when added would further disadvantage the price of Pontook power. Although future power needs of New England appear more likely to be for base power than for peaking power, the investment ratio for a 262,500 nuclear (base) power of $125/kw has not been listed above because such an installation is not, strictly speaking, an alternative to the Pontook project.
† On June 26, 1967, the Corps of Engineers' New England office issued an unfavorable report on the construction of the Pontook Dam.—*The Editors.*

Rudolph W. Gilbert

NOTES FROM A
WILDERNESS LAYMAN

It is a refreshing experience to find myself in the role of a layman. Imagine yourself receiving an invitation to address a convocation of eminent theologians—Jesuits, Neo-Orthodox, and God-is-Dead theologians—and you will have some idea of my mixed feelings when I received Dr. Gilligan's flattering invitation.

I did not have the grace to refuse; and so, with what I hope was a proper show of humility, I accepted.

The flattery of the invitation and the pleasant prospect of being here would not have been enough to overcome my fears, and my feelings of inadequacy. I come really to make a small payment on a large debt—a debt I realized only in recent years that I had incurred.

The dedicated and intelligent work of the Sierra Club has not been well enough known. I am pleased to think this is being remedied, as evidenced in your growing membership. As time goes on, and the nature of your concern is more generally understood, many will come to acknowledge the debt we owe you.

The layman has a role to play in this wilderness worship and the larger work of conservation. We need the prophets and the high priests, the scientists and the legislators, but you also need the congregation, the public. And we both need the dialogue.

I would like to share with you one man's experiences because I think they may be rather common to many, and may indicate where professional and layman meet.

I became conscious of conservation early in life. I was born on an old-fashioned diversified farm in Iowa. My father raised cattle and horses, hogs and chickens, and sometimes a few sheep. Each year he plowed more fertility and mulch back into the soil than he took out in crops. To this day I find it difficult to put chemical fertilizers on my garden—I would rather go to a friend's ranch and bring in boxes and sacks of barnyard manure. And my father planted trees. He was a notoriously soft touch for the traveling nurseryman.

With that as a little background, you can imagine my feelings of shock and disgust when I found myself on the edge of a conversation back in 1932 in which a city man was telling of his proposed venture in farming. He would, he said, buy up farms, preferably those lying adjacent to each other, pay as little down as possible, then tear down the fences, work the land to the road for three or four years until the soil was worthless, and then let the land go back to whatever institution held the papers. Hitchhiking around Iowa, I saw evidence of this kind of operation. I am happy to say this man did not stay with farming very long. I never envied him the tremendous success he realized later in the field of radio and electronics, but was always thankful that his great energy and ingenuity found another channel of expression. I realize corporate agriculture has become much more enlightened since those dark days, largely through the assistance and incentives of federal farm programs.

I came to what might be called wild country much later, when I went to Colorado in 1945. Even then, I must admit, I was held at arm's length for a time, but the high country soon became more friendly, and we found our second home at an elevation of 9,500 feet in the Blue River Valley in Summit County, just west of the Continental Divide. While living there might be considered primitive by some standards, it was really very comfortable and certainly not a wilderness. But something like wilderness was close to our front and back doors.

Examining the topographical maps, we saw that the source of the Blue River was two lakes. The lower lake was easily accessible from the end of a road—a gentle, picturesque climb, with plenty of evidence of mining in earlier days. I inquired about the upper lake. The natives seemed not too aware of it—or perhaps, and understandably, they were reluctant to share it with an outsider. In a way we had to discover it for ourselves, and that was good. The path was steep but open, the kind on which you not only have to, but want to stop often to look back and see the very different view from each pause. The lake changes, the trees become a forest and then a carpet, and other peaks emerge on the new horizon.

I remember well the first time I made the climb. Coming up over the last crest and catching the first glimpse of a little lake surrounded by the bare and rocky peaks of the Divide and the Ten Mile Range, I confess my eyes stung with tears, and I could not blame them altogether on the wind.

The last time I was at the Upper Blue Lake eleven years ago I had a strange feeling as I turned and looked before beginning the descent— call it a premonition. I had no notion it would be the last time I would be there. I knew I would come back to Colorado for visits and I was sure I would make the climb. It was not a difficult one, and happily it would be some years before time would take its toll on heart and leg muscles.

When I did return to Colorado in a couple of years and mentioned going to the Upper Blue, I was told there was a road now and I could drive to the shore of the lake. Well, that was disappointing, but I took comfort in learning that the road was on the other side of the lower lake and the river. I could ignore it and still take the trail. But then they told me a dam was being built at the lake to store water to be diverted to the eastern slope for the growing city of Colorado Springs and the Air Force Academy. I did not make the climb; I probably won't again. I am afraid the tears might come and the throat tighten, but now in the poignancy not of beauty, but of anger and regret.

If I believed in premonitions, I would know why I felt as I did that last time I turned and looked, when the clouds were hanging low among the peaks, and it rained before I got to the lower lake. Now I know this seems insignificant, and even though I may have succeeded in conveying something of my personal feeling, you are justified in saying it is just personal. At first I was inclined to accept it as that—and indeed, it is essentially personal, but it is something else as well. You see, for a good many years I thought the encroachment of civilization on the wilderness was the necessary price we had to pay for progress. I read Thoreau early enough, but, like many of my generation, I took him too personally. The appeal was too romantic, and more than a little self-indulgent. I thought I shared some of his concern, but did not see it as a viable social, economic, and political concept, as well as a personal philosophy and a religious concern. Becoming aware of the work and philosophy of the Sierra Club and various societies concerned with wilderness, I came to realize this was not just a personal feeling, not a selfish indulgence, but something essential to the character of America and her people.

How many areas, many of them much larger and more spectacular, will go as the Upper Blue Lake went? And will it make a difference except to a few old cranks and young fanatics who seem intent on standing in the way of progress, who think there are things more important than a regular increase in the gross national product and the population of cities?

In passing, let me observe that a citizen's concern with conservation is naturally general rather than specialized, and it should be intelligent. This is why I wanted to share with you my personal pilgrimage as the son of an Iowa farmer who diversified his farming and planted trees, spending an interlude of a few years in Chicago, attracted to the high country of Colorado, with another short year in Chicago before coming to the Pacific Northwest, to a city (Spokane) where we still have some choices, to a state (Washington) with tremendous variety: lakes, ocean shore, much semiwilderness and a good deal of genuine wilderness, marine, forest, mountain, and even some desert wilderness, and a few wild rivers. I think you can see why my interest in conservation, still in the process of becoming informed, is deeply rooted and inclusive. It includes the fertility of the farmland. And it includes recreation and wilderness—a distinction you people wisely make.

As one comes even to the edge of wilderness and yet knows he must live and make his living in the city, he comes to understand the whole earth as his home, and that knowledge and tools and machines are part of our at-homeness on this earth in the twentieth century. Without the knowledge that the sciences give and the refinements that technology brings, we would be less at home than we are. We would have less wilderness, and our cities would be more of a human jungle than they are. From the disposal of waste to the transportation of goods and people, technology is essential to the preservation of space and livability in the city and in the rest of the country.

With all our other concerns, we now have to be concerned about population pressure. It is a problem facing not only a few continents, but the world—and not least our own cities and our own countryside. The statistics spell out the problem; the knowledge and the techniques are here to meet it. The most difficult task remains: to articulate an ethical and social philosophy that will give us direction and motivation to solve the problem.

As a wilderness layman, and as one whose vocation is religious, I cannot but see living as a whole, a possible achievement of the whole man in the whole environment—or as nearly so as possible. Just because we are becoming so urbanized and so dependent on technology, we must nurture as much as possible wholesome and creative responses to the earth—respect and wonder, as well as knowledge and use. To this end, wilderness is essential. We must have the chance to relate to the earth, the creatures of the earth, and the elemental forces, not as we have refashioned the earth by our machines, our dams and roads and houses, but as it is there in a natural state. Parks, campgrounds, picnic areas, slopes for skiing, and lakes stocked annually with fish are important. I do not deny their importance. The need for them is great and will become greater. But this is not enough for America and her people. We can do better. Wilderness is essential, and the qualities that issue from wilderness experience are necessary.

Quality in relation to wilderness reservations is a central theme of this conference. I am sure it would be very useful to make qualitative distinctions between various kinds and areas of wilderness, and between wilderness and semiwilderness and recreation. But when I think of quality, I have to think of qualities of experience. This does not mean that quality is purely subjective, that it is only a state of mind or an emotional response. True, the experience is one's own, but it is *of* something—in this case the wilderness. What I really talk about, then, is the quality of a wilderness experience, or the qualities of wilderness experiences.

Not altogether arbitrarily I choose three. There are many others that could be singled out, and many that have been the subjects of discussion over the years in these conferences. Many of them are more specific, and perhaps more useful. The three I choose are general values or qualities, and they apply to many experiences. I feel that they find a particular expression in a wilderness experience. They are youth, adventure, and peace.

First, let us make a distinction—I think a valid one—between the frontier and the wilderness as each has entered into the general experience that we might call America. The frontier, I submit, was Puritan and Promethean in quality, in its attitude toward the earth, in its land ethic. The land was there to be settled, developed, used. The disciplines of hard work and saving for capital investment were necessary. They made their contribution. But the frontier was also harsh and confining. This aspect of the frontier is vividly portrayed in such books as O. E. Rolvaag's *Giants in the Earth* and Hamlin Garland's *Main Travelled Roads*. It is there also in some of the novels of Ruth Suckow, Willa Cather, and Marie Sandoz.

Wilderness qualities, on the other hand, I would call pagan and Dionysian, without, of course, the frenzied and superstitious qualities we popularly associate with those words. However, even as we must not forget the positive values of Puritanism, so, I think, we should be aware of the temptations of the pagan concept. It can lead to a sentimental romanticism or to escapism, and it can even express a misanthropy—not often, not necessarily, but possibly.

The qualities of wilderness experience are also rejuvenating in a way that goes to the very soul of one's being and to the very roots of a culture. To suggest what I have in mind, let me recall James Fenimore

Cooper's "Leatherstocking" tales, and particularly an observation that D. H. Lawrence made on them. The point to remember is that the novel dealing with the early life of the hero, Natty Bumppo, was the fifth and last of the tales. It was *The Deerslayer,* and most people find it to be the most interesting as Lawrence found it the most fascinating. He wrote, "The Leatherstocking novels go backwards from old age to golden youth. That is the true myth of America. She starts old, old, wrinkled and writhing in an old skin. And there is a gradual sloughing off of the old skin, towards a new youth. It is the myth of America."

I think there is an element of truth in this, romanticized though it was by Cooper and overemphasized by Lawrence. It is the essential truth of wilderness. The past is very present in the wilderness, but it does not dominate the present. The river is old, and you can feel its oldness by the channel or canyon it has made with the aid of wind and sun and freezing winters. But it is there very much in the present, still working, in the wilderness, still wild. The past is there in a very different way in the wilderness than it is in a museum. In the museum the past is dead and with great effort we have to make it speak to the present, but in the wilderness the past speaks immediately to the present, and even with some of the wildness of youth.

Likewise, experience in the wilderness is new each day as it is not in the city. I am convinced this is not just because we are away from a routine and perhaps on vacation. The longer we are there, the more conscious we become of the newness of each day, and of each night. Youth, adventure, and peace—in a wilderness experience they harmonize, as so many things do: past, present, and future; solitude and companionship; night and day; storm and sun; effort and relaxation; learning and being. I think this is the reason a wilderness experience gives a sense of wholeness. It is therapy—something more or other than you get in a crowded campground or picnic area, on a ski slope, or at a stocked lake on the opening day of fishing.

A wilderness experience is more than solitude. Being alone in a city or in a crowd—and there is no place one can be more lonely than in a crowd—a person may be driven in on himself, not always to find strength but often in sheer self-defense. He must close his ears to the din, turn his eyes from the flashing neons, perhaps even hold his nose. Being alone with trees or stream or desert and the myriad things going on there actually tempts a person outward—out through his eyes, his ears, his muscles, even through his nose. He is invited to be aware of the subtleties of sound, scenery, and weather. Every day is new in a wilderness, in a way that it is not in a city. Every day is an adventure.

If companions are about, on the trail or around the campfire, there is again a communion—not always in conversation, in ideas—but in awareness and fellow-feeling. Have you ever thought how a circle of people comes natural to a campfire? In its warm light you are looking in the faces of your companions of the way, and not just at the backs of their heads, as you do on Sunday in church or in a lecture hall.

Youth and adventure blend in peace if peace is understood as strength, inner strength, if it is understood as being at home and feeling at home, as possessing your soul even in struggle. Nature has been secularized, as Dr. Harvey Cox reminds us in *The Secular City*, and is therefore neither to be cajoled nor appeased, but understood. In wilderness, nature is not something to be forced or seduced, but met and understood on its own terms. You have not conquered a mountain when you have climbed it. You have not subdued a stream when you have forded it. You may settle a frontier, but you come to terms with a wilderness.

The peace I speak of comes from adventure and memory—a memory that is deeper than historical records. This quality of peace is a perspective on time that comes from a sense of newness, the newness of each new day, and a sense of that which is more ancient by far than man himself—older even than life itself. For the mountains, desert, and sea are there to remind you whence you and all life came, and whither thou goest.

The temptation to quote has been great throughout the writing of this paper. Others have said what I have wanted to say, and have said it so much better. Indeed, everything I wish I had said, had I been able to say it, was said in the publication of the Seventh Biennial Wilderness Conference. But even in that rare collection I did not find one of my favorite quotations—something said by Donald Culross Peattie, and quoted by Oscar Riddle in *The Unleashing of Evolutionary Thought*:

"I say that it touches a man that his blood is sea water and his tears are salt, that the seed of his loins is scarcely different from the same cells in a seaweed, and that of stuff like his bones are coral made. I say that physical and biologic law lies down with him, and wakes when a child stirs in the womb, and that . . . these are facts of first importance to his mental conclusions, and that a man who goes in no consciousness of them is a drifter and a dreamer, without a home or any contact with reality."

These facts you might learn from books or surmise from a microscope, but you understand them as you walk the ocean shore, climb the trail, or wander in an Alabama swamp.

FROM THE FRIDAY AFTERNOON DISCUSSION

Sigurd F. Olson: One of the ideas that has been expressed in this session is how wilderness, the frontier, and the pioneer experience has affected American life. I call this collectively a feel for the land. All wilderness people will know what I mean. I did not say, "love for the land," though there is little difference, but rather an inherent feel for the land. Americans through their four-hundred-year history have developed this feeling to a high degree. What is meant by this? All we've been talking about is encompassed by it—solitude, natural beauty, timelessness, space, vistas, freedom, and even a cosmic perspective. It includes a sense of oneness with the earth, the feel of belonging and the fullness which Reverend Gilbert mentioned. It embraces all these things, but it is difficult to talk about them, because we're so deeply, emotionally, and spiritually involved.

Up in Alaska they have a saying that "you can take a man out of the bush, but you can't take the bush out of a man." We might take Americans out of the wilderness, which we are doing. They predict 90 per cent of us will be living in urban communities within the next decade or two. We are almost there now, but even so you cannot take the wilderness out of us; it is simply there. None of you would be here today if it were not inside you. It is a characteristic of us all because of our close involvement with the frontier. It is part of us because for four centuries we fought this wilderness, battled our way across the continent, subdued it, and now we are trying to change it, and mold it to our particular needs. The feel of the land is in us and the feel of wilderness is in our blood.

One thought has occurred to me, a suggestion I have made to this group before, that we had better raise our sights if we are going to save this wilderness. We are talking too much about camping trips, canoe trips, the physical challenges, the actual participation. Reverend Gilbert did not do that. I know how he felt about the Upper Blue Lake—that came from his heart as it comes from all of our hearts when we see places of beauty and wildness despoiled. These things are important. They are part of the very air we breathe, part of our feel for the land.

Everyone who has spoken so far has intimated that wilderness is a spiritual experience. The more I think of wilderness, the more I see battles going on and on, the surer I am that it is a spiritual experience we are fighting for. I am not going to try to tell you what a spiritual experience is, for you know it is involved with happiness and a sense of fullness and with all that makes life livable and worthwhile. If wilderness does that it is a spiritual experience.

I believe that the way America is going—and we are the most potent industrial and technological civilization that this earth has ever spawned—if it keeps on going, it is gradually going to put more and more pressure on wilderness. Our last reserves are going to be more and more precious and rare. But we are faced with the impact of technology, computerized existence, the machine, divorce from the wilderness, from all of nature, into artificial, urbanized complexes. We are faced with it, but what is it going to do to man? The stakes are so high, the threat so desperate, we can no longer think of wilderness as being a minority need, a need of 2 per cent of the population. I feel that the wilderness is the concern of all Americans and all humanity, that if we do not save some wilderness mankind and his spirit will suffer, and life will not be so happy for future generations.

My only suggestion to this conference is to consider, as wilderness battlers, ways and means not for reaching each other—we are converted—but reaching the other 98 per cent of the people. Make the wilderness so important, so understandable, so clearly seen as vital to human happiness that it cannot be relegated to an insubstantial minority. If it affects everyone—and I believe it does—then we must find out how to tell the world why it affects everybody. Only when we put wilderness on that broad base will we have a good chance of saving it.

I did not agree with this morning's speaker, Anthony Wayne Smith, who said we are faced with disaster because of the way a government agency behaves. That is not the disaster we are facing. I figure we are just plain lucky to have men like Ed Cliff and George Hartzog and others in there pitching and feeling much the way we feel. What would happen if we did not have men of their calibre guarding our interests and doing their best to save what they can? But I know there is more wilderness to be saved and we should not concentrate only on what we have, because the demands in the future will be so great that what is safe now will not be enough then. We should consider all possibilities for adding to the present wilderness system.

Adan Treganza: The cultural significance of wilderness as seen by Roderick Nash contrasts markedly with an anthropologist's view of this same wilderness as inhabited by the American Indian. The historian's approach is through analysis of pictorial art and written documentation; the anthropologist studies the remains of ancient village sites, sifting through dead, unrecorded knowledge retrieved from mounds and remnants. He transforms it into contemporary meaning, bringing the past into focus with the present, giving perspective to man, time, and his natural world.

I can certainly agree that most Americans are not aware that their brief and shallow traditions have been built upon multiple cultural backgrounds stemming from the Old World of Europe. There people were, and are, born to deep-seated traditions, where cultural patterns have been long since fixed, where resources are limited, and "open space" is a nonexistent word. To the so-called European Americans, the Indian had no culture; he was a savage and he stood in the way of "progress." But actually, he had a deep cultural tradition dating back to 20,000 B.C.

The American Indian has already lost the race for time and space, through the ruthless activities of his contemporary brother, modern man. Every effort should be made to preserve what is left of the fractured living Indian cultures and their archaeological past, especially in the Far West where there is a little fragment of survival. A few rare Indian groups have tried to keep their traditions alive and in many cases have formed Indian societies constituting intertribal organizations. This unfortunately mixes cultures and ceremonies, but it is an honest attempt for survival of a way of native life and a way of thinking.

The contemporary Indian has been reduced to the status of a minority group on the one hand, and yet he has been set up as a kind of national symbol or shrine on the other hand. Hollywood has climaxed these two extremes by creating an image of the Indian as either the "bad guy" who attacked wagon trains and handed out to General Custer what he deserved, or the "good guy," like Tonto, who understood the white man's ways but still remained an Indian. As a small reward the Indian was placed on a five-cent coin complemented by a buffalo on the opposite side, both of which are almost extinct. I wonder why there have been no commemorative stamps on American Indian culture.

What is left of American Indian history? Virtually nothing except a handful of archaeological sites. All knowledge had to be transmitted orally and visually through applied technology, mythology, and religious ceremonies, for he had no form of writing. This is no reflection on his mentality. His knowledge was equal to ours if not superior in his understanding and appreciation of wilderness. No one knew the wilderness more intimately than did the American Indian, the "true wilderness person." As club members you are learning about wilderness, but the Indian lived it.

The proposed destruction of Lawrence Hines's Androscoggin River is similar to what is occurring all the way from New Hampshire to the Far West, especially in central and northern California. I can speak in a knowledgeable way since for the last twenty years I have been involved in salvage archaeology connected with similar projects financed primarily by the Department of the Interior through its National Park Service. The areas where archaeological aid is given are in proposed reservoirs, canals, or any other construction that could result in the destruction of Indian or American historical remains. To this end the Corps of Engineers and the Bureau of Reclamation make contributions of money through the National Park Service so that about 10 per cent of the archaeological remains in project areas can be salvaged. This is always far too little to accomplish the recording and preservation of historic and prehistoric remains. Though grateful for their aid, I do not feel they should be responsible for supporting archaeology. We should ask Congress for separate aid to cover the protection and restoration of national archaeological sites.

The California Division of Beaches and Parks also gives support as far as their funds permit. But accompanying the federal and state aid is an implied justification for their projects, many of which destroy natural landscapes. Basically they are engineers dedicated to doing an efficient job on a money–time basis, and the wilderness or record they flood and demolish is rarely considered as a social responsibility. A surveyor's eye goes from one elevation and red flag to the next; what stands between these points is a mechanical problem devoid of feeling.

Archaeological sites are rare and fast disappearing under the impact of the population explosion. A present example is the wholesale destruction of the historically important waterfront and bay area of Monterey, California. Though not a wilderness in the sense of unspoiled landscape, it is now a spoiled area from the point of history and prehistory—and for what? So some tourist can get faster from Monterey to Pacific Grove, a distance of a mile. The time saved by the traveler can never justify the historical time that has been destroyed—a record of considerable interest in California and national history. I am so glad I sketched and photographed the old key shop near the wharf. It is now gone.

Recreation areas around a newly created reservoir, though better than nothing, do not substitute for the loss of wilderness or historic and prehistoric remains. The proposed destruction of the Androscoggin as a wild river is a case in point. Another prime example is the flooding of Round Valley and the town of Covelo that will result if the proposed Dos Rios Dam is built by the Corps of Engineers on the Middle Fork of the Eel River in Mendocino County, California. There are over four hundred archaeological sites in this region that have never been excavated; they contain nearly the total history of an important group of California Indians.*

There are antiquity laws that prevent excavation on state and federal lands without a permit. Recently, Ordinance No. 1589 was passed by the Board of Supervisors of Marin County, California, forbidding destruction of archaeological sites by any means unless a permit is obtained. This is granted only if the grantee will guarantee a sixty-day stay during which controlled excavation is permitted. The archaeological importance of the area is determined by a committee of professional anthropologists. This is a gratifying step forward; some comparable law should be enacted by all local municipalities of the fifty states.

I am sympathetic with the remarks by Reverend Rudolph Gilbert because he has expressed feelings we all share in different ways. There is no separation between Creator and our natural world. We can find a wonderful world if we will emerge from our human psychological cocoons, observe and participate in the fascinating aura of nature.

The book *Ring of Bright Water* by Gavin Maxwell, the story of an otter, expresses in detail what Reverend Gilbert has said: that some people are born into nature through a happenstance of personality construct and accident of birthplace. I believe Reverend Gilbert and I see a total world, a world of unlimited areas of exploration and contentment, because we both grew up in it. Other people, to their great pleasure, find this world of wilderness later in life. The opportunity for participation exists in various degrees and dimensions for those who desire to seek it. Any individual, at any age, can become a part of the natural world in which he lives.

Certainly no one is closer to the understanding of nature than man, and it is through his technology, which we call, in part, culture, that he has modified, improved, and is destroying the planet earth. The anthropologist has a great deal to contribute to future wilderness confer-

* Representatives of the Sierra Club's Redwood Chapter testified in opposition to the Dos Rios Dam at field hearings in December, 1967.—*The Editors.*

ences, assuming the Sierra Club wants to consider the American Indian, past and present, as part of our natural heritage.

I should like to suggest three sources that may open a new area of thinking about wilderness. One is Dr. James Down's book, *The Two Worlds of the Washo,* Case Studies in Anthropology. One "world" depicts a group of California and Nevada Indians who were a part of a true wilderness area and who placed economic values upon natural resources. The "second world" of the Washo depicts what has happened to this same group of Indians when they became exposed to Caucasian culture and were forced to adapt to a difficult ecological niche—one of deprivation and ultimate extinction through loss of identity. It is a study both in cultural and economic contrast. It is a sad ending of a culture, just like the sad ending of many parts of our wilderness.

The second example is a paper by Dr. Robert F. Heizer, Kroeber Anthropological Society Paper No. 13, *Primitive Man as an Ecological Factor.* It explores both the economic attitudes and conservation practices of aboriginal American Indians of the West and presents a good contrasting picture of a present dilemma—how land should be used and at what cost.

The third paper, one of my own, represents an extension of our thinking on how culture operates and affects in time the natural landscape. It is *Horticulture with Irrigation Among the Great Basin Paiute: An Example of Stimulus Diffusion and Cultural Survival,* Anthropological Papers No. 26, University of Utah, Department of Anthropology.

Peggy Wayburn: Thank you very much, Dr. Treganza. We appreciate your contribution. Speaking of archaeological excavations, I just wanted to tell you that the excavation at the Bodega Bay headlands is known as "the hole in the head."

Mr. Olson: If the saving of wilderness is a spiritual thing, I'm going to pose a question to Reverend Gilbert. This is not a curve ball, either, because I am a minister's son. My father was a Baptist minister and I was raised within the confines of the church. I know a little bit about what a pastor's family feels and has to cope with—including the missionary barrel.

If the preservation of wilderness is the preservation of the spirit of man, and I think in its broadest connotations it is exactly that, and if the church is concerned with saving souls and guarding the spiritual life of mankind, then why doesn't it get into this battle all over the land and put its weight behind the whole effort? If we had ten thousand preachers with your eloquence and your feelings, there would be no doubt about it. Do you suppose it would be possible to sell this idea to the rest of the clergy, get them to follow you and work with you, and put this idea across to denominations all over the country?

Reverend Rudolph W. Gilbert: Yes, that is very much what I had in mind when I put myself in the class of a layman. As a layman I am here to learn and to express my concern. I am a professional in another field. I have an obligation to relate my concern to my professional capacity. This is what I think we have to do. I am delighted, Mr. Olson, that you put me on the spot, that you gave me the challenge, because we have captive audiences every Sunday morning, and in most churches they do not tell us what we have to say. So at least once a year—at least—we can take a Sunday morning and put this into the service. There is the feeling of the desire to be at home with nature in the whole tradition of mankind, not only in the Judeo–Christian tradition, but in the traditions of all the religions of the world. Of course, one Sunday a year is not enough. We should do it many Sundays in order to make people aware, and that is precisely what I had in mind. I am delighted that you caught it.

Mr. Olson: Thank you. I am glad you agree. I think the time has come for doing this sort of thing, not only through the churches but through other agencies as well. People for the first time are becoming aware of the importance of this enjoyment. Ten years ago you would not have heard anyone dare to raise a voice about water pollution, air pollution, or any of the other necessary things we must deal with. The climate is ripe. For the first time we have not only industrial figures, but figures in the executive branch of government speaking out about these things. A few years ago it would not have been possible to mention the words "natural beauty" before an audience and expect to get by without being called a pansy or an aesthete. Now we can actually mention it without being stoned. Beauty has become accepted, legal, and attainable. But with all this surge of interest, I think the time has come for us as conservationists, as well as for other interested groups and agencies, to sell the idea of wilderness to all the people. I believe the people are ready for it, but we have not figured out yet how to go about it. We have got conviction and brains, however, and I think we can do it.

I have a question for Dr. Hines, who has touched on something all of us have come up against time and again. How do you put a value on an intangible? How can you sell government agencies on not damming the Androscoggin? Why do these things have to be shoved down our throats when we don't believe in them and haven't a weapon to fight with? I know you have given this matter much thought, Dr. Hines, but do you have any idea of a new approach to this problem? Is there any-

thing new we can come up with to meet the continuing problem? Anyone knows that, in the last analysis, it is often a matter of dollars and
cents for the material; for the intangibles, only guesswork.

Lawrence G. Hines: I think there are a number of comments that
could be made. In the first place, it is possible, of course, to get a better
kind of quantification of the values than it sometimes appears in benefit–cost studies—quantifications in terms of the costs that are foregone
as a result of the building of the dam or other construction in a wilderness area. It should be recognized, however, that it is not so necessary
to overbalance the agency study with conflicting evidence as it is to
present a systematic appraisal of the nature of the agency study. In
other words, it is not necessary to come up with an equally strong contrary economic argument in quantified terms to justify not building a
dam. It is sufficient to demonstrate that the agency study is, at best, an
incomplete measure of the economic validity of that kind of an investment.

Mr. Olson: Thank you, Dr. Hines. You still have not answered my
question. At some future committee hearing in Washington or elsewhere, sooner or later this will come up and as usual it will hit us between the eyes. We will try to talk about wilderness values, and how it
makes people feel, and how unhappy we will be without them; they
will look at you and realize that you must have spent all of your life
back in the woods, because you don't really know the facts, and you
don't know what makes this country go. They will be very polite, very
kind and will pat you on the back, and they will tell you it was a very
fine statement; but in fact it didn't mean a thing!

Dr. Hines: Value can be ascribed to certain kinds of experience.
This is essentially the approach that Marion Clawson and some others,
as you well know, have suggested.
   I am less than enthusiastic about this approach because it tends to
place all experiences on essentially the same basis. For example, it is
possible for a government agency to impute a value in terms of user
days for the impounded water facility created in damming a wilderness
stream. It will also, of course, acknowledge a cost for the destruction of
the wilderness experience opportunities. But in terms of numbers of
users, the impounded water development will generally accommodate
many more than the wilderness area. As a result, crude (i.e., unad-
justed) quantification will favor the greater number to be generally expected from the development. At this period in the use of benefit–cost
analysis, uncritical support of quantification of recreational or wilderness benefits may be harmful to the cause of wilderness preservation.

Mr. Olson: Don't you think that brings us right back to the original premise you mentioned earlier, that we must condition the American people and somehow get the point across that the preservation of wilderness—large, small, natural areas, whatever you want to call them —is a matter for all Americans, all humanity, and only when we sell that idea will we be able to answer the dollars and cents arguments? I really believe this is the important thing, and we all must work harder to sell the whole idea of spiritual values and the intangibles to the American people.

I would like to ask Dr. Nash this: Einstein said that wonder is the most valuable attribute of man—the beginning and the end of all his research into the unknown. If wilderness means wonder, and we must reserve wonder at all costs, why was it that in the early days Americans were not so much impressed with wonder as they were in trying to re-create the old European scene?

Roderick Nash: I think we have to understand this fact: the first colonists were not Americans; they were transplanted Europeans. They thought about wilderness as Europeans, which meant that they regarded it as a physical and spiritual wasteland to be conquered and fructified in the name of civilization and Christianity. This attitude was entirely consistent with the traditional Judeo–Christian belief that the natural world was "given" to man for his personal exploitation. The idea is found, for instance, in *Genesis* 1:28.

The point is that the early Americans had little in their intellectual heritage to suggest that wild country was anything but an enemy. Moreover, the colonists really did not have time to wonder at the wilderness. They were too busy surviving and desperately trying to reproduce the familiar old European scene of which you speak. In this scene was security, comfort, and success; in wilderness was hardship and danger. Transformation of wilderness into civilization had to be the primary task of the Virginia and New England pioneers, just as it was the primary task of the subsequent waves of frontiersmen.

In sum, it took centuries to dilute the hostility toward wilderness produced by the frontier situation. Appreciation of wilderness, as Sig Olson knows well, is characteristic of highly civilized people, not pioneers. Cities, not log cabins, in other words, have been the source of the wilderness movement. So here we are now in the San Francisco Hilton!

Mr. Olson: I think Dr. Nash answered the question very well. I would like to conclude my participation by just quoting from a Spaniard in Puerto Rico who said: "The greatest achievement of modern man is to look at wilderness not as a savage, but through the enlightened eyes of civilized man."

Dr. Nash: That's the point.

Moderator Wayburn: There is a question here for Dr. Hines that asks, "Can your river still be saved?"

Dr. Hines: Well, obviously, I hope so. I think the river can be saved. [See footnote p. 80.] There is a small vocal group that is trying to save it. At the present time the Army Corps of Engineers has issued its cost–benefit study of the river and has since withdrawn it for revision. If the river is to be saved from this project, it can be done at a number of points:

(1) Through state legislative action that we in New Hampshire hope to do. As you know, there is a great preference in New England for carrying on affairs in this manner.

(2) Having the governor refuse to accept that project, although this is not likely. State governors have authority to reject Army Corps projects.

(3) At the level of congressional authorization and appropriation— where assistance from Maine to California will be urgently needed.

Moderator Wayburn: A question for Reverend Gilbert: "It seems you are equating the wilderness experience's pagan quality with a concept of an organized church. May I submit the possibility of individual communion with God in the wilderness? Do you think such would be in conflict with one's role as a Christian, Jew, Muslim, Hindu, or other religion?"

Reverend Gilbert: I would like to equate a wilderness experience with a church experience. I would not insist on it, because I think quite often a religious experience is lacking in church, whereas it is often present in wilderness. Religion means a kind of personal relationship to whatever we call the source of our being—whether it is something deep inside, or something in nature, or something outside and above nature, or the idealized community. There is a personal relationship in a wilderness experience.

And yet I would not want to eliminate the social quality of a wilderness experience. As I mentioned, the campfire lends itself to a circle, and people go out to each other in a physical setting like that. Also, as a culture, as a people, we need to sense wilderness, and this sense of wilderness gives culture a focus, or at least a vitality. In a way, I think it does for our way of life as a people what it does for the individual.

Just the presence of wilderness, the vague knowledge that it is there, does something. When I was cut off from the Upper Blue Lake, something went out of my life. And this would still have been the case had I not returned to Colorado, but instead had learned, from a distance, of its alteration.

Now there is another area very dear to me that was saved just in the nick of time—the Upper Priest Lake in the panhandle of Idaho. It held very precious personal memories for me. It has been saved as wilderness, or semiwilderness. At least there will be no buildings on its shores. Knowing that gives me a feeling of security, shared I believe by many in the inland Pacific Northwest. Whether I or others go there or not, we will have this feeling of enchantment and security. We could go there if we had to. God, for some, is someone to call on in time of trouble. So, also, is the wilderness for others.

Moderator Wayburn: The last question is directed to Dr. Nash. "Does the love of nature require the exclusion of man?"

Dr. Nash: This is a serious problem, perhaps the most serious facing wilderness preservation today. Since its inception in 1949 this conference has concerned itself repeatedly with the probability of wilderness being loved to death. It is the great irony of the preservation movement that for decades the Thoreaus and Muirs and Marshalls exhorted Americans to go to the wilderness. It now seems they have succeeded, but perhaps too well. The city people, like myself, come in such numbers as to threaten the existence of the naturalness they seek. It is no secret that in many parts of the Sierra Nevada, grass for stock and firewood are becoming scarce. Campers even race each other for desirable campsites; the late arrivals at a meadow or lake are faced with "no vacancy." Clearly, something is wrong here, but what can be done? Rationing? Some have thought that charging a fee or limiting the number in an area and their length of stay must be used to save wilderness from its enthusiasts. But there's a rub here: such regulation creates an artificiality that, to me at least, vitiates the meaning of wilderness. As soon as you tell me that I'm limited to three and a half days at, say, Reflection Lake, and then I have to get out because another party is coming in, I am in a hotel, not a wilderness. Perhaps wilderness preservation will come to depend on total human exclusion, yet I would resent this too.

 *Part Three*

Banquet *April 7, 1967*

PRESENTATION OF THE JOHN MUIR AWARD
George Marshall

WELCOME TO CALIFORNIA
Robert H. Finch

ADDRESS
Orville L. Freeman

Dean E. McHenry, Master of Ceremonies

The Seventh Annual John Muir Award
1967

Presented by the Sierra Club to

Sigurd F. Olson

 in gratitude for the superior quality of his contributions toward preserving unspoiled a living part of the American heritage of wilderness

 in recognition of the excellence of his writing and leadership in conservation that we believe will truly make a difference a hundred years from now in the face of this land and in the mind of man

 and in appreciation of his role in assuring that America will remain more beautiful than it otherwise could have been for those who come after us.

His achievement carries forward the historic work of John Muir in rescuing for our time those primeval places epitomized in the great national parks.

George Marshall

President

Facsimile of award presented at the conference

George Marshall

PRESENTATION OF THE
JOHN MUIR AWARD

The John Muir Award was established by the Sierra Club in 1961 as its highest award for outstanding individual accomplishment, over a period of years, in fostering appreciation, interpretation, and preservation of scenic and wilderness values. Sigurd F. Olson's name is being included at this time in the following list of distinguished individuals who have received this honor:

First	William E. Colby	1961
Second	Olaus J. Murie	1962
Third	Ansel A. Adams	1963
Fourth	Walter A. Starr	1964
Fifth	Francis P. Farquhar	1965
Sixth	Harold C. Bradley	1966
Seventh	Sigurd F. Olson	1967

Robert H. Finch

WELCOME TO CALIFORNIA

I am here tonight, on behalf of the state of California, with the pleasant task of welcoming all of you to this critically important and, we hope, productive tenth biennial Wilderness Conference.

It has been said accurately that California is an almost perfect microcosm of this whole nation in terms of the mix of industry, agriculture, urban and suburban use of land, as well as diversity of population.

This is, of course, a simplification, but in addition we must look at the emerging "slurbs" that are marking the face of America today. One stretches from Norfolk, Virginia, north to Boston, Massachusetts; a second spreads under the belly of the Great Lakes from Pittsburgh over to Milwaukee. These cross state lines. The third helps to make my point, and presents California with a unique opportunity. It runs from San Francisco to San Diego, entirely within one state's borders. We have the only situation where one state government alone has the authority —and accountability—to tackle the growth and direction of the urban explosion and to mitigate the collision course between urban explosion and environmental integrity.

We have so many unique and irreplaceable properties. I hardly need to list these for a group as sophisticated as this, for you know the wealth of resources we are talking about: redwoods, Torrey pines, the California condor, the deserts, and the Sierra Nevada. There is also the special zone of the great California coastline, which contains a variety of unique scenery and recreational opportunity of particular concern to the State Lands Commission. So, as in no other state, there is something in California to excite the interest of every individual who seeks the challenge of the primitive environment.

We acknowledge that actions of the federal government have been the cutting edge in preserving important areas of wilderness in California as well as the rest of the country. Large portions of California's four national parks are preserved in their natural state, many thousands of acres of parkland are presently accessible only by trail, and there are many more acres preserved in the national monuments. The recently enacted federal Wilderness Act establishes that legal mechanism by which portions of our national parks and monuments can be permanently designated as wilderness. And earlier this year we have had significant hearings in such widely separated areas as Lava Beds National Monument in Siskiyou County and Pinnacles National Monument in San Benito and Monterey Counties, with the aim of designating wilderness areas in each of these localities. It now seems probable that portions of these national monuments will be preserved in their natural condition.

The Forest Service, under the Department of Agriculture, has long carried out a splendid program of preserving portions of California's national forests in wilderness status.

Until recently, the efforts of California in protecting its natural treasures have been chiefly in the field of acquisition and maintenance of state parks and beaches. I can assure you that under William Penn Mott, Jr., Director of the Department of Parks and Recreation, this activity will be continued thoughtfully and imaginatively.

Under Norman B. Livermore, Jr., Administrator of Natural Resources, I believe you will see the state focusing its attention on those areas where the unique physical assets appear to be immediately and gravely threatened. This brings us face to face with our problem at Lake Tahoe. Because of the overlapping jurisdictions of two states, five counties, and numerous governing agencies, we find the whole ecology of the magnificent Tahoe basin in great jeopardy. It is now recognized that the principal threat to the basin is caused by the population pressure upon the carrying capacity of that region. The deterioration of the whole area is attributable to overintensive use of the land and space and has a direct impact on the basic purity of the waters of the lake.

As most of you know, in 1965 California joined with Nevada in the creation of the Lake Tahoe Joint Study Committee. There was a series of public hearings that culminated in a report released in March of this year. That report called for the creation by concurrent legislation in the states of California and Nevada of a Tahoe Regional Agency possessing regionwide and bistate jurisdiction. The primary responsibility of the Tahoe Agency would be to preserve and maintain the physical environment of the Lake Tahoe region, including its natural endowment for recreational and residential purposes, but particularly stressing the ecological stability of the entire area. Two identical bills have been introduced in the legislature aimed at immediately implementing the recommendations of the Joint Study Committee. The bills are A.B. 1378, introduced by Assemblyman Don Mulford, and A.B. 1362, introduced by Assemblyman Ed Z'Berg. Both of these bills have wide sponsorship and broad bipartisan support.[*]

Another asset that California has acted to preserve is the very bay at our door. In 1850, before any diking or filling of San Francisco Bay had begun, the San Francisco, San Pablo and Suisun Bays totaled 680 square miles in area. That total today is down to about four hundred squares miles. In response to the public outcry over the steady, piecemeal filling that was threatening to make it even smaller, the California Legislature in 1965 created the San Francisco Bay Conservation and Development Commission (BCDC). The assignment of this organization is to make a study of the Bay Area and prepare a comprehensive and enforceable plan for the maximum conservation and protection of its waters and shoreline. This study is to be presented to the governor and legislature by January of 1969. In the meantime, no filling of the bay is permitted without a finding by BCDC that it will not impair the plan they are formulating.

I think the creation of BCDC is significant for a number of reasons. First, it is a clear recognition by the state of the need to approach regional problems on a regional basis. It is legislative recognition that the bay is a physical asset of central importance to the economy, the ecology, and the stability of the entire San Francisco Bay Area. But, significantly for this conference, it is also recognition of the importance of tidelands and marshlands as a wilderness asset and component. Fish and wildlife, of course, depend on the shallow parts of the bay for feeding and breeding. In 1850 there were approximately three hundred square miles of marshland around the edge of the bay, and today this figure is seventy-five square miles. You, as well as research biologists, recognize that marshlands are in themselves extremely productive. For example, cordgrass, a plant indigenous to marshlands, has seven times the food value of an equivalent acreage of wheat. The continued filling in of marshlands and mud flats could threaten and prejudice the entire life cycle of nature in that bay.

---

[*] Assembly Bill No. 1362 was passed by both houses of the California legislature, and approved by Governor Ronald Reagan on August 30, 1967. A special session of the Nevada Legislature will consider the proposed bistate pact in early 1968.— *The Editors.*

It is to be hoped that the activities of BCDC will be applied in other areas of the state. I am one of three members of the State Lands Commission, which is vested with exclusive jurisdiction over all ungranted tidelands and submerged lands owned by the state. We are assigned responsibility to control these lands and lease or otherwise dispose of them in accordance with the presently applicable provisions of law. Sadly enough, the legislative intent behind most of these laws does not appear to be aimed at preserving these areas in any sense as wilderness. I have observed in the few short months I have served that we really are charged with exploiting the tidelands and other submerged lands for the purpose of extracting oil or other minerals and creating fill designed to permit the erection and maintenance of structures. It is clear that we cannot, within the regulations and authority afforded the State Lands Commission, attack the overall environmental problems of the state of California, and we must have some new legislation vesting an overview function in some entity if we are to guarantee ecological integrity in the state for the years to come.

I am touching on only a few points, because my primary message is a welcome to you here. But I want to make it clear that I recognize the frailties of government at any level when it comes to conservation, and I am sure that to you sophisticates of wilderness protection, any government very often resembles a lumbering beast. It is often as difficult to get government to move as it was for the zoo attendants to get Herman the rhinoceros, who recently escaped from a southern California carnival, out of the marsh. To accomplish this they brought a close friend, an elephant, to coax and entice him onto firm ground. I will simply say flatly that when it comes to the state of California, it may be that you must be the ones to coax the lumbering beast into further action.

We are proud of our heritage in California, uniquely oriented to the appreciation of nature and man's enrichment. We have done much, but we must do more—more in the way of upgrading curricula at every level so that the necessity for conservation and outdoor education is known to each child; more in the way of establishing a realistic and workable gradation from the greenbelts to simple accessible parks to pure wilderness; more in the way of developing balanced systems of transportation that do not submerge all natural environment to the automobile.

California today stands at the peak in what must be called a watershed period: on the one hand, doubly blessed with more than our share of natural resources, on the other hand, already the most populous state in the nation, and facing a doubling of our population in the next twenty years. When historians write of this fantastic era, I think they will agree with Dickens: "It was the best of times, it was the worst of times . . . it was the season of Light, it was the season of Darkness." And we will have to ask, What did we do about it? Did we make a difference? I think we can make a difference. And what we do in this great state of California, charged with this special responsibility, must certainly affect the whole nation. As Richard Armour put it in the closing lines of his "I Loved You, California":

> "So leap with joy, be blithe and gay,
>   Or weep, my friends, with sorrow.
> What California is today,
>   The rest will be tomorrow."

Orville L. Freeman

ADDRESS

I have a long-standing personal commitment to wilderness and its preservation. Like your commitment, mine is the result of experiencing for myself what wilderness has to offer. I have packed and camped in the Bob Marshall, the Sawtooth, and the North Cascades. I have enjoyed the Boundary Waters Canoe Area back home in Minnesota ever since boyhood.

These trips—most of them with my family, others with Ed Cliff and Boyd Rasmussen, one with Justice Douglas, who asked to be remembered here tonight—have reinforced my feeling for the values that wilderness offers to each of us: a sense of timelessness, a renewal of spirit, a going back to our origins—things that are becoming lost almost beyond recall in this seventh decade of the twentieth century. And so I have a deep personal commitment to the values in which this organization has believed so strongly and acted so forcefully since the days of John Muir.

I am also interested in wilderness for professional reasons. As Secretary of Agriculture I have final responsibility for administering our present wilderness system and for recommending additions to it. Those of you who follow the national news know that the lot of a Secretary of Agriculture is not always a pleasant one. The difficulties inherent in the job have been compared to those in crossing the Continental Divide in midwinter with cement snowshoes. And so one tends to savor and grasp every pleasurable decision open to him. Two of these stand out in my mind.

The first was the opportunity to inspect, study, and then *add* eleven areas to the National Wilderness System during my tenure as secretary. Five of the eleven are here in California, including the largest, the John Muir, in the Sierra Nevada. The second decision came out of a nostalgic pilgrimage to the Boundary Waters Canoe Area, which was established half a century ago by the U.S. Forest Service, and where I had roamed as a boy. Here I was able to restore some of the wilderness values that had been lost over the years, by restricting powerboats and snowmobiles and by prohibiting or phasing out timber harvesting in an additional quarter-million acres. This brought the "no-cut" zone to 600,000 acres in the Boundary Waters Canoe Area.

In these actions I followed a long tradition established by previous secretaries and chiefs of the Forest Service. The first federal land specifically described and formally designated for wilderness protection was in the Gila National Forest in New Mexico. Today, about one acre out of every twelve in the national forests is under wilderness protection. These are still the only acres so designated under the 1964 Wilderness Act.

The act was a landmark piece of legislation. This Administration believed in it and helped attain it. I know that the Sierra Club is rightfully proud of its role in helping to build a climate of public opinion that assured passage.

There have been other great conservation acts in the past, but usually they were remedial acts intended to repair an abused resource rather than to preserve it in the first place. For instance, in the early 1900's the Forest Service and the national forest system were created only after wasteful logging practices had all but denuded a continent. In the 1930's, USDA's Soil Conservation Service was created only after much of our irreplaceable topsoil had washed down to the Gulf of Mexico; only after dust storms had deposited much of the Southwest in the East. The Wilderness Act, by contrast, was an action not to repair but to preserve and protect from harm a priceless national asset. It was a rare example of foresight rather than hindsight. It was a notable and somewhat unique chapter in our conservation history.

This morning Chief Cliff reported to you on primitive-area review and administration under that act. He outlined the paradoxes in the Wilderness Act itself and the difficulties that "excepted uses" present in practical administration. I would reinforce several of his points that deserve your special attention.

The first is quantity—and quality. It now appears that we can establish in the national forest units of the wilderness system an area at least as large as and possibly larger than the combined acreage of existing wilderness and primitive areas. This matter of quantity—acreage—

is important. More than fourteen million acres are now under wilderness or primitive protection. Four times as many people are packing into these areas today than ten years ago, and more will use them in the future. And so a great many acres are needed to disperse travel and prevent overuse. Accordingly, in the classification process that we are involved in now, it is tempting to look only at numbers and to overlook quality. I think this is a mistake. Philosophically, I think we should settle for no less than the highest quality wilderness in our national system. The legislation calls for it; our posterity demands it.

As a practical matter, substandard additions to the present system will make it extremely difficult for future administrators to resist the breaching of present high-quality areas with the works of man. If development already exists in one unit of the Wilderness System, it is harder to keep development out of others. For instance, I have resisted for years a mass winter sports development in the San Gorgonio Wilderness. It would cut the heart out of the area. So far I have been successful. But if in the past I had recommended for inclusion in the wilderness system an area containing substantial works of man, it would now be infinitely more difficult to oppose comparable development in the San Gorgonio.

Then there is the matter of maintaining quality in existing areas. Both the Sierra Club and the Department of Agriculture strongly supported the Wilderness Act. Both of us opposed, during its period of gestation, certain of the nonwilderness exceptions that were written into the final act. And both of us, I think it is fair to say, came to the conclusion that the final legislation, even with the problems of administration that Chief Cliff mentioned this morning, was better than no legislation at all.

This was my personal belief. I mentioned earlier that from 1961 through 1964 I added some eleven areas, totaling two million acres, to the wilderness system by secretarial order. But under the laws then extant, there would have been nothing to prevent some future secretary, who felt differently than I, from removing wilderness without even a hearing. For this reason, and others, I felt the compromises that had to be made were worth the cost.

In the very near future this Wilderness Act, with all its good points and imperfections, will be at issue in one of the most spectacular areas of the United States. Those of you who have tramped the slopes of the North Cascades, as I have—passing through successive life zones in a single day, from tall Douglas fir to the twisted brush at timberline—know that I use the word "spectacular" advisedly when I describe this area.

The Cascades are an ocean of mountains, frozen in space and time, wave after cresting wave of stone, dotted with the deep blue-green of alpine lakes, laced with the glacial remnants of another age. If you have seen the San Juans, or the East Face of the Tetons, you have an appreciation of the Cascades—but only a partial appreciation. To call them "America's Alps" understates the case. They are uniquely American, and if Americans destroy their character we will not see their like again.

My poor words cannot capture them. The nearest approximation in print I have seen is the Sierra Club's book, *The Wild Cascades,* in which a combination of photos and text gives a feel for their timeless values. But really to know these mountains one must experience them with all the senses: to hear the wind above timberline, a voice like all the rivers in the world flowing over a thousand miles of granite and green; smell the pine; feel a pebble polished by eons of time. If everyone could do this, even for a day, I am confident that most of the controversy over invasion of the wilderness would rapidly disappear. But unfortunately it has not.

Within this fastness is Miner's Ridge and Image Lake. This ridge is also the site of a valuable copper deposit, placed there, perhaps, by a wise Creator to test whether man could forego material riches for the fullness of the spirit. We may face this test in the very near future, when and if application is made to begin open-pit mining operations within the wilderness. The reasons given for this mine are not so very different from the reasons given for other resource development: the copper deposit is valuable; companies are being encouraged to increase domestic copper production; and, as we all know, there is a war going on. The company owns, or already has mineral rights on, some three thousand acres of land. Many of these claims were patented years ago.

Perhaps some of the same reasons were given many years ago when a mine was opened on the rim of the Grand Canyon. But, in balance, it can also be pointed out that: (1) Our present war effort will not suffer if Miner's Ridge is left undeveloped. Neither will our civilian standard of living suffer. (2) This is not the only undeveloped copper deposit in the United States. Others exist, perhaps less valuable, perhaps more costly to develop. Some are in the Upper Lake States—in areas of high unemployment—where development could both decrease the jobless rate and leave wilderness values unimpaired. It is not a case, in short, of "either–or." It is rather a case of economics, of choosing alternatives; of balancing a priceless, yet intangible, national treasure against ledger sheets and profits.

The decision in this case lies almost totally with the Kennecott Copper Corporation, and not with the Secretary of Agriculture. They own, or have claims on, the land on which the deposit is located. The language of the Wilderness Act and the intent of Congress is clear. They have the right to develop it, if they insist. The scenic values of this area are as well known to the company as they are to you and me. The company can, if it so chooses, ignore these values, gouge out its road, and begin operations. If this happens, I want them and you to know that I will take steps to insure that the highest standards of performance and restoration, under the law, are observed. But I cannot really believe that such an application will ever reach my desk. I urge the management and directors of Kennecott Copper Corporation, who will make this decision, to consider and weigh most carefully the very real and transcendent values that will be destroyed if mining is begun. I further urge that the Sierra Club take every possible opportunity to inform the officers and shareholders of the company, and the American public, of the issues at stake on Miner's Ridge. These issues are not simple. But if they are presented fairly and completely, I am confident that the public interest will prevail.

The issue in the North Cascades presents, in microcosm, some of the larger conservation issues we face across the continent. Ours is a nation of exploding population and expanding standards of living. There is a nearly infinite demand on very finite natural resources. This means pressure for consumptive use of resources such as the copper deposit at Miner's Ridge; it also means the pressure of people on wilderness, which Chief Cliff discussed this morning. It seems to me that one of the best things we can do to relieve such pressure on wilderness is to provide alternatives, to make sure that resources and recreation are plentifully available in nonwilderness areas. Let me illustrate what I mean, first in material resources, second in recreation.

If you're a family of four, as the Freemans are, then each year your family uses an amount of paper representing the annual growth of two acres of timber land. This paper must be produced—for textbooks, the daily newspaper, even for the *Sierra Club Bulletin*. But we do not have to sacrifice our wilderness to get it, nor do we have to saw down all the trees in the national forests. Most forest land in private hands is now producing at only about 50 per cent of capacity. This can be increased radically, given enough public support, research, and funds. Continued support for wise multiple use practices in the nonwilderness portions of our national forests can continue to provide needed timber. Doing so will go a long way toward removing the pressure on the wilderness.

We can also relieve the pressure on wilderness of people. The demand for outdoor recreation is inceasing at a rate about four times as great as population increase. The use of the national forests for recreation purposes in terms of visitors is today almost double what it was when I became Secretary of Agriculture only six years ago. Shorter working hours, higher incomes, a desire to escape increasing urbanization—all these contribute to this trend. This is a demand that we will have to meet, one way or another. The department is trying to help by providing more outdoor recreation both in the national forests and on private lands.

In the national forests last year, in addition to acquiring private holdings within wilderness areas with Golden Eagle funds, we also acquired 18,000 acres in the Sylvania tract in Michigan, another 14,000 acres in the George Washington and Jefferson National Forests in Virginia, and 6,000 more acres in Oklahoma, among others.

The department's Soil Conservation Service, Extension Service, Agricultural Stabilization and Conservation Service, and the Farmers Home Administration, as well as other agencies in the USDA, are working closely with farmers who wish to develop recreation businesses on their own land. As of now, more than 30,000 farmers are devoting parts of their land, diversifying their operation, to income-producing recreational purposes. Perhaps this kind of recreation is not your cup of tea. But many people do enjoy camping in improved areas, or skiing with the help of a chair lift or T-bar, or spending a day at a national seashore area or a week on a farm.

Leaving aside the merits of one particular kind of recreation over another, it seems to me that we wilderness supporters have a real stake in providing other kinds of recreation for those who wish it, if for no other reason than to take the population pressure off the wilderness and primitive areas.

The late Howard Zahniser, former Executive Secretary of the Wilderness Society, put it this way: "The best apparent hope for success in the preservation of . . . wilderness is actually in application of the multiple use principle. To preserve some areas free from timber cutting will require adequate timber production on other areas. Preserving natural areas undeveloped . . . will require adequate provision of developed areas with the . . . facilities needed by the large numbers seeking outdoor recreation with conveniences. . . ."

I am proud of the Forest Service's application of the multiple use principle. In our national forests we offer everything from mass skiing to the solitude of wilderness, with every gradation between. Developed sites—picnic areas, campgrounds, and winter sports sites—occupy but a tiny fraction of the area of these forests yet provide facilities for a very high proportion of the visitors. In all, the national forests received 173 million visitor-days of use last year, nearly half of the recreation visits on *all* federal lands, and more than three times the use received by lands managed by any other federal agency. I commend for your study—and I hope for your support—a continuing, wise multiple use policy as the best long-term hope for preserving the wilderness values we all cherish.

All the things I have discussed here tonight are part of a larger conservation picture. The Department of Agriculture is interested in this larger picture; so is the Sierra Club. The department is responsible for administering conservation programs embracing some 81 per cent of the nation's total land: all the cropland, pasture, range, and 186 million acres of national forests and grasslands. We also administer cooperative programs on much of the private forest land.

These conservation activities account for about $900 million of the department's annual expenditures and engage about half our total personnel, some 50,000 persons. As a matter of fact, by all odds the greatest increase in personnel over the last ten years has been in conservation work.

Of necessity, USDA is concerned with both the here-and-now and the future. Trees that will mature one hundred years from now are being planted in the national forests today. The soil that will feed 300 million Americans in the year 2000 has to be saved today.

In recent months we have been studying, probing, examining that future in a series of exploratory messages entitled, "Agriculture/2000." It came as quite a shock to me as we were writing these to realize that the year 2000 lies no further ahead of us than the year 1934, the second year of the New Deal, lies behind. I would like to discuss with you briefly three of the more important conservation areas that I recently reviewed in "Agriculture/2000: Resources in Action." They are: (1) the quantity of our conservation efforts, (2) a planned land use policy, and (3) preservation.

(1) *Quantity of effort.* At the time President Kennedy took office, in 1961, he inherited a federal budget of roughly $2.4 billion for conservation and natural resource measures. President Johnson's 1968 budget calls for $3.9 billion. This is a 60 per cent increase in seven years. Yet the nation must be prepared to devote much more to conservation than it is currently spending.

This may seem self-evident to those of us in the conservation movement. It is less evident in much of the political dialogue current on the national scene. It seems to me that we have to convince many more people than are presently convinced that a new national park, or an additional wilderness, or the buying of another national seashore area is as important to them personally as is a second car or a larger motorboat.

This is a difficult thing to do, but not impossible. Many of us are convinced already. We cannot do it painlessly, since all these things cost money. But I hope the Sierra Club and like-minded organizations can increase their efforts to present these issues to the public.

Quantity alone, however, isn't the complete answer. We also need:

(2) *A planned land use policy.* Here I think we are sadly remiss as a nation. We need a real, far-reaching planned land use policy. The U.S. Department of Agriculture's Soil Conservation Service estimates that we have some 680 million acres of land in the contiguous forty-eight states suitable for cultivation. This land feeds us now, and it will have to feed 100 million more Americans thirty-three years from now. Planning to preserve this prime farmland is of the utmost importance. Obviously, we cannot exist without the food it produces. But what are we doing? Every day, we are losing thousands of prime acres to subdivisions, highways, airports. We are burying it under concrete or houses, and it is not likely to be jackhammered clear again. More is involved than just farmland. We're also burying land needed for recreation, pushing the open spaces farther away from the urban residents who need it most.

So we need a sound land use policy for the nation, one that identifies land suitable for multiple use and single use, a policy that establishes priorities and makes the best use of a shrinking natural resource. Such a policy would mean building highways, to the extent possible, on unproductive land rather than on rich topsoil. It would mean an opportunity for local communities to identify land needed for future recreation, and provide a way to finance the land *now*, before urban land costs double again, as they did in the last decade.

A policy like this requires information of the type now being gathered in USDA's Land Use Inventory, but on a continental scale and in much more detail. Planned land use incorporates two elements. The first is use—determining the best use that can be made of our land. The second is preservation—preserving land suitable for wilderness, crops, open space, or mass recreation. This brings me to my final point:

(3) *Preservation.* The national forest wilderness illustrates preservation in its classic sense of maintaining a resource in its primeval state. But this is not the only kind of preservation we need. In a somewhat different, and larger, sense, preservation means "preventive conservation."

In agriculture, it means the continued production of abundance without damaging man's ecology. For example, it consists of careful testing of herbicides and pesticides *before* use, careful education in their application, and continuous monitoring of their effects on the environment. All these functions are being performed by department scientists today. It means continuous research to discover biological and other nonchemical methods to control plant and animal pests, basic research in plant and animal genetics to discover resistant strains and species, new methods to control the dangerous byproducts of an industrial society.

In the long run, preventive conservation is much less expensive than restorative conservation. More important, some environments, once blighted by man, can never be repaired, no matter what we do. All our billions, all our technology, can never restore a single acre of wilderness if we fail to preserve it. In short, it means creating—for we do not have it now—an environment in which man "does not merely endure, but one in which he prevails." Some 70 per cent of our population is now crowded into 1 per cent of our total land area. In the city, in the country, almost everywhere he goes, the American is confronted with an environment dominated by his own technology. This is new; no others before us have experienced it on the scale we experience today. The end result is not certain. For man, with all his ability to adapt, for all his domination of the "lesser" species, still is a child of the sea, the mountains, the very wilderness he is rapidly obliterating. We are a nation bedazzled by technology, and addicted to crash solutions. But there are no instant ecologies; no instant wilderness. And so, in the final analysis, we must devote much more of our attention in the future to assessing each new technological development for its ultimate impact on man's environment.

I hope it is never said of this generation, as Stephen Vincent Benét once said of another: "They thought, because they had power, they had wisdom also."

We now have the power, literally, to move mountains. The next few years will determine if we have the wisdom to refrain from doing so.

REMARKS

Master of Ceremonies Dean E. McHenry: The messages we have heard tonight carry a depth and a special significance to all Americans. It is good for those of us who are true believers to come together and rededicate ourselves.

The problems of saving our forests, not just as outdoor museums but also for use of posterity; of saving enough water so that every household in the land can have the well-driller's minimum of a half a gallon per minute per family; of saving the soil that took centuries to develop, and the shoreline and the bay, the fish and game, including our wonderful sea lions of Ana Neuvo Island off the Pacific coast near Santa Cruz; of keeping the air free from pollution; and of preserving good recreational environments—these are our job. We cannot just say "they" in Washington, or "they" in Sacramento, "Why don't they do this?" It has got to be a job that comes out of our own minds and hearts, our own energy and our own persistence in looking after the preservation of what we inherited.

The secretary referred to the hundred years necessary to grow a tree to maturity. Some grow faster, some grow slower, but this is a pretty good norm, I think. It reminded me of a sign I saw in the London subway one summer. Through the courtesy of a beer or ale company, a poster showed beautiful trees planted along a roadway. The inscription on it was: "He who plants an avenue of trees plants not for himself but for England."

 *Part Four*

Forgotten Wilderness

Historically greatest emphasis has been placed on the need to preserve representative segments of forested and mountain areas in wilderness condition. The rapid pace of present development is now bringing great pressure upon the last remnants of isolated lands and waters that were bypassed in earlier surges of use. The natural values of deserts, caves, shoreline, wild rivers, and underwater areas are fast disappearing under human use and exploitation. The need and opportunity to reserve undeveloped portions of forgotten desert and marine environments as wilderness will be explored in this session.

Daniel B. Luten

INTRODUCTION

The infant who crawls from his mother's knee has begun his exploration of the world. But with each foot of separation, his feeling of security dwindles and, sooner rather than later, he returns to establish his confidence before turning away again. (What miniskirts, and the difficulty of reaching them, will do to the human psyche has not yet been told us by those concerned with our minds.) The duality of our nature, which causes us to probe the unknown and then to shrink back from it, is not new, nor is it unique to us.

All of animate life is faced with the problem of securing its future. Each organism has come to have instincts, tropisms, behavior patterns, call them what you will, that direct it and instruct it to seek opportunity, but also to secure its continued existence.

The patterns are almost as diverse as life itself. I have not the time this morning even to suggest them, but they will come in hosts to your mind. Repeatedly, insistently, emerging from among these patterns is a polarity—the search for security against the search for opportunity, nostalgia against wanderlust. These are not essentially at odds, of course. Opportunity fulfilled provides security; security may be a base from which to seek opportunity. Each promotes the purpose of the animal, which is, after all, to survive, first as an individual, next as a lineage.

This polarity is not absent in mankind, even though man is perhaps the most adaptable of all animals and perhaps the least instinctual. The great emigration of men from the ancestral regions of southeast Africa, enduring perhaps a quarter of a million years, ten thousand generations, has quite plausibly modified the human mind, just as their efforts to shape stone tools have shaped our minds and our hands as well. While other animals have been content to conform in most things, to seek opportunity narrowly, man the heretic, the deviant, the nonconformist, has upon occasion rejected his culture and has turned away from his environment.

Inescapably, we are the children of our past. And it is proper to ask, Who in fact were our ancestors? Were they the men who stayed in the settlements? Were they the men who stayed even though the situation, once secure, had become desperate? Or were they the men who moved onward, whether from curiosity, from simple refusal to put up with crowding, or because they were thrown out? Those who stayed raised families, but did their grandchildren die of privation? Those who wandered mostly died of unforeseen hazards but, when they survived, they sired entire tribes.

Whose children are we? I think we are the children of both, and I think this still shows in our nature. Each of us is, in some degree, endowed with both wanderlust and homesickness. How much of each, and of what quality, on this we vary. At one extreme, I may mention John Ledyard, who in the eighteenth century set out by canoe from central New Hampshire to sail with Captain Cook's third expedition, to walk across Russia to Irkutsk, and to die in Cairo on the threshold of exploration of Africa. At the other extreme stands William Ellery Leonard, seared in his infancy by a locomotive and ending afraid to go beyond the limits of a Wisconsin campus.

Whether wanderlust comes first or whether it awakens only when security hard-pressed becomes desperate, I do not know. Whether wanderlust is a search for opportunity only, or for insecurity, I do not know. But when you see, or imagine, an infant venturing from and then returning to his mother's knee, imagine also those ten thousand generations of your ancestors who lived while men were walking from southeast Africa to Cape Horn, and back and forth and in and out and up and down. Because they wandered and survived, it is instinctive in you. That is why you need wilderness; that is why you must seek what is not known.

Let me call on Henry David Thoreau for support with his "Most men lead lives of quiet desperation" and "Our village life would stagnate if it were not for the unexplored forests and meadows which surround it. We need the tonic of wildness. . . . At the same time that we are earnest to explore and learn all things, we require that all things be mysterious and unexplorable, that land and sea be infinitely wild."

But still a question remains unanswered: Is wilderness in the landscape or in the mind? To the boy brought up on the pavements of Brooklyn, the Catskills may be remote and wild. To the boy brought up on the fringe of Montana's statutory wilderness, the mountains are home, the Catskills a cityscape, and Brooklyn a wilderness. Do wildernesses of the mind satisfy the need for wanderlust, or must the need be met on the land? Is wilderness the edge of knowledge? Is it personal or universal, subjective or objective?

We do not intend, I believe, to attack this question today. We have enough without it. Instead we will start from two propositions:

(1) We have been on this continent for three and a half centuries, most of this time narrowly confined to the Atlantic seaboard. We had been here two and a quarter of those three and a half centuries when Thoreau went to Walden Pond. Our traditional views of wilderness have developed, as Roderick Nash told us yesterday, in large measure from the writing and painting of it. For most of our tenure, well-watered, forested valleys rising to wooded hills lay to the west of our homes. Only in the last century have new wildernesses come into our literature and our art: the Mississippi's waterways, the plains, the arid rangelands, and finally the alpine meadows and, rising above timberline, the stony slopes of western peaks.

(2) Three years ago Congress passed an act to preserve certain wild lands in their primitive state. We did this because of the persuasiveness of dedicated advocates of wilderness. Why they are thus dedicated has never, it seems to me, been said clearly. But I have tried to suggest some qualities of human nature itself which may be responsible.

We have now a considerable body of conventions concerning wilderness and we have a legal definition of it. Inescapably these reflect much of these past three hundred and fifty years. But we must not imagine the matter to be settled; we still must ask: Has the literature guided us wisely, or have we overlooked something? Have we defined wilderness broadly, or have we defined it narrowly and in doing so forgotten other wildernesses?

In reflecting on what may have been forgotten, we will think first of the desert, the original Biblical wilderness, and next of the sea's edge. Later, we will recall also the Arctic wilderness, wild rivers, caverns, and submarine and island wildernesses. And we may wonder about a host of others, about bogs, marshes, and even microwildernesses.

We have brought to you today a group of distinguished experts to initiate a discussion of the first two sorts of wild lands that we tend to forget: the desert and the edge of the sea. We hope, with the start they will give us this morning, to come to see more clearly what we wish to do with these places and what we mean when we say "wilderness."

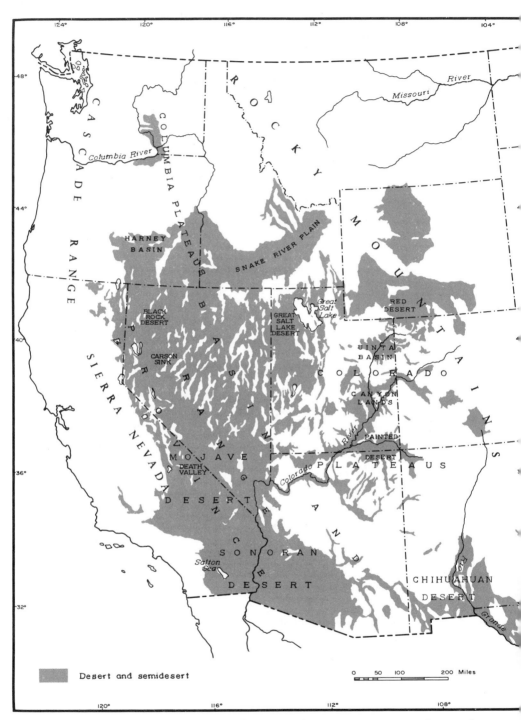

Arid Lands of Western United States (After U.S. Department of Agriculture
map "Major Land Use in the United States," 1950.)

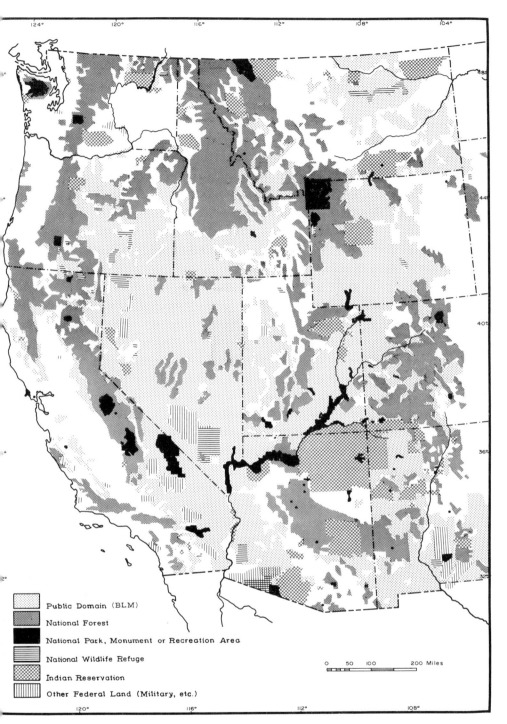

Public Domain (BLM)

National Forest

National Park, Monument or Recreation Area

National Wildlife Refuge

Indian Reservation

Other Federal Land (Military, etc.)

0   50   100   200 Miles

Public and Indian Lands of Western United States (Intermingled private
holdings not shown.)

Charles B. Hunt

VALUES IN DESERT WILDERNESS

In speaking about values in desert wilderness, I use the term "desert" in a very broad sense to refer to lands that are largely barren because water is scarce and undependable. In this quantitative age, it might be more fashionable to define desert with a number coefficient that balances such factors as precipitation, infiltration, transpiration, evaporation, and perspiration. But even if an exact definition could be agreed upon, the facts of desert life are such that it would have to be applied in a general way. By "wilderness" I mean only that the lands are thinly populated; I exclude areas that are densely populated. Unfortunately, man has contributed to making some parts of the desert uninhabitable, for dump sites are much too common in our desert wilderness.

In today's world, "value" usually means one of two economic worths: the worth if you want to buy it, or the worth if you want to sell it. In this discussion I refer to spiritual, educational, and cultural values. In 1936, while mapping geology along the canyons in southeastern Utah, my packer and I had stopped for lunch at a scenic rim point overlooking the Dirty Devil River. We ate in silence. I was wholly absorbed with the view when the packer, an old-time cowpuncher, broke the silence with, "There's just gotta be mineral in those rocks; no piece of country could be so gosh-darned worthless."

The values I refer to are those qualities contained in beautiful or exotic scenery. To many people, the quality is the scenery itself; to others, the qualities include questions and understanding about how all this came to be. Others find their values in the plants and animals and their habitats or adaptations. Still others find some treasure in the historical and archaeological record, like the values ascribed by the historian H. H. Bancroft to the humble Humboldt River: "In the course of westward-marching empire few streams on the North American continent have played a more important part than the Humboldt River of Nevada. Among the water courses of the world it can lay claim neither to great beauty nor to remarkable utility. Its great work was to open a way, first for the cattle train and then for the steam train, through a wilderness of mountains, through ranges which otherwise would run straight across its course. It is the largest river of this region, and the only one hereabouts running from east to west. Most of the others are with the mountains, north and south."

We should mention some examples of our deserts and consider some of the ways their wilderness values can be made available to an increasing population and yet be preserved.

The Dirty Devil country is typical of an extensive part of the Colorado Plateau known as the Canyon Lands section. The plateau slopes west from the rim before rising again to the Henry Mountains in southeastern Utah, one of the several groups of laccolithic mountains on the Colorado Plateau. These mountains have a special place in geological science because of the classic study made there in 1876 by Grove Karl Gilbert of the Powell Survey. Because of the excellent exposures, a number of concepts were developed that are fundamental in geology, and this isolated group of desert mountains, still not very accessible, is referred to in the geological literature of every language. Both the desert by the Dirty Devil River and the nearby forested Henry Mountains are largely public domain lands administered by the Bureau of Land Management.

The canyon of the Dirty Devil River is three thousand feet deep and the mountains, twenty-five miles away, are five thousand feet higher than the plateau. The gorgeous ground colors can be read in the sky on partly cloudy days; the geologic pattern can be seen there as well as on the ground.

A major problem in desert preservation is the location of new roads. The road that the state of Utah is now building to Lake Powell illustrates the problem. When highway engineers plan a road, they seek routes where building costs are least, which is understandable and reasonable, but I submit there are other values besides the mighty dollar that should be considered in planning highways in the midst of such scenery. The most economical route in this area, according to the engineers, is in a broad flat between the canyons and the mountains, a route that misses most of the spectacular views. Knowing the country, I dispute the cost figures projected for alternate routes. Even assuming they are right, I contend that the state of Utah and the United States as a whole would be richer if the highway had been placed along the rim of the Dirty Devil River with its unparalleled vistas in every direction.

This route had been suggested to Utah officials, to the Interior Department, and to the Bureau of Public Roads, but the futility of the suggestions serve chiefly to demonstrate the need for some overall planning so that all values would be considered. Here is a tremendous capital asset that is not returning to us the interest it could.

I should have commented earlier that the name Dirty Devil was given by Major John Wesley Powell. It is the antithesis of the Bright Angel, also named by Powell, and also a tributary of the Colorado River. East of it is Labyrinth Canyon of the Green River, most of which is outside Canyonlands National Park. Why? Probably because these lands may support a dozen cows. Now I am not one to begrudge the cows their feed, but I would like to see such lands protected for visitors to enjoy too. The problem in usage of such lands is not too many roads, but roads in the wrong places.

Another kind of desert terrain and another kind of protection problem is found in Castle Valley, Utah, between the Colorado River and La Sal Mountains. This is a nearly dry, anticlinal valley over salt beds, with colorful stacks or rock monuments of red sandstone hundreds of feet high. The salt beds under this valley have considerable potential mineral value, and *now* is the time, before the deposits are mined, to plan how they might be developed with least damage to this scenery. Dramatic contrast in the desert scene in this region is provided by the La Sal Mountains, which rise to more than 12,000 feet.

A very different kind of desert can be found in the badlands of Cretaceous shale located near Utah's Henry Mountains. The badlands of South Dakota have been made into a national monument, but these lands are much "badder." In fact this particular area, without roads or trails, is the most worthless piece of real estate in the country. It contains no water, and is virtually without animals, vegetables, or minerals. "*No* piece of country could be so gosh-darned worthless!" About one hundred square miles here constitutes a trackless maze avoided by livestock and avoided by people. It is a dried-up Death Valley, which in summer provides a sample of one of the levels of hell. Yet the terrain is so fantastically exotic it has an interest all its own. Moreover, these badlands provided the basis for many of the concepts about erosion and land sculpture developed by G. K. Gilbert in his study of this area. No one would want to camp here, but many would enjoy visiting it. I have recommended to the Bureau of Land Management that consideration be given to erecting signs telling about these badlands and their significance for revealing processes of land sculpture, and building access roads to the *edge* of the area so persons could visit it.

Where formations in the desert are of sandstone, dunes are plentiful. These are always an asset, not just as scenery or scientific interest, but as a place where mom and pop can stop, and the kids can run off some of their accumulated steam. Having been through the wars, both with children and grandchildren, I know that these huge sandpiles have unusual values.

Volcanic formations in the desert arouse interest and stimulate the imagination. Some lava flows are young enough to have been witnessed by Indians. Some lavas have created volcanic necks like the famous pillar at Shiprock, New Mexico. About twenty such necks are clustered on the east side of Mt. Taylor in northwestern New Mexico, and one provides a natural cross-section of a volcano. The Columbia Plateau in eastern Washington and Oregon is the physiographic province for illustrating lavas and their structures, such as columnar jointing, or the pillow structures that develop where lavas enter lakes. This feature can be seen today in Hawaii, where lava flows extend to the sea. Amboy Crater, at Bristol Dry Lake, in California's Mojave Desert, contains another young volcanic cone and lava flow.

Still different kinds of deserts are in the Basin and Range province, found in Utah, Nevada, California, Arizona, and New Mexico; here there are fault-block mountains separated by basins that are structural rather than erosional valleys. In the middle of the valleys are playas, or dry lake beds, which may be mud flats or salt pans. Gravel fans rise from the edge of the playa extending to the bordering mountains. The mountains have a variety of landforms, depending on whether their rocks are Precambrian crystalline, which develop rounded landforms, or rough craggy mountains of limestone and dolomite mostly suited for bighorn sheep, or Tertiary volcanic formations, which form equally rough but more colorful mountains.

Major features of the Great Basin portion of the Basin and Range province are the remains of the great Pleistocene lakes. The largest was Lake Bonneville, in northwestern Utah. It was one thousand feet deep and its shorelines are conspicuously impressed on the mountainsides around the lake. Another large one, Lake Lahontan, was in western Nevada. Even Death Valley at one time had a lake six hundred feet deep. Altogether there were several dozen such Pleistocene lakes in the western desert regions. Great Salt Lake, the residue of Lake Bonneville, is certainly unique, and steps are being taken to make Antelope Island in the lake part of the system of national parks and monuments.

With this brief summary of the several kinds of desert terrain, we might consider now some aspects of desert plant geography. Within each climatic zone are great variations in the distribution of plants and animals, controlled by differences in soil types. Ecologists refer to this as the edaphic factor, but since they really mean the geology, they might as well eliminate the jargon. We begin by distinguishing two very different plant habitats: those where ground water is shallow and provides a perennial water supply to plants—plants that can grow there are known as phreatophytes; and the habitats where ground water is too deep to be reached by plant roots, where the plants— xerophytes—must be capable of surviving protracted periods of drought.

The kind and composition of a stand of phreatophytes faithfully records the occurrence of the water supply and its quality. Around saline playas and lakes the phreatophytes are zoned in accordance with the salinity of the ground water. In a particular environment, each species has its limits of tolerance. For example, in some environments honey mesquite extends to the 0.5 per cent brine line; this is potable water but has strong taste. It has body. Arrowweed extends to the 3 per cent brine line, which is approximately as salty as sea water; pickleweed extends to the 6 per cent brine line, which is the limit for flowering plants. Greater salinities are reflected in zonation of the microflora, algae, fungi, and bacteria.

The composition and healthiness of the other major plant group of the desert, the xerophytes, depends on the quantity of water available for plant growth, which is a function of catchment area and rates of runoff (or infiltration). A simple example may be seen beside most highways in the desert. The growth is considerably better by the road because that strip collects runoff from the pavement. Mapping the different kinds of surfaces on gravel fans quickly clarifies the reason for differences in plant stands found growing there. This has been done in Death Valley where one of the important discoveries of that research is that for healthy growth, plants need water.

Plants also record climatic changes of recent date. In a period of wet years a species may be able to invade ground that ordinarily is too dry for its needs. In a following period of dry years the stand is left as a group of dead plants.

The southern part of the Basin and Range province has extensive cactus gardens, but rather than discussing more plant geography— after all, I am not a botanist—I would make a plea for the establishment of a United States Botanical Survey. Such an organization would systematically map the vegetation of the entire country, starting on public domain lands. The purpose would be to plot the location of existing vegetation and to relate it to the macro and microclimates, to the geology (which includes water supply, surficial deposits, and soils), and to historical and prehistorical vegetative changes. The United States Geological Survey is mapping the geology of the country, and that effort is paying off handsomely. The Soil Survey is mapping the soils, although it is much too restricted to agricultural areas. Some of the money being spent to reach the moon could better be invested in learning more about the world we live on, including the vegetation. Let me stress that the vegetation maps should show the here-and-now vegetation and not some theoretical climax.

While on the subject of desert preservation, I would like to urge the creation of a society for the protection of coyotes—protection against state and federal predator hunters. Mrs. Hunt and I spent seven months last year living in the desert, and at only two of our many camps did we hear the coyotes howl. With apologies to Rachel Carson, I would say that the poisons our government has scattered on the desert have created the silent night.

Among the fast-disappearing resources of desert wilderness are the hunting sites, campsites, and small homesites comprising our archaeological record of the prehistoric Indians. Most of the major sites that have impressive masonry structures have been set aside for special protection, but there still remain many sites that record equally important but different kinds of prehistory. In many parts of the desert the geologic evidence indicates the drying up of streams during the past 1,500 or 2,000 years, and in many valleys the archaeological remains provide evidence of a population shifting upstream as the flow diminishes. The sites also provide a measure of surface erosion since the original occupation. In other examples there is geologic evidence of former springs once surrounded by Indian campsites. At many places, these campsites record abrupt termination of use of these springs and so give a good indication of when they went dry.

These campsites, though numerous, are small. Mostly they are located near water, and the surrounding lands are especially valuable and much used. The Antiquities Act has been successful in curbing commercial exploitation of archaeological sites, but the protection problem has changed. Now we face the problem, not of commercial exploitation, but of the healthy, wholesome American families who enjoy the outdoors. In their search for outdoor respite from urbanization they take weekends for camping and for hunting Indian arrowheads and other artifacts. What is more American than hunting for arrowheads?

Local residents also know of these sites and spend part of their time collecting. In addition, visitors are encouraged to dig the sites and so they stay in the area a while longer. With the rapidly increasing accessibility of the desert this situation—which is widespread—will probably become worse before it improves. The situation might be partially remedied by the excavation and restoration of selected sites in some of these areas and by provision of pamphlets for self-guided tours. Something like this has been done at Painted Rocks State Park, Arizona. Through this kind of education perhaps local residents of desert areas would develop an interest in the protection and preservation of archaeological remains. Possibly this plan would not alleviate the problem, but most emphatically the present system is not working.

I am critical of the way the Antiquities Act is being administered today, for it serves chiefly to add to the paperwork of government administrators who issue permits for bona fide scientific work. This is simply an exercise in self-righteousness on the part of the administrator and on the part of the scientist, because for every professional working by permit there are one hundred amateurs enjoying the outdoor sport of collecting arrowheads and hunting for pots. This is a considered estimate; if anything, it is conservative.

And what about the purple bottle? How old must a tin can or bottle be before it ceases to be litter, with threatened fine for leaving it, and becomes an object of antiquity with threatened fine for removing it? When does junk become junque? And what about collecting fossils and rocks on the public domain?

The present system of licensing the 1 per cent of collecting that is legitimate, and doing virtually nothing about the 99 per cent that is not, is worse than misplaced effort; it diverts thought and attention from the big problem. A much simpler system involving general authorization to universities and museums engaged in bona fide scientific studies could be devised, and the funds and effort saved from the present system could better be spent in educational and developmental programs of the kind suggested, the kind that might win cooperation of local residents in the protection effort.

These are but a few of the values in the desert wilderness and a few of the problems. There are many others. How long, for example, must we tolerate withdrawals of ground water that deplete limited water reserves in order to grow cotton that is surplus? How much grazing is reasonable? The range today, in Utah at least, is in better condition than it was thirty years ago; the efforts in range improvement have not been in vain. How many roads and to where, and, as I have stressed, by what route? Active mining scars the landscape, but to a considerable degree unnecessarily so. Long-abandoned mines are among the most popular places in the desert, for these are the home of the purple bottle. Another problem concerns the proportion of desert that should reasonably be set aside for military reservations where the public is barred.

The greatest asset of the desert is its aridity. This is the main reason the Colorado Plateau has more than two dozen national parks and monuments; given a humid climate, that desert would be without its spectacular landforms. Its colorful rocks would be concealed. The land would be as crowded with people as is the rest of the country. As it is now, our vast desert, still retaining much of its wilderness features, has tremendous value as a rest-haven for the nearly 200 million of our population who do not live there. I have been going there almost yearly for more than thirty-five years; I hope it retains its primitive attractiveness so others may enjoy it as I have.

Walter P. Taylor

PRESERVATION OF
DESERT WILDERNESS

To some it will probably seem a tautology to refer to desert wilderness, for are not the desert and wilderness synonymous? If anybody wants it, why not turn over the desert to him and be done with it, saving our conservation efforts for the mountains, forests, rivers, seashores, and lakes?

I am not sure I can answer this question satisfactorily. I will have to appeal to those of you who have lived or traveled on the desert. Perhaps those gray and barren ranges of desert mountains have a fascination for you as they do for me:

> Something hidden Go and find it.
> Go and look behind the Ranges—
> Something lost behind the Ranges.
> Lost and waiting for you. Go!

We have to concede that a great number of extremely interesting phenomena are associated with these desert mountains and the broad valleys between them. With their erosion, alluvial fans, bajadas, and deeply cut canyons, they tell us of past geological events. Their lost mines and signs of former occupation hint at an interesting history. The keen hunter and the naturalist are sure to be enticed by the variety of desert wildlife. The speculator, the miner, the lumberman, the grazier, the recreationist—all are attracted by the possibility of financial gain.

But then, look a little farther. Closely or remotely associated with the desert mountains are a number of other fascinating features. Rock faults, some of outstanding scientific and historical interest, like the San Andreas that extends at least from the San Francisco Bay region to the Colorado Desert; eroded and grotesquely carved mesas; a wealth of ranges, natural bridges, lava flows, volcanoes, playas, dry lakes, and meteor craters; impressive cliffs; rocks of immense variety—these are the chief ingredients that exemplify the stress and strain of mountain-making and other geological phenomena.

What can we say about desert colors? For the most part they are gray and prosaic when first seen in the full glare of midday, but we are hardly prepared for the brilliance of desert sunrises and sunsets, mountains, cliffs, volcanic necks, and rocks. There are black canyons and grand canyons, not to mention the fleeting vivid colors sometimes seen in the rainbows and highly colored skies associated with desert storms.

It is easy to conclude that in a parched and dried-out land, water should be the *summum bonum*. The story of how plants, animals, and man secure their water supplies within these vast arid regions is of unending interest. Some desert rodents form water chemically within their bodies, eating only dry food. Others know where to dig for succulent roots. The coyote scoops out the sand in some favorable desert wash to reach water. Some desert plants give up water altogether in the dry season and become dormant. Others send their roots down one hundred feet to water. Some plants live on dew.

New discoveries about water and desert relationships are changing previous concepts. On a trip to Palestine, it was reported to us that David Ben Gurion, then Premier of Israel, was starting a fruit orchard at Sede Boqer in the Negev Desert south of Beersheba. And more recently, Robert P. Ambroggi of the Food and Agriculture Organization of the United Nations in Rome has reported in *Scientific American* (May, 1966) the news of extensive unsuspected water sources contained in the Sahara Desert.

No desert naturalist should ever be asked to discuss desert flowers and animal life in twenty-five minutes. We are all highly appreciative of the floral explosions on the desert following the rare showers: cacti, sahuaros, ocotillos, primroses, desert dandelions, verbenas, and others. Though less obvious, the desert animals are equally attractive and interesting. These range from microscopic forms to the insects, amphibia, reptiles, and birds. Mammals are found that range from the tiny pocket mouse to the pronghorn antelope, and to man himself.

Man's usual attitude is that the desert is completely worthless unless it can be used for making money. I strongly dissent from the view that only through commercial development can the desert make its highest contribution.

Like a human being, the desert possesses untapped resources. It may serve not only for the elevation of man's material welfare, but it may also serve for the enrichment of the human spirit. We would do well to remember that the world's dominant religions were born and evolved in desert regions.

Nevertheless, it is a rather melancholy fact that almost everybody who has anything official to say or to do with the desert immediately desires to industrialize it; but to industrialize the desert is to destroy the very thing that many people want. I speak of the increasing thousands in a mobile society who seek permanent or temporary location in the Southwest. The combination of favorable climate, unique beauty, and peaceful solitude is a basic human attraction peculiar to desert areas. Perhaps it will come to you, as it did to me, as a profound shock to learn that all the tremendous desert areas in San Bernardino County, California—largest county in the United States—are zoned for industry.

Possibly some of us are thinking, after all, why worry? Desert and semiarid lands occupy from one-seventh to one-half the land surface of the entire earth, depending on how you define your terms. Isn't our big problem the avoidance of the creation of more deserts rather than the conservation of existing ones?

The answer is plain—both are big problems. It is a sad truth that man's careless management of arid lands has tended to increase the acreage of barren desert. Paul B. Sears's famous classic, *Deserts on the March,* published in 1935, is still pertinent. Furthermore, Egon Glesinger of the Food and Agriculture Organization of the United Nations in Rome pointed out in *Scientific American* (July, 1960) that the Sahara and neighboring deserts in the Mediterranean region already have taken over 1.25 billion acres and are still advancing. It is perfectly clear that the problem is acute of keeping nondesert lands from becoming desert as a result of man's activities. But here we are concerned with the maintenance of some fair samples of natural desert for purposes of study, observation, and enjoyment with a minimum of disturbance.

This will not be easy. For testimony on this important problem we can review some alterations occurring now in our California deserts, which contain about thirty-six million acres, an area as large as the state of Illinois.

First, let me recall some of the activities of the Department of Defense on our local deserts. A basic problem in preservation of desert lands lies in the allocation of hundreds of thousands of acres of desert lands wholly controlled by the Army, Navy, Air Force, and Marines. You will recall that their combined jurisdiction is huge in southern California alone, comprising some eight major installations, and containing 3,099,000 acres (nearly four times the area of Rhode Island). For a while the military was taking over desert lands in the Southwest so rapidly, it appeared that all the unallotted and unappropriated lands in the public domain might go this way. Fortunately, Congress intervened to prevent this.

I would like to call your particular attention to the so-called desert exercises of the department in recent years; specifically to Exercise Desert Strike in southern California, May 13 to 17, 1964. This was a joint Army–Air Force maneuver for which some fourteen million acres of desert land were designated.

In view of the obvious possibilities for harm to the desert and its fauna and flora, the Desert Protective Council publicly declared prior to the exercise:

(1) Under no circumstances should such maneuvers be permitted on lands now in use for general public recreation, scientific study, outdoor education, or similar purposes. Nor should such maneuvers be permitted on lands earmarked for eventual recreational uses—such as the Providence Mountains, Cima Dome, Chuckwalla Mountains, and Whipple Mountains.

(2) These maneuvers should be restricted to the very great areas of the public domain now under the jurisdiction of the various armed services.

The Desert Protective Council informed the agencies involved that the ecology of these arid lands is extremely fragile and in delicate balance.* What actually happened?

Dr. Ernest R. Tinkham of the Desert Protective Council's committee appointed to investigate Desert Strike reported a good deal of damage to the desert lands affected. For example, "In the wild region fifteen miles from Rice . . . we found a cache of live ammunition partly buried in a mound of coarse sand. The cache contained not only boxes of ammunition, but machine gun belts, some of them six feet long, loaded with blank, but lethal, bullets. In an area fifteen to twenty miles south-southeast of Essex, the military had wrought much havoc to the desert landscape. The destruction of desert vegetation was widespread. Mojave yuccas, cholla cactus, Larrea and other native plant life had been uprooted and dragged into heaps. . . . Ration cartons, cans, and bottles littered the area. Farther along, approaching Essex from the

* See *Exercise Desert Strike, A Post-Mortem,* Desert Protective Council, Inc., P.O. Box 33, Banning, California 92220, November, 1964.

east, large bivouac areas had been almost completely denuded of their plant cover."

In a letter to the Desert Protective Council, Verl Martin of the Desert Nomads wrote, "Desert Strike cost the American taxpayer some fifty-four million dollars and thirty-four lives. . . . In the areas I have checked over, Desert Strike has left the sectors in a most deplorable condition."

Roger Stinchfield, supervisor of Mitchell Caverns State Reserve, said, "Another phase of destruction, which is prevalent in a maneuver of this size and scope, and which many people ignore or do not realize, is the vast damage done to the wildlife of the area involved. . . . We can attest to many of the animals' being killed. It seems that the shovel-nosed snake was mistaken for the deadly coral snake (not found in this area), and the entirely harmless chuckwalla was mistaken for the Gila monster. Both these reptiles were sought out and slaughtered for this reason. As a matter of fact everything that crawled was immediately killed. . . . I hope this report . . . will be of some help to stop future destruction of the flora and fauna of this great desert country."

The Desert Protective Council commented, "Again we have tragic proof that to the men of the Pentagon the unique deserts of our Southwest are indeed expendable." The worst of it is that the uninformed general public probably would agree with them!

One more incident bearing on Desert Strike may be cited. Recently Congressman Charles H. Wilson of Los Angeles called for a complete inquiry by the Department of Defense into the alleged abandonment of large quantities of explosives and equipment in the deserts of California, Arizona, and Nevada. In one case before the Municipal Court in Alhambra, California, a man was charged with possessing TNT and a tear gas bomb. When arrested, he claimed that literally millions of dollars' worth of equipment had been abandoned by the military, including explosives, booby traps, machine gun parts, rocket fuel, and aerial bombs.

It is of interest that a large portion of California's great Anza Borrego State Park has been closed to the general public because of the danger of unexploded ammunition abandoned in Desert Strike. Mr. Harry C. James, former executive secretary of the Desert Protective Council, kicked a few loose rocks out of the way of his camera tripod in order to photograph a smoke tree. "Directly under my tripod was the ugly egg-shaped nose of a mammoth unexploded shell."

The sorry exhibit of desert impairment by the Department of Defense is indeed dramatic. But aside from the wastage of human life, the combined destructive aspect of our ordinary peaceful pursuits in the long run may be even more injurious to the desert than military actions. Let me give you a quick and incomplete inventory.

First, the real estate developers are indictable on several counts. Those fair-haired entrepreneurs insist that our entire gross national product and indeed the future of civilization rests on their activities. Their heavy machinery often eliminates all desert vegetation and animal life and reduces the pleasing irregularities of the landscape to a monotonous plain. Usually these aggressive pioneers of dollar making know nothing of desert ecology, its climate, or its moods. Some have actually placed subdivisions so that desert winds carried sand from nearby dunes into the very midst of building areas, filling up swimming pools, piling up sand to the level of the window ledges, and rendering tracts uninhabitable until extensive alterations were made.

Those of us who in recent years have traveled roads over the Mojave and Colorado Deserts have been unfavorably impressed by another kind of shotgun development—the slummification of the desert by jackrabbit homesteads. Fortunately, the purchase of these lands from the federal government has now been eliminated.

Outdoor advertisers comprise another large class of desert decimators. In rearing their huge and expensive billboards along well-traveled desert highways (San Gorgonio Pass to Palm Springs, California, is one with which many of us are familiar), they not only render desert travel more dangerous, but tend to conceal wide expanses of some of our most outstanding desert and mountain scenery.

Roadside zoos with their wretched and despairing caged animals help to make a paltry mess along our desert highways. Curio dealers are also not free from blame. Those who depend upon sales of the commercially popular denizens of the desert—including horned toads, Gila monsters, chuckwallas, and desert tortoises among animals; cacti, ocotillos, Joshua trees, and many others among desert plants—exercise a continuously disintegrative effect.

In many instances those modern authoritarians, the highway commissions and road builders, official and unofficial, have sinned against the desert and against those of us who love it. While nobody objects to a few well-chosen roads to insure the safe and timely crossing of the desert, the construction of expensive new roads, paralleling excellent existing highways, can be vigorously challenged.

I must include in this discouraging inventory the cement plants and other manufacturing enterprises that are polluting the desert atmosphere. We householders of metropolitan areas have felt that the desert could provide escape, at least for a time, from the all-pervading smog of our coastal areas. But how much longer will this be true?

The gorgeous flora of the desert has been brought to favorable public attention by artists like Jane Pinheiro of Lancaster, California, as well as by leading periodicals, professional writers, and photographers. It is astonishing how enthusiastic the general public is over the colorful desert flowers appearing after good rains. But according to leading botanists and ecologists, the arid-lands flora has been so depleted by grazing animals, especially sheep, that many are gone. In some instances it is difficult or impossible for the experts to determine exactly the composition of the original flora. The problem of protecting a fair representation of native desert plants is critical.

Some of my most likable friends are officials or owners of the great electric power companies. But the shattering work roads and unsightly utility poles of these gigantic corporations all too often march straight across the desert with little regard for the native beauty of the landscape, despoiling forever some of our choicest scenic wonders. From the standpoint of attractiveness, the engineer's straight line is usually not the shortest distance between two points!

I have not mentioned the prospectors and pseudominers, who often have taken advantage of the antiquated basic mining laws of 1872 to hold desert lands for other purposes. Deserted mining camps are often the most unattractive features for hundreds of miles in any direction, virtual tin can dumps—trashy, unkempt, neglected, melancholy reminders of past activity. Many of their dangerous "glory" holes are left open and their abandoned and rusting machinery left standing.

The latest contributions to despoliation of deserts comes from the fertile minds of the machine makers: the dune buggies with their accompanying drag racers, tote goats, and motorcycles, the Hell's Angels type of community invaders that import raucous noise and poison gas into God's great silent desert. Must we infect everything with our vaunted technology?

Closely akin to the drag racers are the speedboat operators who invade and enthusiastically monopolize our few desert lakes and seas, such as Lake Havasu and Salton Sea, driving away the wildlife and changing peaceful environments into roaring urban infernos.

No list of desert destroyers would be complete without the predatory-animal hunter hired by government or private agencies to kill those interesting desert denizens, the coyote, the bobcat, the wolf, the mountain lion, and, often unintentionally, other carnivorous species. I should add that these so-called benefits are sometimes questionable even for the western stock ranchers who put political muscle into these eradication programs.

Finally, I should mention the careless tourist who, unfortunately, misses the point of all his vacation leisure and glorious mobility. These travelers often line our desert highways with waste paper, cans, tires, discarded containers, human feces, toilet paper, garbage, and liquor bottles. Local construction workers, truckers, business travelers, and transients contribute mightily too. But the careless tourist is as guilty as the other desecrators of our mountain, river, meadow, seashore, and desert heritage. Here is the trusty and true architect of "God's own junkyard." I do not think any one of us is free from guilt in this matter of conservation cleanliness and scenery.

Surely some of our generous and inspiring desert values are worth protection in their natural condition for our benefit and for future generations. We need a John Muir of the desert. Today nearly all these desert values are seriously threatened. If adequate attention is not given to them immediately, they will disappear, as some have already, to the great loss of humanity. There is an urgent need for a few vast— not token—wilderness areas in the desert where nature can be left on her own, and where man may commune with the country as God made it; but where he should not remain or introduce his noisy machinery, his ugly commercialism, his asphalt jungles, his garish billboards, his midways, his gambling hells, his liquor joints, or other reflections of his sophisticated civilization.

To preserve our attractive earth, we must give more effort to intelligent consideration of man's activities and to exercising disciplined restraint. We can agree that the desert includes a wide range of objects of intense interest, some of them commercial, others recreational and inspirational. It is for us to see that the others are given their share of support and protection.

It has been pointed out that the dominant religions of the world came out of the deserts. There are unfound resources in the desert, just as there are in every human being, which we ought to be able to utilize. By the way, our sincerest appreciation should go to the tenth biennial Wilderness Conference for affording attention to our vast reserve of desert wildernesses. The unique values of these regions have not received adequate emphasis in the past.

Just one last word. Basic to any kind of conservation, including desert preservation, is the assumption that man can and soon will learn to regulate his own population so that it will not overtax or destroy the natural resources on which he depends. Failing in this, there will be no need for concern, for not only the resources, but man himself will be lost forever. If we cannot solve this most difficult of all problems, Homo sapiens can count on joining the dodo, the passenger pigeon, the dinosaur, and the saber-toothed tiger in total extinction.

Boyd L. Rasmussen

EXPLORING DESERT RECREATION

Perhaps I should open these remarks by discussing population trends. You already know that in 1967 some 3.6 million babies will be born in this country. This will move the population of this nation past the 200 million total. But I suspect that anyone attending this tenth biennial Wilderness Conference is well aware of this population explosion. You probably know its direct and indirect influence on the remaining wild lands of America.

For my part, I think it is more significant that a director of the Bureau of Land Management (BLM) has been invited to discuss public lands at a wilderness conference. I commend those organizing this meeting for recognizing the coming of age of the remainder of a once vast public domain—a national heritage that years ago included lands now within our priceless parks, forests, wildlife refuges, and our new national recreation areas.

The 458 million acres of unreserved public lands *are* coming into their own. They have to, in face of mounting population pressures. One result of the people explosion is new legislation, new laws that recognize for the first time that these lands have value for recreation and other purposes. One law passed in 1964 gives BLM temporary classification and multiple use authority. We have tools now that we did not have under the Taylor Grazing Act. Now we can classify lands for their best use in the public interest—and this includes classifying lands for wilderness.

But I used a term just now that is new to a lot of people, including our own, in discussing the public lands—wilderness. The Wilderness Act of 1964 does not apply to public lands administered by BLM. The reference to wilderness preservation in the Classification and Multiple Use Act, then, is very significant to us. It means that Congress has recognized the potential wilderness values in the remainder of the public domain in the western states and Alaska.

Where do these relatively unknown wilderness values of the public lands fit into the future? I do not need to tell you about the overcrowding that is taking place in many of our national parks and seashores. Some of the national forests are beginning to experience mass use far beyond earlier expectation. And because more and more people are discovering the spiritual and physical refreshment of a wilderness experience, the solitude of wilderness may become increasingly rare as the years pass on.

Ultimately, we must look to other lands for solitude—if solitude is our medicine. And as growing industries place greater demands on the resources of these lands, it is only reasonable that we look to areas where the recreationist and the developer have little reason to compete.

At the 1966 Annual Meeting of the BLM National Advisory Board in Sacramento, Michael McCloskey of the Sierra Club made a significant statement about the recreationist of today: "Recreationists want to feel that when they got there they have gotten to something worthwhile seeing. . . . If you come on an arduous journey and you turn off on a side road of a progressively lower and lower character, you get a sense of discovery: a sense of adventure develops, a sense of uniqueness occurs when you have found something important, when you are not just one of millions who will pass that point, even though undoubtedly others will be there and have been there."

I would like you to come with me today on an imaginary trip exploring some of our deserts—to see the opportunities they can provide for those who seek a measure of solitude in their recreation, and some of the problems that BLM administrators have in protecting these lands. The desert stretches for hundreds of hot, thirsty miles across the western United States. Let's begin by defining what we mean by the term, desert. Mainly, we mean a region where precipitation amounts to less than ten inches a year. It can be much less. In the West, rainfall—or snowfall—varies with altitude. The higher mountain areas often get enough moisture to show a lush contrast with the drier valleys below. Only a few thousand feet of elevation can take you from desert to green forest.

Of the five desert regions we will discuss today, one is the Great Basin, a desert that covers most of Nevada and some of Utah, with fingers that reach into Oregon, Idaho, Wyoming, and Colorado. To the southwest is the Sonoran Desert. It begins in Mexico, reaches north into California and Nevada, and covers most of Arizona. A third desert region is the Chihuahuan, which, like the Sonoran, takes its name from a Mexican state; it extends north into New Mexico along the Rio Grande and Pecos rivers. One of the driest deserts in the world is the Mojave, in California and Nevada. It includes Death Valley, the lowest point in the United States.

For one who thinks of Alaska in terms of Eskimos dwelling in igloos, the fact that much of Alaska is desert by precipitation standards may come as a surprise. North of the Brooks Range, on the bleak Arctic slope, precipitation averages less than four inches a year. South of the Brooks, lands range from desert to semiarid.

For countless years, man has looked upon the desert as a place to be feared, distrusted. But now, with much of the rest of the land filled to capacity, our deserts loom as a new frontier in recreation, a place where you can still find room to roam.

The greatest part of our American deserts remain today in the public domain, leftovers that no one wanted in the rush west. Responsibility for these lands rests with the Bureau of Land Management, which looks after some 170 million acres in the West and nearly 290 million acres in Alaska.

Until quite recently, BLM had very limited authority from Congress. By law, BLM could manage lands only for wildlife and domestic livestock. But as some of you know, in 1964, three history-making laws were passed. One gave BLM interim authority to classify its lands for multiple uses—including wilderness and recreation. Another 1964 law allows BLM to sell lands for needed community expansion; another set up the Public Land Law Review Commission to review all federal land laws, and recommend what should be done about them.*

And so, today, the men and women working for BLM are active managers of the public lands. This is a new era for the public lands and for those responsible for their management. And this is a new era, too, in cooperative relations between the federal government and local communities. As we develop new policies and procedures for our recreational resources, we are aware that our deserts have wilderness values. We are aware, too, as we go about our job of classification and management, that deserts are fragile lands—lands that should be labeled "Handle with care." I would like to be able to tell you what our final policies are going to be regarding our deserts, how we are going to

* The Classification and Multiple Use Act, which was due to expire June 30, 1969, has been extended by the 90th Cong., 1st Sess. (1967) to December 31, 1970. —The Editors.

meet the demands for them, and what we will do to maintain the wild environment. We are not that far along. However, we know this: the deserts of the West are filled with strange and unique things—plants and animals, mesas and canyons, things that have no dollar value at all but are priceless in their own way.

Early settlers who came from the East found the deserts hostile barriers to be crossed. Coming from a land of abundant water, they learned the desert had to be met on its own terms. But people have met the desert on its terms. Perhaps 25,000 years ago, the first nomadic hunters ventured into the Southwest. Two thousand years ago, the first farmers arrived. We call them the Anasazi—a Navajo word meaning "the ancient ones." The Anasazi built a culture that was successful for more than a millennium; their descendants, the Pueblo Indians, still live in the Southwest. The history of the Anasazi can be traced through architecture. Beginning with simple mud huts, they gradually came to mesatop villages of pit houses partly below ground, partly above. At ruins such as Alkali Ridge in southeastern Utah, you can still find the outlines of pit houses, lined with slabs of rock. By A.D. 1000, Anasazi architecture had matured. North America's first apartment houses— made of fieldstone instead of brownstone—rose to four stories. The crowning glory of Anasazi culture came with such monuments as are found in Mesa Verde National Park in Colorado.

On the public lands we still find petroglyphs (rock writings) and pictographs (paintings on rock) that give us other clues to life among the Anasazi. While most archaeologists refuse to speculate on the meanings of the ancient drawings, you can learn much about these desert dwellers from the unique animals they drew. One cannot help but wonder if some drawings portrayed imagined spirits, with their small heads and grotesque tapering bodies. You can theorize, too, that strange geologic formations in the desert must have had spiritual meaning for the ancient ones.

Archaeologists date the Anasazi buildings by tree rings, matching growth rates of trees that were cut a thousand years ago and more. From these, we know that the Anasazi culture began a decline about the time of the Magna Carta. Perhaps a subtle shift in climate, sustained drought, made it impossible to farm the higher mesas. By the time of Columbus, the watchtowers stood empty, the fields fallow.

On a cliff near the entrance to Canyonlands National Park, an Indian recorded a footnote to history on a wall already bearing the doodlings of the centuries. A man on a horse—an animal unknown until the coming of the Spanish—closes a chapter in the story of the West.

There is a lesson to be learned from the partnership between the Anasazi and their land, even though the land finally defeated them.

These ancient Indians did meet the desert on its own terms; they lived for more than ten centuries without altering the balance of nature in their surroundings. But history didn't stop with the retreat of the Anasazi. Spanish rulers came and stayed for three hundred years. The cattle empires that followed the Spanish brought changes that continue today. In simplest terms, the one product of an arid land that has ready cash value is grass. For years Uncle Sam was an absentee landlord. Use of the range was for the taking; if land was grazed too heavily, there was always more over the hill. The days of moving ever westward for grass are gone, but scars left by too many livestock remain and much of the land is still deteriorating. We have come to recognize that our deserts are fragile; there is a delicate balance that can easily be upset. Yet they are vast and primitive, alive, alluring, and challenging.

When the Taylor Grazing Act was passed in 1934, Congress made its goal "to stabilize the livestock industry." The act did recognize wildlife values, the big game animals that must share the forage with domestic animals. But in the three decades since, population in the West has doubled. It continues to soar. Interstate highways have reduced coast-to-coast driving time to fit the average vacation, and there is hardly time to read a good book on a transcontinental flight.

So it is BLM's job now to look at these so-called forgotten lands in new terms, for values that have new meaning in an increasingly mobile nation. For those of us who spend our days in a bumper-to-bumper existence, open space has value. And if you can look as far as the eye can see without meeting another soul, so much the better.

There is life in the desert, but there is no insurance policy written for it. In fact, the odds for survival are slim for most desert life. In a good year, when there is moisture, the desert can become a floral carpet. Bright-colored flowers decorate the usually drab landscape, bringing it alive. Each desert is different, each has its own charm; certain plants and animals seem to characterize our five desert regions. The Joshua tree could almost be a symbol of the Mojave Desert, patiently drawing moisture from the soil over centuries of life. In California, along the transition zone between the Sierras and the Mojave Desert, the strange yucca is called "the candle of the gods." In a good year, with a little moisture, the ocotilla celebrates with a bright red trumpet, a touch of color on the Sonoran Desert. Covered with thousands of spines, the cholla stands out on the landscape. The cholla of the Chihuahuan Desert blooms in midsummer, with fat red flowers that beckon to the passing bumblebees.

In Alaska, BLM manages millions of acres of land that might be called a green desert—where total precipitation is similar to southern deserts, but permanently frozen ground prevents the water from soaking in. The migratory caribou must move from summer to winter range and back again to find enough forage in the barren north country. And on the west coast of Alaska, along the Bering Sea, Eskimo herdsmen tend reindeer, a close relative of the caribou. The BLM and the Bureau of Indian Affairs are cooperating in a program to improve management of imported reindeer. The Reindeer Service is staffed with Eskimo herdsmen who look after an experimental herd of several hundred animals near Nome.

Plants in our desert of the north show adaptations just as the southern ones do. The little Arctic cotton plants must grow quickly to bloom in the short growing season.

But back to our more conventional deserts—for here is where we face the pressures of more and more people. It is here, in a context of multiple use management, the BLM must plan the role these great desert lands should play in the coming outdoor recreation explosion.

There are questions yet to be answered. One question is access. Deny it, physically or legally, and use is restricted to only a handful of determined people. Should it be? If we encourage use, problems appear. Litter, for example, that would soon dissolve or rust away in wetter climates, lingers for years in the desert.

Another of BLM's big concerns is with archaeological values that can be destroyed by thoughtless pothunters. Often Indian burial sites are vandalized by people who seek pottery, which finds a ready market in roadside curio shops. One way to protect fragile ruins is to erect fences. But do we really preserve a historic ruin by enclosing it with a fence?

The capacity of fragile lands for carrying people may be astoundingly low. Roads wash away into gullies or drop over hillsides eroded by flash floods.

In many places, man has conquered the desert and has made it lush with water from rivers miles away. Nowhere has this conquest been more spectacular than in the Imperial Valley in California, which produces many of our winter vegetables. But trying to conquer the desert is a gamble, and sometimes man has gambled and lost. In the same Imperial Valley, many a farmer was unequal to the task. By scratching away the protective cover, he surrendered the land to water and wind erosion.

The pattern of land ownership in the desert and on other public lands is often an accident of history. One problem facing BLM is the checkerboard ownership remaining after years of homesteading, desert land entries, mining claims, and wholesale grants to states and railroads. The public lands are what is left, the Swiss cheese that is sometimes more holes than cheese. BLM still manages about a fifth of the nation's land area, including Alaska. Now, with the new multiple use classification authority, the bureau can take the initiative. We cannot do the job alone. By law, local communities must have a voice in land classifications, must help us determine the short- and long-term goals for these lands. We need your help and the help of all interested citizens in determining the best uses of these lands.

The public lands have many faces, from the deserts of the Southwest north to the Arctic. Questions are endless, answers elusive. But nowhere are the resources more fragile than in our deserts. Time will not stand still, and choices must be made. We hope the public will take an interest and help share the burden of making these choices.

Kenneth S. Norris

THE PRESERVATION OF MARINE WILDERNESS

Before discussing preservation of marine wilderness and some of the problems and opportunities there, I would like to speak about our deserts. The University of California established a National Land and Water Reserve System in 1964 with the idea of preserving for teaching and study a mosaic of California's diversity, the greatest of any state in the union. This effort will encourage the protection and understanding of mountain, desert, and seashore areas.

The problems in protecting the deserts, I think, are even more difficult than our previous speakers have described. They are particularly apparent to those of us who are trying to find areas where one can carry out undisturbed experimentation, observation, or teaching. It is literally true that around the Los Angeles basin, for example, there is a zone of vandalism that extends for a couple of hundred miles out from the Los Angeles City Hall. Almost all of us who have tried to carry out experimental work on the desert have had our fixed field equipment torn up or destroyed, even in places that seemed exceedingly remote. I think this points up the tremendous pressures on this fragile habitat. The deserts are incredibly sensitive, since they take so very long to reconstitute, once disturbed. There has been indication that the evidence of even relatively minor disturbance may remain after more than one hundred years.

Now let's look at some of the problems of preserving our aquatic world of the seas. To preserve inviolate any sample of an ecosystem, one needs to know the broad outlines of its dynamics. Only with such knowledge at hand can one sensibly place boundaries or regulate use. For example, the cycling of life and nutrients of a pool is dependent upon the importation of upstream decaying vegetation; the entire character of that pond might change if the nutrient sources themselves were not included and protected in the preserve. Realization that one must know broad ecological dynamics to develop preservation policy brings some surprises and novel views when considering marine wilderness. While the broad framework of ecological relationships in the sea is similar to that on land, in detail it is often strikingly different. For instance, competition for space and tight integration of communities are demonstrated in both milieus. However, on land, dispersal by reproductive products—seeds, spores, and pollen—is typically a plant method; in the sea, animals and plants alike are apt to fill the environment with overwhelming numbers of reproductive products.

Let us press this comparison a bit further, just to emphasize some peculiar differences. We can then consider how these features and differences may affect preservation policy.

The atmosphere of the sea is water. Most organisms, plants and animals alike, have a density quite close to that of the water, at most a fewfold different. On land our bodies are about eight hundred times as dense as air, and most other animals and plants bear about the same relationship in density. Thus, organisms of a great many kinds float in the sea; reproductive products in countless numbers and fragmented organic material float; and even the largest animals adjust their buoyancy and float along with little effort. The moving water is at once the source of most food for bottom-dwelling creatures and the means for their dispersal. This allows thousands upon thousands of species to survive by the simple expedient of pumping volumes of water through tiny traps of one sort or another, in the assurance that a fragment of usable decaying organic material, a reproductive product, a larva, or a tiny adult organism will be trapped often enough for growth and survival to proceed.

In air, flight is an effort; only the tiniest spores or ballooning spiders achieve effective densities low enough to be wafted for long distances without effort.

When we drive a new piling into the muck, or drop a bargeload of rocks onto a new breakwater, they enter the water nearly clean of macroscopic life, but once the water wafts the toxicity of creosote or mineral dust away, the organic soup of the sea starts a subtle and rapid colonization. In a few days' or even minutes' time, tiny larvae of seaweeds and worms, barnacle nauplii and tiny crustaceans settle. Many cement themselves in place, some attach by threads they themselves produce, and some simply intertwine themselves among the other settlers. In no time, seemingly, a complex community of organisms covers the new habitat, and within a few weeks this community grows in physical dimensions until it supports little fish scattered regularly over the encrusted surface, vying with their fellows for space. The miracle of succession has taken place, and continues in flux as long as the community lives. Seasons change its composition in both subtle and obvious ways. The shift of an ocean current may send it into a decline that provides raw materials for a new succession of different creatures that are adjusted to the new water mass. The same degree of change will occur if somehow the piling or breakwater becomes sheltered from sea swell and comes to lie in calm water. This happens often along our shores by man's agency.

The point is that the sea is a soup of reproductive products and, given an adequate place to settle, most marine organic communities can reconstitute themselves far more quickly and completely than is the case with terrestrial communities. This, of course, requires reestablishment of original habitat conditions, and in many marine situations this is unlikely. Man's alteration of the basic habitat is apt to be complete in bays and estuaries. On land, to destroy a community by human intervention very often dooms that community forever, even if the basic habitat is restored. There we are faced with a now-or-never necessity of saving what is left while it exists at all. This is the kind of problem that brings out the ferocity of the conservationist in confrontation with developers.

The significant difference noted for the marine environment reflects two important things: first, we can often take a less than pristine water environment and by human endeavor clean it of the exuvia of our society, and expect it to reconstitute, providing the water (atmosphere) is not itself polluted; and second, we can manage some habitats with much more ease than is the case on land, while still expecting them to survive in essentially primordial condition.

This demonstrates the similarities between marine and terrestrial preservation problems; namely, one must look first to the preservation of the habitat—the soil and the air, the bottom and the water—if one is to achieve meaningful long-term preservation.

It is a platitude to say that there is great wisdom in ancient cultures, but there is at least one example we can use here. No people were more oriented to the sea than the ancient Hawaiians who came to their islands across the Pacific and who derived much of their sustenance from it. It came as a great surprise to me to learn that these people were extremely numerous on their lovely island chain before the advent of white men—almost as numerous as the entire population of the islands today. Some say 450,000 is a reasonable population estimate. They were scattered on all the islands and were great fish-farmers as well as fishermen of the open seas and reefs. With all the pressure of their society upon the reefs, these limited coral circlets were rich with fish life when the missionaries arrived, and it is no credit to Western civilization that they have seriously declined in productivity since then.

The Hawaiians preserved the productivity of their reefs by a rigid "kapu" system, which meant that emissaries of the kings watched the reef populations and when the animals and plants showed signs of declining, that portion of the reef was made "kapu." Fishermen stayed out upon pain of death, sometimes for several years, while the reef reconstituted itself, and meanwhile they worked elsewhere. By rotation of areas under kapu the reefs throughout the islands were kept in healthy condition and a store of prime reef areas was always a source of reproductive products for the reconstitution of other adjacent areas.

It seems to me that we conservationists can consider this ancient tactic as a modern lesson. I am not advocating the death penalty for poachers, though watchful protection is clearly essential and deserves our strongest support. As a matter of fact, such control is one of the most troublesome aspects of marine wilderness preservation because these areas are extremely difficult to patrol.

The obvious lesson is that management of marine reserves is wise and possible, and it allows an unusually complete rapprochement between the recreationist and the conservationist. Such a program has been initiated now in Hawaii under the imaginative leadership of State Senator Taylor Pryor and is called the Blue Belt Program. It seeks to revitalize the zoning and management of subsurface terrain using modern methods of population estimate and management, much as the old Hawaiians did, but within the framework of present day agencies and laws. It will work in Hawaii—except in a few deplorable instances—because the water and the bottom terrain are as they were centuries ago and only await sensible management to bring them back to full productivity. Such a system can support the recreational activities of a large population without serious change in community composition or decline in numbers. But to succeed, such a plan must have both informed surveillance and enforcement of protection in closed areas, and must also operate in clean seas.

Thus, our prime problem in saving marine wilderness is what we might call underwater smog—the spread of pollutants that have destroyed large areas of underwater wilderness. Pulp mills throw their poisonous discharges by the thousands of tons into the sea, primary outfalls along our coasts dump wastes such as nondegradable detergents into the sea, and cycling and recycling pesticides occur in alarming levels in some marine organisms. One looks with uneasy concern at areas marked "chemical dumping grounds" on coast and geodetic charts. For example, one such area exists in the Santa Cruz basin off southern California. My concern here is that this basin, along with others in the area, contains such still, uniform-temperature water that precise reversing thermometers (accurate to thousandths of a degree) might be calibrated there. It could become a toxic pocket to bleed poisons into the surrounding sea for many years, since adverse effects cannot be stopped quickly.

Our prime concern is that the seas are not unpollutable and that a variety of features of the undersea weather and environment may lock or channel pollutants, and thus magnify their expected effects. Currents sweep debris alongshore, strong thermoclines (temperature stratification) may cause warm outwash waters to slide over the surface and thus hit shorelines miles away in essentially pure form. We must watch our rivers, even the intermittent ones like the Los Angeles River, since they pass through polluted lands of the continents, picking up pesticides, simple debris, or even radioactive materials.

No marine environments are more vulnerable than our few remaining bays, estuaries, and mud flats. Many forms of tampering by man in these areas can be disastrous. Because very little salt water marsh or mud flat land is now protected, it is only by rapid and dedicated work that any of it can be saved. Even if a portion of a bay is saved, it can still be subjected to incompatible activities by neighbors. The prime destroyer of flats that have become very high priced land throughout most of western North America is the marina developer. Marinas spread oil and in the confines of a restricted body of water this may quickly spell intolerable pollution. Dredging may change current and tidal patterns and shift sedimentation. Tidal flux may change when the bay entrance is dredged for easy movement of vessels, and so on.

Some bits of marine wilderness worthy of our concern should also be mentioned. One such bay is the Laguna de Ojo Liebre, or Scammon's Lagoon, of Baja California, Mexico. This locale is certainly one of the marine areas most deserving of preservation of any in the world, for it is the prime breeding and nursery lagoon of the California gray whale. This peculiar, primitive, baleen whale is the only whale that chooses shallow inland waterways in which to breed. During January through March this lagoon hosts hundreds of whales in one of the most remarkable biological events known. Forty-foot whales float quietly in the calm water, only the thin black lines of their backs showing, often with fourteen-foot calves at their sides. One may walk down the sandy beaches and be startled to see one of these monsters hurtle almost free of the water to crash back again in a welter of foam. This lagoon is endangered: it lies in the Vizcaino Desert where the constant sun evaporates sea water so effectively that adjacent Guerrero Negro Lagoon has become a major salt producer, and Scammon's is contemplated as the next production area. A Mexican national park at Scammon's would, in the long run, pay much bigger dividends than would an anchorage for a salt works.

Our experience shows that these shy animals will vacate the lagoon if much disturbed by man. One can read in the history of San Diego Bay, California, that in the middle 1800's it was considered dangerous to cross the bay in a skiff during breeding season for the gray whales. Now the whales only enter this crowded bay as occasional strays and doubtless quickly regret their action.

Scammon's Lagoon has other biological attributes too. It harbors tens of thousands of sea birds—migratory brant, curlews, willets, and many others—some nesting on its sandy islets. It is a pocket of warm-water fish and invertebrate life, and many species find their northern limits in its waters. It has the majesty of silence, of sun on dunes, of shallow water rippling over eelgrass beds while rays fly along beneath the surface. It should not be allowed to disappear because of the thoughtless acts of man.

Closer at hand, the last major salt water lagoon in southern California, Point Mugu Lagoon, exists yet because it is part of a naval base. But it is so little cherished that major dredging projects can be carried on without consultation with biologists over the damage that would and did result. Untreated effluent water continues to empty into the lagoon from Calleguas Creek, even though its pollution-producing effects are well known. We thank the Navy for saving the lagoon, while at the same time we wish they really understood the rare treasure they hold with apparent carelessness. The lagoon has a very rich fauna, long studied by the famous marine biologist husband-and-wife team, George and Nettie MacGinitie. One of the very few coastal populations of harbor seals breed there. It is an increasingly important way station for migratory waterfowl and other birds, particularly as similar places disappear rapidly under the spreading megalopolis.

San Francisco Bay, so vast and seemingly untouched such a short time ago, is all but destroyed; yet there are things to save. I hope the present preservation efforts of organized local citizens, among whom Mrs. Clark Kerr is especially prominent, will prevail. Myriads of birds still migrate through this region, and salt marsh still exists in portions of the southern bay and in San Pablo Bay.

Special efforts are needed to preserve some of the native biota and conditions in northern California bays such as Humboldt Bay, and those farther north in Oregon and Washington. The need for strenuous and urgent preservation efforts in Puget Sound, in Washington, is also most evident. We must never underestimate the pace of change; it rises stealthily to overwhelm us. I am continually reminded that Los Angeles had slightly more than five thousand people in 1870, less than one hundred years ago. Thus jogged, it is hard to be complacent about time.

What of other kinds of marine wilderness? One that deserves special mention is the rocky intertidal reef. What a delight for children (and adults) to crouch by a clear pool and to watch the busy hermit crabs scurrying about among the shell fragments, or the multicolored undulating skirts of swimming nudibranches, or to watch an anemone unfold after a touch, or to watch the shy octopus pile debris outside his front door. The lessons to be learned are as deep as those known to any biologist, and nowhere is there a better place to teach or learn about wild things. Conservationists must recognize that they must teach what they cherish or lose by the default of an ignorant generation to follow. I envision this as one of the most important things that we can do in our Natural Land and Water Reserve System in the university. We hope to bring on a future cadre of people as concerned as we are.

I envision zoned reefs where marked trails, often dipping below high-tide line, will wind past plaques affixed solidly to rocks. These explanatory markers would point out sessile and mobile life of the seashore, and provide a system where, with proper techniques, one can touch and look and hold living things for a time. Nearby, a section of reef could be closed, patrolled, and posted appropriately to explain how this allows the reef to live and recuperate while people can continue to enjoy parts of it and learn from it. Explanations through trails, plaques, and literature are greatly needed, as very few people understand what they see in the pools, or know the fascinating stories of nearly every shoreline creature.

One marine locale, the Point Conception–Point Arguello coast of central California, has seldom been mentioned as worthy of preservation. This stretch of coast, much of it under control of Vandenburg Air Force Base, is one of the sharpest faunal and floral breaks in the marine world. To the north the cold water of central California, containing its customary species, bathes the shores all year long, while to the south the summer eddying of warm water brings its species northward. Within the narrow band of fluctuating conditions, the two points touch. Here life reaches its geographic limits for hundreds of species and tells the many-faceted story of what limits organisms to this or that water mass, or shoreline. It is a major and little-known outdoor laboratory.

Subtidal reefs should be preserved, too, in a way similar to the preservation in Virgin Islands National Park, or similar to the plans for management in Hawaii. Heavy usage of these reefs is increasing, even where cold water discourages most divers. The Hawaiian Islands National Wildlife Refuge, a little-known and vast stretch of true marine wilderness, is now at the crossroads. Under consideration for wilderness status is the entire stretch of atolls, islands, and reefs from Nihoa Island, French Frigate Shoals, Pearl and Hermes Reefs, Laysan to Midway Island—the northwestern tail of the Hawaiian chain. This wild region harbors pristine bird rookeries, the nesting grounds for the rare central Pacific green turtle, the last remaining herds of the Hawaiian monk seal—one of the world's rarest animals—and a magnificent biota beneath the sea surface. It is wilderness in the truest sense of the word—remote, wild, and clean. This conference should support its inclusion in the wilderness system.

I will not dwell upon the mechanics of preservation except to say that marine areas are largely under the jurisdiction of state or federal governments, though the shore above high-tide line often is not. Effective conservation requires that these needs be recognized by laws, departmental rules, and use plans such as the recently issued *California and the Use of the Sea*. It especially requires the thorough cooperation of state and federal fish and game agencies who are responsible for policing these areas. Units like underwater reserves are difficult and expensive to patrol, and we must realize the burden each new reserve brings to these agencies.

As everywhere, the sea forces its challenge upon the already laden shoulders of the conservationist, but much can be done. Preservation of some representative zones of sea and seashore can only be maintained by constant vigilance and by education of the next generation in the wonders of the underwater world.

FROM THE SATURDAY MORNING DISCUSSION

George E. Lindsay: First, I should disqualify myself as a discussant because to be a discussant one should be objective, and I cannot be but subjective about desert wilderness. Having observed the changes in the Mojave and the Colorado Deserts during my time—that Dr. Taylor recounted—and the change in Baja California and the Gulf of California in the last two or three decades, I feel very strongly about the use and preservation of these areas.

There have been many general statements in this unusually stimulating group of presentations. We recognize the necessity of the tonic of wilderness, and we recognize that in the deserts, scars are conspicuous and very slow to heal, and that the desert environment is terribly sensitive to spoliation. It has been said over and over that the ecology is frail, the habitat is frail and difficult to reconstitute.

Many years ago, William Beebe spent a week out at the Ord Mines in the Mojave Desert near Daggett. He was just relaxing for a week. The first day he shaved and threw away the razor blade in the sands, and it was not concealed. It glittered every morning until he picked it up. It did not rust. Nothing breaks down in the desert, and the litter remains. This made a lasting impression on him, and influenced his actions and thoughts of desert beauty from then on.

Professor Hunt introduced us to the geography, geology, and biology of the desert areas and recommended strongly that overall planning to consider all of the values should be a part of and should precede any development of the deserts. He has also made a fine recommendation for the protection of coyotes from state and federally sponsored decimation, and judging from some of the questions that have come in I think we could start initial action on this problem.

Dr. Taylor spoke of specific and critical problems in desert preservation including predatory animal operations. I think it is heartening to know that the fifty-dollar bounty on the mountain lion has recently been removed in California. But I recall the time when we were anxious to preserve a subspecies of mountain lion that roamed the lower Colorado River while at the same time anyone could have gotten fifty dollars for shooting one. The plea for a John Muir of the desert is entirely appropriate.

Mr. Rasmussen has given us the heartening word that public lands can be classified for best public land use, including wilderness. We are further encouraged by his report of current investigations of public desert land use enabled by the Multiple Use Act of 1964. With his color slides, Mr. Rasmussen gave a beautiful visual review of the deserts managed by the BLM. And, while I am particularly interested in the deserts, I certainly was interested in Ken Norris' presentation of the necessity of preserving marine wilderness, but I will reserve further comment on that.

Cadet Hand: I have enjoyed the morning's discussion. I do not profess to know much about deserts, but at least I do, now, know a great deal more about their problems.

I was particularly pleased with Dr. Norris' comments about the marine environment and some of the needs for wilderness preservation. I wish we had time for me to say each of those words over again with more emphasis and drive them home so that each of us could go away convinced that this is something that must be attended to.

One of the things that Ken did not say was what areas along the California coast, except the Point Mugu Lagoon and the San Francisco Bay region within the estuary, he would put into marine wilderness. I am not sure that Ken and I could agree where it might best be done, nor am I sure that if we could agree on an area, and convince all of the authorities that one would have to convince, that we would have accomplished our goal. One of the reasons I say this is because there is in this state a great deal of concern about the use of our waters by the Water Quality Board and by certain parts of the California Department of Fish and Game.

There is urgency, too, stimulated by the federal agencies that have been asked to assist this state in waste elimination programs. I am sure you have heard about the master drain that is coming out of California's Central Valley and perhaps will dump its commercial, industrial, agricultural, and domestic wastes into the Sacramento River and the bays at Antioch. That plan received much opposition because there are obvious problems that such a drain would create. A re-evaluation now speaks of a master drain outfall at Antioch that would pick up both the Central Valley wastes and all the Bay Area wastes, and would take them out to sea somewhere, instead of dumping them inside the bay.

The impact of this is nearly unthinkable, and biologists find themselves in the extremely difficult position of not having the facts and figures, of not being able to state in precise terms where the effluent would go, and of not knowing what its impact on the sea and its biology would be. However, the San Francisco Bay region provides an example of just what can happen as a result of local runoff of effluents. There is no question in the minds of many biologists that for thirty or forty miles both south and north of the Golden Gate there is a demonstrable impoverishment of the marine fauna in the shallow waters. We have seen in the last few years the nearly complete demise of the Dungeness crab industry in this region. No one knows for certain yet why this has happened; however, there are very good reasons to suspect that the crab has fallen a victim of man's use of insecticides that has reduced the crab's ability to reproduce itself and survive in the marine environment.

I regret that the coast of North America is already despoiled perhaps to the point where there is no suitable area for a proper marine wilderness. We have to look as far away as Professor Norris' suggested Scammon's Lagoon in Baja California where the great gray whales breed, or to the Hawaiian Islands where there are still some essentially unpolluted and undisturbed areas.

This is a sad commentary on this "great society" that we call the United States of America. If you do not believe that we are destroying the world in which we live, someday take a stroll on a piece of beach that is hard to get to in California. Go north to Shelter Cove in Humboldt County where the bulldozers are now angrily tearing at a beautiful piece of seacoast to develop a new bit of land for the enrichment of a few. Leave that nasty sight, walk north about forty miles along the shore where nothing but your own two feet can give you access, and discover that for every ten feet you walk you pass another piece of plastic: blue, white, green, and red detergent, soap, and bleach bottles littering the beach and indeed the beaches of the world. I have been on an uninhabited Pacific island three hundred miles from the nearest land; there again plastic bottles are found on its beaches.

I think it is high time we all make a most intensive re-examination of the world around us. It is well to think about preserving marine environments, but before we can accomplish this effectively, we must have a full appreciation of the total needs of our society. We must understand the total ecology of the area we seek to preserve and we must be prepared to modify our own activities to guarantee that the preserve be a meaningful one.

Moderator Daniel B. Luten: Mr. Rasmussen, what can we do specifically to help the Bureau of Land Management establish wilderness areas?

Boyd L. Rasmussen: First of all, BLM land must be classified under the Classification and Multiple Use Act, and we are in the process of classifying all our lands now. Approximately seventy million acres have been classified for multiple use management, and twenty million more have been proposed and are under review [these figures have been updated to December 31, 1967—*The Editors*]. As these areas come up for classification, you can express an interest to your local BLM people, your state director, and those who represent you in Congress.

Moderator Luten: How do you impress the Appropriations Committee that desert national parks need more funds? Is writing letters to congressmen effective enough, or should some more drastic move be taken? If so, what?

I would like to answer this question myself by saying a congressman's most sensitive tentacles are pointed in the directions of the letters from his constituents, and particularly when the letters are articulate enough to suggest that the person who writes them might be persuasive with a lot of voters. Any congressman can hear this message very clearly.

Now a question for Dr. Taylor: What provisions, if any, are there for clean air regulation on the deserts? This would cover primarily cement plants and other mineral refineries that dispose of polluted dust (frequently referred to by company officials as "steam") into the atmosphere.

I hope we can all tell the difference between steam and dust; they appear quite different in the desert and the San Francisco Bay area.

Walter P. Taylor: I do not know of any effective regulations that have been put into effect to cut down air pollution on the desert. This will require more study and a great deal more attention from bodies like this wilderness conference. One possibility is that counties could zone the desert against certain industries that pollute the air.

Moderator Luten: Professor Hunt, will you explain the significance of proposals to exploit oil shale to the conservation of wilderness?

Charles B. Hunt: The problem of the development of the oil shale resources in a basin in northeastern Utah and northwestern Colorado was touched on in that part of my talk about a canyon underlain by salt beds of potential mineral worth [see p. 126]. What is needed, in my view, is some advance planning that would recognize that this resource is going to be developed. I might comment here that the oil shale reserves are tremendous, something like 150 times all the oil that has been produced to date in the entire world. It is going to be tapped. The problem is: how can it be tapped with the least damage to all values concerned?

I would like to comment further on resources. The problems of minerals, mines, and mining occur in appraising the effect of a mining development proposed on any piece of land. What should be considered is the relative value of the mineral deposit. I was involved with this in discussions on Death Valley, which, as many of you know, is still open to mining. The best formula I could come up with in distinguishing between a valid entry and one that ought to be blocked was to ask whether the deposit is of national significance, either because of its size or because it may be a critical or strategic substance. If it is simply a deposit that will be valuable to the owners but is not of national significance, then I think in any of these reserved areas there ought to be a hard look before any entry is granted.

The oil shale deposits are so huge that they are not only of national import but of world import, and the best that can be hoped for is that there will be overall planning.

Moderator Luten: Mr. Rasmussen, when the military takes over public lands for new bombing ranges, as along the highways east of Tonopah, Nevada, and in Panamint Valley, and in and near Moab, Utah, is the Bureau of Land Management consulted?

Mr. Rasmussen: We prepare a report on all withdrawals of this type. The final decision is not made in our office; it is made on the basis of national needs and is made considering our reports.

Moderator Luten: Dr. Taylor, where would you suggest military maneuvers be held? Where should bombing sites be located? Do you know of less valuable sites? Assuming we still have a need for military preparedness, is it a matter of zoning and adjustment?

Dr. Taylor: There are 3,099,000 acres already held by the Department of Defense in the deserts of southern California. I think there is some question whether some of this tremendous area should not be returned to civilian use or nonuse.

There is also the inescapable question of guidelines for the use of lands under military control. Certainly such use of desert lands as that which occurred some years ago in the Anza Borrego State Park in San Diego County of California should never be permitted. As you will remember, a large area within this state park has been made inaccessible to the general public as a result of contamination by unexploded ammunition left in the area. At the least, the military should be required to leave every area used by them clean of explosives and free from every form of trash or rubbish or any other kind of extraneous material. Detailed and rigorous instructions should be set forth for the proper care of desert vegetation, animal life, and terrain. These instructions should call attention to the fragile character of desert resources and should insist on as little disturbance as possible.

Marks of heavy machinery are visible for many years on the desert. Great wisdom and sensitivity are called for in administering these great public areas in behalf of our people now and in the future when our children, we hope, will use them.

Some of our soldiers and officers are exemplary conservationists but, like the general public, too many are lax and uninformed. Many of them know little about nature and less about the desert. All should be given effective instruction, which would tend to build up their sympathetic understanding and interest.

It is extremely important for Congress to hold a tight rein on the military in their use of public lands because recent history demonstrates the military's appetite for more and more land. If the Department of Defense were given a free hand, apparently the only limit on its acquisition of public lands would be the extent of public lands available. It is of the greatest importance that conservation organizations keep in close touch with Department of Defense plans and do all in their power to bring about wise decisions.

Moderator Luten: Two questions for Mr. Rasmussen. First, what should be done to establish wilderness on Bureau of Land Management lands? Second, how can conservation groups help in the identification and classification of BLM wilderness?

Mr. Rasmussen: The first step leading to establishment of wilderness on BLM lands is the classification of these lands for retention and management. Wilderness could be established in areas classified for retention. The classification work is a cooperative program between the local BLM people, local governments, and local citizens.

Citizen groups all over the country should be interested in the public hearings held on each classification for retention or disposal. We are in contact with most of these groups that have headquarters in Washington to keep them advised of the dates for hearings. At these hearings you can submit an oral statement or a written statement for the record.

The bureau is intrigued by the opportunities for primitive area management on the public lands. We will recommend areas to be managed as wilderness where this use appears to be the most suitable, and in these cases wilderness will have priority over other uses. Instructions now being prepared for the field offices will present criteria and procedures for identification and proposal of wilderness candidate areas. Their recommendations for segregations will be included in their proposals.

Moderator Luten: Another question for Mr. Rasmussen is: What is the most restrictive classification the 1964 act permits?

Mr. Rasmussen: The most restrictive classification would be to segregate BLM lands for agricultural purposes.

Moderator Luten: Now a question for Dr. Taylor: Lake Havasu City will eventually have a population of over sixty thousand. Most of these people like motorboats, water skiing, etc. Do we have any right to deny this kind of development with its multimillion-dollar economic impact and its answer to the wants of the residents and visitors? Could you generalize to cover possible similar developments?

Dr. Taylor: This question is of a good deal of interest to me, as my son-in-law is one of the promoters of Lake Havasu City.

Do we have the right to limit the people who want to water ski and run their motorboats over everything? Should we turn over the administration of lakes like Havasu, Salton Sea, and the rest to the multimillionaires?

That is a question that probably each man must consider for himself. We actually do exercise the right as a government to restrict the activities of mechanical contrivances. We do not allow certain kinds of machines in the Boundary Waters Canoe Area on the Minnesota–Canadian border. As I understand it now, airplanes cannot carry hunters and travelers into that area.

In Yellowstone Park, we restrict motorboats to certain portions of Yellowstone Lake in order to safeguard the interest of wildlife in that great area. I think we have to face the fact that as our population increases—now about two hundred million, soon to be four hundred million—we are going to have to restrict more and more. We cannot afford, as I see it, to turn over the drawing of the regulations and the administration of such areas to the developers. The rest of us have got to be included in usage and control considerations. I have confidence in the people of this audience, and others like you, to work out proper and fair regulations that will safeguard not only the recreational interests of all, but will protect remote areas that perhaps ought not to be invaded. Nature should have some chance to survive. The same principles should apply to the desert.

Moderator Luten: Let's turn our attention now to the second "forgotten" wilderness to be considered in this program, the nearshore marine environment. Dr. Hand, the control of school field trips is a must. Moss Beach, a few miles south of San Francisco, is a child-made "desert." What can we do about it?

Dr. Hand: I could talk about that for quite a while, but I will try not to. I think Moss Beach is an example of an unstated agreement by a lot of biologists that it is perhaps better to select one area and concentrate on it—and in the process almost ruin it—than to indiscriminately ruin many locations.

The fact remains that for about thirty years as many as two thousand students have arrived at Moss Beach in a single day, and yet Moss Beach has remained an extremely useful piece of seashore for class work. It no longer has all the common species, but a sufficient amount remains to make it useful and interesting.

It would be interesting to know just how many starfish, and I suppose it may number millions, have been carted home by well-meaning students only to discover that within twenty-four hours they were decaying so obnoxiously that it was hard to get close enough to them to throw them away.

The suggestion that Dr. Norris made for setting aside an area for regeneration is one solution to this—if you have several places equally accessible as Moss Beach. It seems to me the fact that Moss Beach is still selected by classes from Stanford, the University of California, San Francisco State College, junior colleges, high schools, grammar schools, and so forth is evidence of the ability to rejuvenate. Perhaps it is best to select an area like this and let it be trampled to death, without spreading this same destructive effort over the whole seashore.

Moderator Luten: Dr. Norris: Please comment on the whale population today. If they are declining, why and how can we deal with the threat of their extinction by the demands of the dog and cat food industry?

Kenneth S. Norris: There is no question but that the whale stocks of the world are declining—with a few exceptions such as the California gray whale, which is under international protection.

The limits of catches are strictly those set by economics at the moment; even though we have an International Whaling Commission, which supposedly regulates these affairs, it is not strikingly capable of regulating the acts of its own members. This simply means that when the whale stock declines to the point at which it is no longer economic to send out a processing boat and a fleet of catcher boats, then the fishing stops—and one hopes this is prior to the demise of the whales.

The real danger lies in the selective hunting of whales. Some are more desirable than others. The blue whale, for example, is larger and is a more important take; hence it is hunted more relentlessly than any other. If a gray whale should happen to be in the midst of a group of the blues and is killed, it is a regrettable mistake. Not yet exploited here—I have never understood why—are local stocks of small whales and porpoises for the dog and cat food industries. Sometimes they occur in many thousands along our shores. I think they are in need of recognition in our statutes. This should be done after some study of their biology.

Dr. Lindsay: Dr. Norris and I were discussing the California gray whale, which is the kind that migrates south along our coast, en route to Scammon's and other Baja California lagoons where they breed and calve. Once there were about fifty thousand of these wonderful animals. Between 1840 and 1870 they were decimated by California shore stations and by whaling vessels anchored in or off the Mexican lagoons. They did not have a chance, because the whole population went by or to the whalers. By 1900 they were given total protection by the International Whaling Commission. But again they are endangered, threatened by the commercial development of Scammon's Lagoon and the possibility of the establishment of a whaling station in an area where the whales congregate. The Bureau of Commercial Fisheries of the federal government this year gave a permit to slaughter one hundred specimens over a three-month period for "scientific purposes," and these are in addition to fifty-two more taken in 1966. I think this is difficult to justify on a scientific basis. Certainly, speaking as a biologist, I do not agree with their research use.

Dr. Theodore Walker who, like Ken Norris, has been studying gray whales, has made a very strong plea that one kind of whale, the California gray whale, be left undisturbed so that we can understand its population dynamics.

Moderator Luten: I would like to add a comment concerning the plight of the blue whale. We have all heard of guilt by association. There we see a case of extinction by association. The population of blue whales now being far too small to support Antarctic whaling expeditions, the economic support comes from the fin whales and sei whales, but the blue whale inadvertently gets caught in the same net and suffers by virtue of its association with more abundant whales.

Now here is a question for Dr. Hand. What do you think about dumping old cars offshore to form new fish habitats and new recreational islands or peninsulas?

Dr. Hand: That is being done at places in our state, here in California, and elsewhere in the country. Car bodies and all manner of things are being placed in the marine habitat. As Dr. Norris explained, when you put almost any object in the ocean, it very soon accumulates a particular flora and fauna. A new habitat is created, and this is basically very good management as long as these things are not placed in main navigational channels or on grounds where fishermen expect to use their dragnets. With some careful thought about location, it is really an excellent idea.

Moderator Luten: There is one last question, for Dr. Norris. What would be the administrative procedure for establishment of marine preserves and for their placement in the National Wilderness Preservation System?

Dr. Norris: Inclusion of marine areas in the wilderness system requires the same procedure as for any other area. For lands that are presently held under jurisdiction that allows this designation, there must be the preparation of a plan by the administering agency, the scheduling of hearings, and the securing of congressional and Presidential approval of its inclusion. As far as the establishment of other preserves is concerned, this, of course, depends entirely upon the various agencies involved, from state beaches and parks departments through other agencies such as my own group within the University of California.

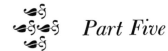 *Part Five*

Luncheon *April 8, 1967*

INTRODUCTION
Caspar W. Weinberger

REMARKS
Norman B. Livermore, Jr.

WILDERNESS AND THE PROPOSED FEDERAL
DEPARTMENT OF NATURAL RESOURCES
Frank E. Moss

Caspar W. Weinberger, Chairman

Caspar W. Weinberger

EXTRACT FROM INTRODUCTION

In observing the growing interest in wilderness attested to by the growth of these conferences, I am struck by a basic paradox. If everyone in this room were turned loose into one of our wilderness areas at once, how long would that area remain such? In facing this paradox now, perhaps the solution is simply to reserve more wilderness areas to meet this expanding need.

I have been asked why it is that at all the wilderness conferences so many of the leading speakers are also leading figures in government or politics. I think it should be apparent that the cause of wilderness is not only very good politics, but the cause of wilderness and conservation is a very necessary element in the whole effort to improve the quality of life. In looking at the quality of our speakers who embrace this cause, it is evident that politics is not necessarily the dirty business so many people automatically seem to feel it is.

Norman B. Livermore, Jr.

REMARKS

If anyone had told me a few short weeks ago that I would be sitting here at this head table as a bureaucrat, I would have shot him. But here I am, a bureaucrat, speaking to my old Sierra Club friends. One of the first questions that has been asked of me since I have taken this tumultuous change in my career is how I feel about shifting from being treasurer of a lumber company up north to being an administrator in Sacramento. And my reply: "After the numbers of experiences I have had in the mountains, nothing bothers me much."

In the few moments available, I would like to mention just three things.

The first I speak of with both amusement and nostalgia at least for Dave Brower and me, for it will surprise you to learn that this is the eleventh Wilderness Conference rather than the tenth as your program lists. I hold in my hand one of my most prized possessions: a post card issuing an invitation to a meeting that was held December 3, 1940, here in San Francisco, under the auspices of the San Francisco Bay Chapter of the Sierra Club, titled, "A Program and Discussion of Our Remaining Wilderness, Stressing the Enjoyment and Necessity of Wild Places." This, at least to my knowledge, was our first San Francisco Wilderness Conference, and those of us who helped organize that meeting in 1940 certainly did not in our wildest dreams envision that later these conferences would grow to their present size and eminence. As an aside, some of you might be amused to know that this first meeting was held under the friendly auspices of the Pacific Gas and Electric Company in their auditorium on Market Street.

If I may be permitted to get a bit serious, I would like to take time to stress the next two points, neither of which will be new to those of you who know me. First, I would like to make the strong suggestion to you and to future Wilderness Conferences that you watch your terminology. To me, wilderness is big wilderness. I believe the original Forest Service definition was that a wilderness had to be 100,000 acres or more. There are many possible definitions, but I do feel, and feel strongly, that the effectiveness of the word wilderness has been diluted by using it in too small a sense. As a specific example, one of our most eminent San Francisco conservation writers in last Sunday's newspaper raised the question: "How much of Pt. Reyes National Seashore should be wilderness?" I simply say to you briefly, but I hope emphatically, none of Pt. Reyes can be wilderness; it is simply too small. It can be wild, yes; but a wilderness, no.

The second and last point I would like to make is to urge you, with all the strength at my command, to put at the very top of your list of projects (and this suggestion applies both to the Sierra Club and to this conference) the stopping of the proposed Minarets Summit Road. I have here in my hand the saddest newspaper clipping I have ever seen. It describes plans to build this road, with endorsement by three California senators, fourteen California assemblymen, and one congressman. I understand it is also supported by Secretary of the Interior Udall. Completion of this road, in my opinion, would be the greatest tragedy since Hetch Hetchy. The John Muir Trail is the very heart and soul of the wilderness concept, both in California and elsewhere. To what avail would success be in other great preservation causes such as the redwoods, the Cascades, the Grand Canyon, and the proposed Golden Trout wilderness, if the crown jewel of them all, the High Sierra and its John Muir Trail, is bisected by a road?

I say, stop that road! *

* The proposed Minarets Summit Road, which would bisect the longest continuous wilderness trail in the nation, is still being debated at presstime.—*The Editors.*

Frank E. Moss

WILDERNESS AND THE PROPOSED FEDERAL DEPARTMENT OF NATURAL RESOURCES

I particularly welcome this opportunity to address the 1967 Wilderness Conference of the Sierra Club because it allows me to thank all of you personally for the magnificent work you have done in conservation since the club was founded by the great John Muir in 1892.

For seventy-five years you have been dedicated to preserving American beauty. Your farsightedness in launching this crusade; your commitment to preserving the spiritual values of nature at a time of frenzied industrialization and production of material wealth; your valiant affrays in defense of "the eagle and the mockingbird of the wilderness" —all these and more attest to your importance in the stream of American society.

I must also mention your handsome publications. One of my favorites is *In Wildness is the Preservation of the World,* with quotations from that apostle of the wilderness, Thoreau. These publications bring to many an urban dweller a world unknown—a world filled with nature's magnificence and majesty. The imagery and inspiration of them is held quietly, to be recalled in days of stress, smog, noise, and the blare of ordinary living in an uglified, crowded, industrialized, workaday world. Many who ponder your beautiful books may never see in person the wonders they depict, but to know that such places do exist— and in America—is to be reassured of our heritage and of our common life with nature. If parents do not view the wonders, the Sierra Club has helped to assure that their sons may, because the beauty will be saved from generation to generation. The Sierra Club is and has been a missionary, a bold, a wise, and a salubrious influence on the United States.

When one reflects on the controversies that occupy the political man's mind and activities, it is more than a little startling to realize that the conservation of the country's natural resource base is not one of the most intense. To you and me, it appears that reason and sensitivity would naturally dictate the preservation of such things as the giant coastal redwoods, as Indian pictographs in the Canyon Lands of Utah, as the bleak central coast range habitat of the nearly extinct California condor, as the ruggedness of the North Cascades, as the aquatic life of the Everglades, and as the glistening untrammeled world of seashore.

The logic of saving what can be saved of America's wilderness should be obvious, for the reason that it is not a renewable resource. If man shrinks and destroys the primeval, he can never recreate it. It is gone forever. But there are user groups in politics and society at large who do not take the "forever gone" view of their actions. It is only in recent years that the bird watchers, the photographers, the campers, and the climbers are making themselves heard above the chain saws and the bulldozers. They have determined that we shall not be overwhelmed within sterile horizons.

I am encouraged, as I know you are, to find signs all over America today that indicate a turning away from perpetual exploitation, perpetual destruction, perpetual overdevelopment of the American earth. There is a growing awareness among the citizenry that to conquer and to alter and to utilize for profit every square mile of the United States is not to create the best possible homeland for Americans. This message, I can assure you, is coming in strong to the members of Congress. Certain user groups, who have appeared to believe in economic growth at any price, are presently listening to the organized, sophisticated, and articulate conservationists like yourselves, who stand firm for what the future society must include in its master plan. What is left of America's wild beauty is a central objective of modern conservation. I am hopeful that we will not need to say a century from now what Thoreau said a hundred years ago: "Thank God they cannot cut down the clouds." This is not to say that all natural resources development should cease. Obviously, man's economic well-being and achievement of the good life require metals, timber, water, energy, and fuel supplied from our natural resources bank. What I do say is that discrimination and judgment must prevail. Both wilderness and development are valuable. Neither must be throttled.

The pendulum, having swung far toward unchecked economic exploitation, is now swinging back.

One of the permanent and notable achievements of the Eighty-eighth Congress was its adoption of the Wilderness Act. That act extended protection to a vast acreage of national forest land that had already been classified as wild, or wilderness. It also provided for review of other lands in the national forest system, the national park system, and the fish and wildlife refuge system. This review is to determine which of these areas could properly be classified for inclusion in the wilderness system.

The Sierra Club cannot afford to slacken its vigil nor lessen its endeavors to get the bills for wilderness reclassification passed. Your opponents from within and from without the Congress continue to press their philosophies with slogans of "sterile bondage," the "freezing of vast acreages in static preservation," "full development under dynamic, multiple use management," "ecological purity is a dream of the past: 'civilization' must have priority," and many, many other charges.

On January 11, 1967, in Chatham, Massachusetts, a public hearing was held on a proposal of the Bureau of Sport Fisheries and Wildlife to classify a small offshore island in the Atlantic Ocean called Monomoy as "forever wild." Monomoy is a permanent home for no human beings. It belongs to the yellowlegs, plovers, sanderlings, and other shore birds; to the Canada geese and the black ducks; to the warblers and the terns. Over three hundred species of birds have been observed on this ornithological wonderland. The hearing on Monomoy was important not because practically nothing on the island will be changed, but because if the preliminary proposal on it is ultimately approved by the Congress, the island will be permanently protected from the automobile causeway that some wanted to build between it and the mainland. No yacht harbor will be constructed, and the beach will not be overrun with vehicles. It will be for the far-stretching future a wild place where visitors may come by small boat to fish, stroll the sands, watch the birds, collect shells, picnic—and then leave Monomoy to the wash of the Atlantic and the probing of the sea winds.

I mention Monomoy because it is the first proposal that the Bureau of Sport Fisheries and Wildlife has made under the 1964 Wilderness Act. The Forest Service is developing similar proposals for what are now called "primitive areas" in the national forests. The Interior Department is working on proposals for every roadless area of five thousand acres or more within the national parks, wildlife refuges, and game ranges. Since there are more than 150 such areas, and the law requires that at least one-third of them shall be reviewed within three years, the deadline for the first fifty hearings will be September, 1967.

The Sierra Club will have a lot of work—and bearing witness—to do in the next few months. You will find countrywide support and participation by interested citizens who are resolved that they will have a hand in determining the uses to which America's yet undeveloped land is devoted.

The President, in transmitting to Congress the Second Annual Report on the Status of the National Wilderness Preservation System, called the maintenance of our existing wilderness system a "priority program of the federal government." He stated that "the period of expansion and exploration, the great era of successive western frontiers, has now become a part of our American past." Recalling that past, the President noted that the pioneer of our American history regarded the wilderness as a foe to be conquered, but today's pioneers have a new purpose: "To preserve some remnants of that wilderness from the onrush of modern civilization." The ax and the plow that made farms and pastures out of the seemingly inexhaustible forests have been replaced by the more subtle pressure to preserve and to keep. This is the result of an upsurge of determined public opinion that demands "that we maintain our wilderness birthright."

One paragraph in the President's statement pinpoints a problem that I feel particular concern about solving. This is what the President said on February 14, 1966: "Legislation is one thing; administration is another. The executive branch must fulfill its responsibility with common sense and imagination."

We in the Congress have accomplished a great deal in conservation legislation. The Congress has appropriated millions and millions of dollars to carry out that legislation. Resource agencies in great number have been created in just about every department of the United States government except the Post Office. The Congress has approved proposals for saving land, forests, mountains, rivers, seashores, fish, wildlife, lakes, wilderness, white water, minerals, and even clean air.

Despite all this legislation and concern, despite all this expenditure and good intention, the facts are that in many areas our air is filthy; our rivers, lakes, and streams debris-strewn and polluted; our landscapes hideous with billboards and old cars; our national and state parks are noisy and crowded and smoky; our redwoods 80 per cent gone; and our soil and forests bulldozed and covered with houses and concrete highways.

Last year I made a proposal in the Senate to establish a Department of Natural Resources. The bill did not go anywhere last session; I have reintroduced it as S.886 in the Ninetieth Congress on February 7, 1967. I am hopeful that this embodies an idea whose time has come. It is my conviction that the place—one of the places—where we have gone wrong in our conservation efforts is that we have lacked a coordinated, synchronized effort in all the federal departments and agencies where responsibilities have been widely delegated, and then jealously guarded, and never looked at as pieces of a whole plan to save our national habitat. Like the ecological unity in nature, I am persuaded that we need unification of natural resources management in government.

There has been no dearth of strictures about current methods of dealing with natural resources problems. In the legislative acts of the Congress, goals for conservation have been clearly enunciated. Agencies, bureaus, commissions, committees, and councils almost unending, have been created to help attain the goal. Yet all this activity and delineation of purpose have not been adequate to assure us that our renewable and nonrenewable resources will be adequately managed to meet the prodigious demands of this generation and those to come.

As the President so wisely said, legislation is one thing, administration is another. In past years, any suggestion that the methods by which we handle our resources should be reorganized has met vehement opposition. The opposition has come not only from those interests that directly obtain economic benefits from literally eating the nation out of house and home. The functionaries of the agencies have strenuously objected to reorganization too. This is ironic, inasmuch as the agencies were created to preserve and protect the public interest and to keep our small part of the planet in condition for our health and enjoyment. The departments concerned with natural resources were created to deal with problems of our land, forests, minerals, and waters not only in terms of what economic gains could be derived from them, but to save our heritage of natural beauty and wide open spaces for pleasant living. In some cases, however, this goal has been lost in the building of ever-widening empires of overlapping, fractious, duplicating, and contradictory bureaucracies.

The problems of the management of resources have today become too urgent to permit the organization and direction of them to be bogged down in the old status quo thinking of federal administrators or to be dissipated for the private gain of business organizations and individuals. I guess it is our long background of pioneering that has lashed us to the juggernaut of perpetual growth—industrial growth, population growth, material wealth growth—so that we are only in recent years waking up to the fact that the enslavement of more and more of our natural riches means there will be less and less of them free for our children and our children's children. We are even thinking sometimes that more and more material wealth, and more and more people, are in acute conflict with our own notion of the good life. Unless we stabilize our population we may not be able, in the long run, to save our wilderness and wildlife.

One of my favorite conservation stories is about Uncle Joe Cannon. He was that venerable and intransigent Speaker of the House of Representatives at the time President Theodore Roosevelt was launching an American conservation movement. On hearing about Roosevelt's plans and requests of the Congress relating thereto, Uncle Joe commented firmly, "Not one cent for scenery." But Cannon's law has been repealed. The law of "appropriative rights" that has been applied to the programs administered by the federal agencies must also be repealed.

The prerequisite to federal—or national—leadership in natural resources conservation is a permanent and coordinated department that will deal with all aspects of policy and program as a whole. Natural resources are interdependent in nature, and it seems to me that this concept must be applied to man's management of them.

It will take considerable soul searching and give and take to reach a meeting of minds in Washington, as well as all over the country, to bring all of the natural resources activities into one federal department with one head.

Organizationally, what I propose in my bill evolves something like this: the Department of the Interior would be redesignated the Department of Natural Resources, and the Secretary of the Interior would be redesignated the Secretary of Natural Resources. The Under Secretary of the Interior would become Deputy Secretary of Natural Resources. There would be two Under Secretaries in the new department —one an Under Secretary of Natural Resources for Water, and the other an Under Secretary of Natural Resources for Lands. Several bureaus and agencies would be transferred either into, or out of, present federal departments: the Bureau of Indian Affairs and Office of Territories would go to Health, Education and Welfare. The Forest Service would be transferred into the Department of Natural Resources, where it and the Park Service—which is already there—would not only work out a modus vivendi on the methods of conservation about which they now disagree, but would be parts of the same department with the same overall objectives. To illustrate the present conflicts of purpose between the Forest Service and the Park Service, we may take the case of the North Cascades in Washington state. Writing recently in the *Atlantic* magazine, Paul Brooks calls it "The Fight for America's Alps."

The principals in the struggle over which agency shall have the controlling interest in these wildest, most rugged, and some say most beautiful mountains in the United States, are the United States Forest Service of the Department of Agriculture, which presently controls them, and the National Park Service of the Department of the Interior, which would like to develop them into a national park. The Forest Service is supported by lumber, mining, and hunting interests, while the Park Service has the backing of most national wildlife, park, and wilderness organizations. Secretary of Agriculture Freeman has called the North Cascades "one of the most magnificent areas in the world," and others believe they offer an opportunity for the most beautiful wilderness park in our entire national park system.

However, the rock-bottom conservation issues concerning the North Cascades are (1) whether the Forest Service will compromise between the lumber interests and recreation; or (2) whether the Park Service, carrying high the banner of recreation, will compromise to omit some of its customary "improvements" in park-forest areas, so that in the end the North Cascades may be saved for use and wilderness; or (3) whether they will be yielded for timber and developed recreation. I will not go further into the involved and difficult questions that could be laid out in this case. I have only brought up the North Cascades question as an illustration that is contemporary with my concern about similar questions throughout all areas of natural resources management.

The functions of watershed protection and flood protection now in the Department of Agriculture would also be moved into the Natural Resources Department. The civil functions of the Corps of Engineers now in the Department of the Army would likewise be moved into the new department, with the provision that in time of war or other national emergency, the functions of the Army Engineers would be transferred back to the Secretary of the Army's authority for the duration of the emergency.

It is a kind of folly that presently permits the Corps of Engineers to plan a one hundred million dollar flood-control project in the Rio Grande watershed of New Mexico, while upstream in the watershed there is extensive erosion that is causing sedimentation that will move downstream unchecked to fill up the reservoir, while the Soil Conservation Service of the Department of Agriculture and the Bureau of Land Management of the Department of the Interior debate their jurisdictions.

And it is certainly a kind of folly to permit the Corps of Engineers to imperil and destroy in the Florida Everglades what the National Park Service has preserved and guarded. A great battle is taking place on the southernmost tip of Florida. The dredges and the bulldozers and the earth-moving machines that the Army Engineers have employed to build a canal along the northern edge of the park have drained or cut off water supply to vast marshes and everglades and thus have pushed back and have even eliminated many birds, fish, amphibians, and animals, some of them of dwindling species.

The canal carries barges from an aerojet plant in the area producing rockets for the space operation at Cape Kennedy. It is now proposed to remove the plug which is holding salt water out of the canal, and to allow it to flow through. The salt water would spill over into the area of the park that has most of the roseate spoonbills, the wood ibis, the great white herons, and the few alligators that have retreated there. Local drainage authorities say let the water in—they doubt it would do much harm. Director of the National Park Service George B. Hartzog says that it would destroy the delicate balance between fresh water and salt water that is the biological base. *There is no referee.*

The nonmilitary functions of the National Oceanographic Data Center now in the Department of the Navy would be transferred to the new Department of Natural Resources. The sea grant programs now under the National Science Foundation would be moved into the new department.

By administrative action the water pollution functions of the Department of Health, Education and Welfare have been transferred to Interior. My bill would add air pollution functions also to the new Department of Natural Resources. The Secretary of Natural Resources would, under provisions of my bill, be the only official whose approval would be required before the Federal Power Commission could issue a license for a project that might affect the comprehensive plan of any river basin commission developed under the Water Resources Planning Act.

At the end of each calendar year, the Secretary of Natural Resources would submit to the President and thence to the Congress a report on the year's departmental activities.

Speaking idealistically, I think that such an administrative and organizational regrouping would bring all resource-related agencies together in a way that makes sense. President Johnson has said, "The executive branch must fulfill its responsibility with common sense and imagination." I would hope that a Department of Natural Resources might help considerably in doing just that. In such an organization, after the initial protestations, some of the rivalry and confusion would undoubtedly be eliminated. In future, the department could in unity determine whether a reclamation project is to be built in a certain location or whether it is to be a power project alone; whether a storage reservoir is to be built or scenic landmarks are to be left untouched; whether a wilderness area is to be turned into a teeming mass recreation park with "improvements" or whether it is to be left forever wild as nature made it; whether public lands that are primitive or wild are to be turned over to mining, grazing, and timber cutting, or whether the deeper values of the trees and mountains are to be regarded as permanent retreats for an increasingly urbanized population. One hopes it would solve—or resolve—some of the disputations about power projects between the corps and the Bureau of Reclamation and the uses of public lands by the Forest Service and the Park Service, to cite but two examples that have gotten a lot of attention.

I am compelled by pride, or in defense, to point out that all this could be accomplished without setting up a new federal agency. It would be essentially no more than an ingenious reshuffling, with a single, sound purpose built into an existing department with a new name—to make the federal government make sense in its natural resources policies and programs.

I am an advocate of the virtues of competition, but among government agencies where prolonged jurisdictional disputes keep important matters unresolved and hanging fire for indefinite—and critical—periods, I am all for cooperation and coordination. The nation can no longer afford this exercise in agency muscle-flexing. I am not saying that all blame for past contentious tie-ups can be laid on federal administrators and agencies, because the facts are that each one of them has been assigned specific missions and responsibilities in acts laid down by Congress. And I can think of no program that is without considerable merit. Under scrutiny of a judging eye, the programs generally are excellent and of essential worth. However, I do say that the fragmented approach has dissipated many effective achievements that could have been realized from the same activities.

You are an extraordinarily concerned and wise organization, and I ask you frankly: Do you know where you might go in the federal departments to find out just what the overall natural resources plan is, or where we are right now, or where we are going to come out vis-à-vis our natural resources? I think not. Someone has likened the situation to a symphony orchestra where all the musicians are first-rate but have no conductor.

With a federal Department of Natural Resources, combining in a harmonious relation all aspects of natural resources programs, I believe there would be productive repercussions on other levels. States, local bodies, representatives of industry, agriculture, labor, conservation groups, and just plain citizens would find less bewilderment and confusion if they could see the pieces of the patchwork quilt of conservation sewn together. They too would understand just what it is we are attempting to accomplish in conservation, in the utilization and preservation of our land, water, forests, minerals, and wildlife. There would undoubtedly be some bruised feelings arising from such a consolidating move into a Department of Natural Resources, but in return for a little suffering about old allegiances and hurt pride, we might be able to achieve a long-term yield that would more than repay our transient short-term adjustments.

To return specifically to wilderness preservation, to which this group is especially dedicated, I am of the opinion that such a reorganization plan as I have laid before you would be of benefit in achieving your high-minded goals. A federal Department of Natural Resources should have within its capability the power to relate conservation practices and development to each other, just as nature has related the resources of soil, water, forests, wildlife, and wilderness in a noble and interdependent whole.

It is my conviction that despite the work of conservation groups like the Sierra Club, the resource conservation programs of federal, state, and local agencies, and the vast appropriations and multitudinous conservation bills of Congress, the United States is still undergoing a progressive deterioration of its natural resources. It is my further conviction, as I said on the floor of the United States Senate on February 7, 1967, that the trouble is that "we have allowed competing interests for the use of our limited resources to block any overall development and protection plan. Every resource management agency is surrounded by competing agencies, each striving to utilize our waters, minerals, and land for its own particular clientele." Consequently, it turns out that when important decisions are to be made—such as to dam or not to dam a river, to cut down a two-thousand-year-old redwood or to let it stand—we frequently have no policy at all to deal with the question. It is with thoughts—and facts—like these in mind that I have offered you today my proposal for an effective resource management reorganization. I hope that you will give it earnest and critical thought.

Of the various labors I have performed in the Senate of the United States, the most congenial ones have had to do with all phases of conservation—the establishment of parks and recreation areas; the development of mineral and water resources; and the conservation of wilderness and wildlife. As a native westerner and one who loves and finds the deeper meanings of human happiness in great spaces and natural, rugged beauty, I conclude my visit with you by repeating the eloquence of Wallace Stegner, with whom I went to school at the University of Utah, on the mystique of primitive areas and the importance of intangibles to human development and joy:

> Something will have gone out of us as a people if we ever let the remaining wilderness be destroyed; if we permit the last virgin forests to be turned into comic books and plastic cigarette cases; if we drive

the few remaining members of the wild species into zoos or into extinction; if we pollute the last clean air and dirty the last clean streams and push our paved roads through the last of the silence, so that never again will Americans be free in their own country from the noise, the exhausts, the stinks of human and automotive waste. And so that never again can we have the chance to see ourselves single, separate, vertical, and individual in the world, part of the environment of trees, and rocks and soil, brother to the other animals, part of the natural world and competent to belong in it.

We need the wild country available to us, even if we never do more than drive to its edge and look in. For it can be the means of reassuring ourselves of our sanity as creatures, a part of the geography of hope.

I salute you, members of the Sierra Club, for helping to save for all Americans the wonder of our wilderness.

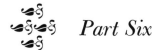 *Part Six*

The Quality of American Wilderness

The reservation of wilderness areas under present public law and regulation does not automatically insure their preservation. Recreational and scientific use, the dynamism of ecologic processes, protection from fire and insect epidemics, and activities adjacent to wilderness units, can have a severely disrupting influence on the wilderness environment that was intended for preservation. In addition, current laws and regulations of the various agencies involved are often not adequate to maintain wilderness conditions. Whether wilderness requires that any prescribed set of natural conditions be maintained depends on one's understanding of the meaning of wilderness and what provides its quality. This session will examine what wilderness quality means to experienced users, and problems of retaining that quality.

Albert E. Burke

A WORLD WITHOUT WILDERNESS

There are very few places in the world that can compare, either in quality or in character, with what there was on this land base of ours for those early settlers to start working into our way of life. We do not dare ignore the imprint of the wilderness into which we moved, for in our time we have become potentially dangerous to the rest of the world.

Our experience in using land and resources is unique because the content of our wilderness was unique. When we go into other parts of the world and begin talking from our experience about what they ought to do in their aid programs, we are terribly dangerous because most of the rest of the world has not had the margin of natural resources to play with that we have had.

In 1883, in the Dakota Territory, there was an incident that illustrates how the expanse and abundance of the new land on this continent provided a unique margin for error. One day, a farmer was plowing the sod on his homestead, turning it over to prepare it for crops as he had done back where he had come from. He became terribly uncomfortable with the feeling that somebody was looking at him and, sure enough, there was a Sioux Indian on a horse staring at him as he went through the routine of plowing the land. The Indian just stood there looking at him. Finally it got under the skin of the farmer. He turned to the Indian and very roughly asked him what he wanted.

The Indian stated his business. He muttered three words and then left. Those three words revealed the reality of the world in which the land rush took place. The three words were "Wrong side up." That's all he said, "Wrong side up." That Indian was not a scientist. He had absolutely no idea about the more than eight thousand years of experience that human beings had had using land of all kinds, all over this planet, with results that had destroyed some civilizations. That Indian knew nothing about what happens when you turn the sod cover over and expose the bacteria so that the sunlight can kill it and otherwise oxidize the soil so that in effect it loses its binding properties and blows away. But he did know on the basis of the wisdom of generations, who lived in very close contact with the land in North America, that this land should not be plowed. It should not be turned wrong side up.

What happened to that region in the late 1880's you can still read about in your newspapers. Until a recent set of rains came, drought had destroyed about one-half the crops. And in our time, with the government pushing as hard as it can to get as much as we can off the land, this becomes as serious a problem as it was then. But now the margin for error is gone and we can no longer ignore what we do to our land and its resources. The point is that what we have done on our land has conditioned everything we think and everything we do.

When I say our experience has made us dangerous to the rest of the world, it is because of an interesting experience that happened to me while I was teaching at Yale. I have had many foreign students in my classes over the years. On one occasion I invited two students from Jordan to come to my home for a weekend. It was at that point in time when we were quite concerned about the impression that foreign students were getting about the United States and we wanted to give them some idea of what Americans were like in our own homes. When we got around to a discussion of their impressions of the United States, what they told me bears on that word dangerous. They said that they were impressed more than anything else by the fact that Americans really seem to believe that the process that gave us the good life began with the right ideas. It was what men believed that explained what we did with the resources that were available to us, and made us what we are. They posed a very simple question: "What would have happened if those early colonists had landed on the east coast of Saudi Arabia instead of the east coast of North America? What kind of lives would your ideas have made then?"

The east coast of North America, my part of it in New England, has averaged between thirty to fifty-five inches of rainfall every year I have lived there since 1949. The result of this is quite clear to see against evaporation rates and a number of other important items. There is a forest cover on the land, which in the beginning contained a good deal of wildlife. It also was easily worked by the people who had primitive tools. Whatever it was they needed—their shelters, their tools, their transportation—a good deal of it was out there in those woods.

In that environment there is also something called a glaciated landscape. A glacier does some peculiar things to the land over which it passes. As it melts, the stuff that it carries in solution will be dropped in peculiar ways: some of it, the heavier stuff, in one place; the rest of it, the lighter stuff, in other places. In New England there are small pockets of good soils that, as was proved in time, could be worked best by small units of labor.

Thomas Jefferson used to talk about something called the individual family farm. The individual family farm and the rugged individualism ᵗhat we associate with it came out of a very specific kind of environment, a wilderness environment, which did things to people. The ideas that we developed there were then carried clear across the land to affect what we did with our dry lands as well. And it was the farmers who came from areas that had a great deal of rainfall who were doing the things they had previously done in Europe where there was also a considerable amount of rainfall. These farmers moved out on the Great Plains where there was very little rainfall, and they accomplished exactly what the Indian warned would be done. They turned the soil wrong side up, and we have been paying for it, periodically, ever since. But the settlement of this continent and its prosperity did not falter because of the mistakes made in the Great Plains. The land was so extensive that we could afford to learn from mistakes made in certain regions. The country as a whole could still thrive.

I must stress that I am not trying to suggest that environmental determinism is the explanation. I am simply stressing that what we call freedom is very much the result of a unique experience. It is the result of elbow room that provided a margin for error and many other factors. When you deal with a society that has neither elbow room nor the other conditions similar to ours, you cannot speak to it in terms of our experience. You must find some way to deal with its problems given its own full set of circumstances.

Put our colonists down on the east coast of Saudi Arabia where there is practically no rainfall, no forest cover, no game in the woods; where there are no materials for building shelters or tools or the rest; where in fact the only way to provide for survival is through a communal cooperative effort to dig the wells, the ditches, and the reservoirs that make it possible to irrigate the land—in that kind of place a rugged individualist becomes downright dangerous and would be kicked out of the community rather than respected by the community as he was in our early history.

The important thing here is that we have to remind ourselves from time to time about the realities of what made us as we are: it was that wilderness in which we began, it was that wilderness that left its stamp. We must understand it so that we can communicate with ourselves and the world around us. This is the idea of a gentleman named Elbridge Gerry, whose name is signed to the Declaration of Independence. He made the important statement that periodically a people must go back to their roots to refresh themselves so that they will understand what they are.

I am not trying to suggest that in the good old days the farmers and the founders had all the answers to the problems we know in our time; but they had all the right questions about all the timeless values. If you read the basic papers you will find that into them they put such questions as What is the good life? and What is the nature and the destiny of man? and Is there, indeed, a supernatural being that lays down laws to which all men must conform? That is not quite the way they put their words. Instead, they talked about promoting the general welfare, insuring the domestic tranquility, and the rest. But they set down values that have not been realized fully because I am not entirely certain they can be realized in the same way from place to place. The important thing is to go back to refresh our roots, to understand what we were so that we can understand what we are.

How do you do this? I ask this question with more than a little academic interest. I have tried for sixteen years in the communications media to talk about just such things, because in many ways what we do not understand about the geographical and cultural realities of the world around us explains why we have failed to get the best results from the 150 billions of dollars that have been spent so far trying to help other people help themselves. I have found we cannot do this because of a problem that we face not only regarding our wilderness roots, but regarding everything else.

There is a strong message in the record of the constitutional debates and the *Federalist Papers*. The founders were concerned about power: how it would be checked, how it would be balanced so it could not be abused. Never in the history of this country has the problem of power been so great as it is today. You can read the evidence on any financial page of any newspaper in this country. In 1964 there were sixteen hundred corporate mergers, which means that the power to make decisions in the economic sphere had now been reduced by that much. In 1965 this was raised to twenty-two hundred mergers, and the process goes on. Those who have the power to decide what will be done in relation to wilderness or anything else are now few in number. They are few in business and in industry. They are few in government. They are few in politics. Unfortunately, they may not be the ones with the knowledge.

As our reserve of wilderness dwindles and we forget the true nature of our heritage, it becomes acutely important that those few men of power today be informed of the realities and uniqueness of our short history and of the consequences of the policies they promulgate in a world without wilderness.

This is a pressure-group state. Senator Moss, in his fine speech here, has told us what must be done. Conservationists must set up a pressure group of their own and they must set about informing the men of power in industry, commerce, government, and politics of the influence of wilderness on the quality of American life.

The most important power of all is the power to inform. This reminds me of something that happened two years ago when a man was appointed to a position of authority and power in the Columbia Broadcasting System. Interviewed one day about what the television industry would do now that we had orbiting satellites that would provide for instantaneous communications on this planet, his comment was that he was frightened about the prospect—the idea that we, as the leading nation, one that had placed this satellite in orbit, might have to say something to the world around us frightened this man. He did not know what to say.

I found the interview to be nothing short of frightening—certainly amazing. Considering the fund of knowledge that is available, considering the things we know, considering the problems there are to be dealt with, that any man with that kind of power in the communications media would be afraid that he might not have something to say is a pretty accurate reflection of how the power in that industry is used today.

I know at first hand how difficult it is to get men with great power to talk about issues, even if they may know something about them. No matter what the issue is, it is disruptive, and men with power justify their positions as corporate employees by the degree of harmony they can preserve in their companies and not the degree of disruption of things as they are. Yet what conservationists suggest is that areas of the United States be set aside and not used, as Senator Moss put it, to make a profit, or for utilitarian purposes. This will obviously change things, and it is impossible to talk about such things on the air unless you can get the men who have the power to make the decisions to agree to this. Only men in business and industry can do it. They must be persuaded of the importance of going back to our roots for refreshment and that the availability of a reserve of wilderness provides the means for this refreshment.

I can sum it all up by saying that a nation that will not explain itself to its own people, or to its own children, or to the world around it, really does not need any enemies. It has no future.

Estella B. Leopold

ECOLOGICAL REQUIREMENTS
OF THE WILDERNESS ACT

In discussing quality in American wilderness, it is important to recognize that biological naturalness is a very important aspect of quality. Biological quality as found in original wilderness communities is a value we can ill afford to sacrifice or compromise in reserved wilderness areas. The maintenance of biological naturalness, through management if necessary, clearly becomes a primary objective in wilderness area protection.

What happens ecologically to our wilderness tracts once they are safely tucked away in the National Wilderness System? If we leave them completely alone, do they remain the same through time? Many references to the healing powers of nature imply a bland assumption by many that letting nature take its course will automatically provide a natural balance in the plant and possibly in the animal communities at hand. Although the nature-heals-all hypothesis may be valid in some vegetation areas where climax is self-maintaining and relatively stable, it certainly is not true in many others, for example in fire-maintained climaxes. In order to maintain highest biological quality in wilderness areas, especially those involving unstable communities, active management definitely is required.

The Wilderness Act sets forth our objectives in protecting wilderness tracts by defining wilderness as an area "retaining its primeval character and influence." Of enormous importance is our interpretation of the words "primeval" and "natural condition" in the act. Secretary Udall's committee appointed to study management of the national parks has suggested that restoration of the natural primitive scene in the parks should be taken to mean restoration of the condition that prevailed when the area was first visited by the white man. This interpretation of natural conditions has been accepted by a wide number of American botanists, like Norman Fassett, John T. Curtis, Hugh Raup, and E. Dyksterhuis. This interpretation of natural that has now been accepted by the Department of Interior has the advantage of being objective, and certainly is in keeping with the spirit of the Wilderness Act.

In considering a definition of primeval communities (as opposed to those altered by man), we should discuss their chief characteristics. In my view these include extensive species and structural diversity of native plants, and high organic productivity. These three are linked closely in the functioning of the natural ecosystem—linked in such a way that the sacrifice or compromise of one will negatively affect the other two values. These concepts are basic in studying examples of unstable communities that have been overprotected and undermanaged by man.

The Wilderness Act recognizes the need for management programs, for it states that wilderness shall be "protected *and managed* so as to preserve its natural conditions. . . . Each agency administering any area designated as wilderness shall be responsible for preserving the wilderness character of the area. [Emphasis added.]" However, the Wilderness Act comes at a time when established fire-control practices have already altered the primeval character of plant communities and vegetation in many different wilderness areas, and when research on how to reinstate the original character of these communities has scarcely begun.

There are methods that can be used to reinstate and maintain each protected area in its primeval condition. First, we must determine what the primitive conditions and influences were or are in each area. Actual investigations would utilize historical records, age-class distributions and the so-called relict-site method to determine the actual size and nature of the original flora. Through these techniques, the differences in structure and flora between the present and the original plant communities can be recognized for a particular area. Through research, we must devise effective management techniques that will attain and maintain an approximation of the original scene.

These methods are not easily pursued. From the beginning of the wilderness concept in 1924, administering agencies have been protecting wilderness, not managing it in a basic biological sense. Management has kept out nonconforming uses, offered fire control, and moved to control overpopulations of some game species. What the Wilderness Act now calls for in the way of management is so new that it requires a new set of research programs to find out what to do and how to do it in each area. Only the Park Service is launched on such research, even though almost three years have ensued since passage of the act.

The following case histories indicate that complete fire control as a general goal of our administering agencies has resulted in unnatural ecological conditions inside several wilderness or de facto wilderness areas. The examples demonstrate that fire is a natural component of the environment, and plays an important role in maintaining a wide variety of plant communities. The extensive ecological changes resulting from the exclusion of natural fires can be considered as undesirable under the Wilderness Act because by definition the resultant changes are not natural. In addition they are undesirable because they create thick, junglelike forest stands where open, parklike ones stood before; the general effect is depressing, not uplifting.

Deep in the heart of the Southwest, far from any major city or highway, lies the magnificent mountain massif called the Mogollon Range. In the deeply dissected and richly forested Mogollons of southwestern New Mexico, with arid flat lands on either side, lies our first established federal wilderness, the Gila. Deer, black bear, Abert squirrels, mountain lions, elusive turkeys, and three species of quail are among the abundant native game that call this area their home. During the 1920's several conservationists, including Senator Clinton Anderson and Aldo Leopold, convinced officials in the Forest Service that some part of this range should be set aside. Mainly through these efforts, the first formally established wilderness preserve, the Gila Wilderness, was established by the Forest Service in 1924. (It is now threatened by the proposed Hooker Dam that would flood about five to seven miles of the impressive Gila Gorge on the west side of the wilderness.)

The ponderosa pine belt, which is the main timber type below the high spruce-aspen zone in the Gila Wilderness, had originally a consistent savannalike structure—an open woodland with a lot of space between the high crowns of the pines and the well-developed grassy understory. Scattered shrubs were mainly along watercourses. According to stockmen and ecologists who saw it in the thirties, the vegetation was, in effect, a fire climax, for there were frequent lightning-caused fires that burned through the understory but almost never climbed to the crowns of the ponderosas. These ground fires served to clear out the organic fuel on the forest floor and to reduce brush in the stands.

Forty years of assiduous fire control by the Forest Service has allowed greatly increased accumulations of fuel on the forest floor. The result is replacement of grassy meadows by stunted pine trees; increased shrub and brush growth; and replacement of parklike pon-

"No, I don't smell something burning. Now go back to sleep."

Drawing by Lorenz; © 1967 The New Yorker Magazine, Inc.

derosa woodland by thick stands of stunted "doghair pine" too thick to
penetrate by horse. The annual average number of lightning-caused
fires in the past decade within the Gila Wilderness is sixty, and the Gila
Forest, in total, has from three hundred to four hundred lightning-
caused fires in "bad years" and two hundred to two hundred and fifty
in "good years." The widespread prevalence of lightning strikes is very
conspicuous to those who have traveled through that country and have
seen the lightning scars on many medium to large ponderosas.

Unless something else is done, complete fire control now is obliga-
tory, for the additional ground fuel, all sizes of brush and small pines,
contribute greatly to the heat of modern fires in this region; now almost
any fire may become a crown fire and may cause conflagration. Four
enormous forest fires on the Gila Forest occurred between 1951 and
1956 and wiped out over eighty thousand acres of timber in the wilderness and primitive areas.

Fire control is now immensely expensive; it cost about $1.8 million in
the last decade for the Gila Forest alone. In the light of these facts, is
complete fire control in fire-climax communities a good idea? The lack
of ground fires in such a forest deprives it of its most attractive features
and makes it susceptible to conflagration. The shrub and brush layers
that develop in fire-protected areas vastly decrease the carrying capacity for game and ruin much of the woodland habitat for turkeys and
quail, which prefer parkland to dense forest.

Under the auspices of the Forest Service fire control program, a whole series of roads and an airstrip have been built in the Gila Wilderness, many of which are outmoded since the use of helicopters is the efficient way to fight fires there. The airstrip was used for fire control during only one year, 1959.

Applying the management technique of prescribed burning in the Gila Forest will not be easy now, but once instituted, the immense effort to control fire there will become far easier and much less expensive. The new wilderness policy prescribed by the act seems to call for it.

Though the U.S. Forest Service has conducted research on prescribed burning in the western United States in recent years, most of it is directed to the study of burning cutover slash, not in standing pine woods as in the Gila National Forest. As the fuel piles up year by year, it seems time for the Forest Service to develop a regular program of prescribed burning in managing ponderosa woodland in the Southwest.

Controlled burning in fire-climax pine stands of the Southeast has been the subject of much careful research during the last twenty years. The research has in part been carried out by the Forest Service, but primarily it was developed by private investigators (for example by staff members of the Tall Timbers Research Station in Tallahassee, Florida) and by the states. Extensive experimentation in the brushlands of California and Arizona under the auspices of several land management agencies and universities has led to the successful use of prescribed burning for purposes of reducing fire hazards and improving wildlife habitat. A vast literature contains good leads on methods of carrying out small and large light burns. Many of the rules of burning may have applications in the Southwest:

(1) For light, easy-to-manage burning, soil and duff should be damp.

(2) Burn from highly combustible areas toward low combustibility.

(3) Burn really inflammable mixtures downwind.

(4) Burn under steady air drift, after 3 P.M., when inflammability is low.

(5) Generally do not burn during the dry season; light burns may be achieved in April.

(6) To burn isolated jungle islands, burn when dry.

At Sequoia–Kings Canyon National Park, California, biologists noticed that the survival of sequoia seedlings was exceedingly limited; however white fir seedlings were succeeding in large numbers. Fire control has been in effect there since about 1925, and interestingly the thick stands of the white fir reproduction postdate 1930. Three years ago the Park Service contracted with a scientist at San Jose State College, Dr. Richard Hartesvelt, to study the problem. He determined that sequoia seeds were sprouting all right, but because they lay on top organic litter piled so deeply, by the time their roots got down to permanent moisture, their strength was spent. White fir seedlings were more able to probe the thick litter, and by being more shade-tolerant, were shading out surviving sequoia seedlings, which were growing slowly indeed. Dr. Hartesvelt arranged with the Park Service to have some eight acres of forest floor litter scraped up and burned carefully, and to have white fir and brush removed. The next crop of sequoia seeds sprouted and survived very well. Wildflowers began to proliferate; reports indicate the elegant-looking experimental sequoia grove was reminiscent of John Muir's description of the open-structured stands.

Hartesvelt's discovery that sequoia is a fire climax amazed botanists because they have always considered sequoia woodland to be an ultimate or climax in local plant succession. John Muir's observations of annual spring ground fires creeping through the big trees should have clued us in years ago. It now appears clear that natural ground fires have played an important housecleaning role in reducing litter, encouraging the herbaceous understory, reducing brush and crown fire hazard, and in establishing new sequoia forests rather than white fir.

The Park Service reports that fire hazard in many parts of the Sequoia–Kings Canyon National Park, including the General Sherman grove, is building up to exceedingly dangerous levels. Consequently it plans to extend Dr. Hartesvelt's work by using prescribed burning on a larger experimental area in the park.

It took us about forty years to appreciate the fact that if we do not manage with fire at Sequoia–Kings Canyon National Park, we will not have sequoias forever. Carefully planned research and cautious management such as the Park Service is now engaged in can save the day for the big trees.

The Everglades National Park, which is the third largest national park and the only one established in North America to preserve a semitropical swamp wilderness, is without question the most serious preservational problem the National Park Service faces today. So little is known about this complicated area that the only scientist in residence at the park, Dr. Robertson, feels unsure what the original vegetative structure and pattern may have been before the area became a park. The local ecological problems are now many decades old, and some of these revolve around fire protection.

The mature pine woods or pine islands of this park are in many cases now supporting a heavy young understory of hardwoods and palmettos. According to Robertson's observations, ten to fifty years of fire protection for pine stands is enough to establish a continuous hardwood understory. Despite great odds, and little support or encouragement from the Park Service, Dr. Robertson carried out a great deal of research on the invasion of pine woods by hardwoods, and by 1958 he was able to inaugurate a program of prescribed burning for hardwood-control in the park. This was the first venture by the National Park Service into the use of prescribed burning to manage vegetation.

Robertson has discovered that a single fire merely trims the hardwoods and does not kill them. Immediately after the fire there is a great bloom of native herbaceous flora and temporary prominence of grasses; but after two or three years, the hardwood seedlings recover and the area looks exactly as it did before. He also found that the intensity of the fire is a direct function of how long it has been since the last fire. The hottest fires eliminate much of the prominent vegetation, including the pine forest. He concludes that under natural circumstances there would have been fires at least every two years in this vegetative type in the park. Natural fires of this frequency would have been only ground fires, not crown fires, and would have succeeded in holding back the hardwood succession and encouraging the herbaceous flora understory.

Robertson and Park Service personnel observed about fifty natural, lightning-caused fires between 1951 and 1961 in the glades of the park. Robertson also reports there can be no doubt about the role of natural fires before the white man because of numerous ash layers seen in fossil peats. He concludes that pine savanna is a natural plant community in the Everglades National Park and that its maintenance requires the frequent application of fire. In the interest of restoring at least simulated natural conditions, the Park Service will expand its burning and fire research in this important national park.

While I have given examples of ecological effects of fire prevention in only three plant communities, an amazingly wide number of plant communities and types are known to be stabilized by fire, including Douglas fir, western white pine, sugar pine, lodgepole pine, eastern white pine, paper birch, long leaf pine, loblolly pine, pitch and short leaved pine of New Jersey, ponderosa pine, and *Sequoia gigantea*, as well as most American prairies. By maintaining increasingly effective fire control for the last fifty years we have altered the original environments for these species or types in most of the areas where they occur, with the possible exception of the southeastern pineries where burning is an accepted management tool. There are few wilderness areas that do not involve these species or types.

Management of land, including management of wilderness tracts, is a scientific matter, not just an administrative problem. Research can provide a scientifically based management plan for every unit in the National Wilderness System.

A pertinent comment on the desirability of wilderness management is contained in the report "Management of National Parks and Equivalent Areas" by a committee of the First World Conference on National Parks that met in Seattle in 1962. Fifteen members of this committee represented eight nations. In the estimation of many biologists, this report suggests a firm basis for not only park but wilderness management:

> Few of the world's parks are large enough to be in fact self-regulatory ecological units; rather most are ecological islands subject to direct or indirect modification by activities and conditions in the surrounding areas. These influences may involve such factors as immigration and/or emigration of plant and animal life, changes in the fire regime, and alterations in the surface or subsurface water.

The report goes on to say that there is no need for active modification of climax communities that tend to be relatively stable, and that under protection tend to perpetuate themselves indefinitely, such as large tracts of tundra, tropical rain forest, and tropical plateaus. "However, most biotic communities are in a constant state of change due to natural or man-caused processes of ecological succession. In these successional communities it is necessary to manage the habitat to achieve or stabilize it at a desired stage. For example, fire is an essential management tool to maintain East African open savanna or American prairie."

This international committee, as well as the committee appointed in 1963 by Secretary Udall to study policy in management of national parks, has stressed the fact that management in national parks should be firmly based on the programs suggested by field research that is carried out by qualified personnel. However, the technique of wilderness management is limited by the Wilderness Act, which prohibits permanent constructional modifications to the land; for example, permanent roads would be inappropriate but temporary modifications such as fire breaks may and should be used in order to accomplish the objective.

To determine if the three administering agencies are prepared to undertake the management requirements of the Wilderness Act, let us look at the fiscal status of their biological research. We should keep in mind that each unit in the wilderness system must be treated separately, for each contains its own plant and animal communities and has its own special problems. In fiscal year 1967, the U.S. Forest Service is spending the largest proportion of its budget on biological research—11.3 per cent. The Bureau of Sport Fisheries and Wildlife, which has jurisdiction over all wildlife refuges and game ranges, comes next with 7 per cent. The National Park Service is spending only 0.03 per cent. The Bureau of Sport Fisheries and Wildlife and the Forest Service have in their employ hundreds of well-trained scientists, many of whom do full-time research. The Forest Service maintains several ecological research stations. The Park Service, on the other hand, now has only six scientists for full-time biological research, and although it has contributed land for a research station and helps administer another, it has none of its own.

But personnel, research stations, and proportion of budget allocated to research do not guarantee that an agency is going to get the job done. For example, the Park Service with a small research staff and budget is now well launched on its studies for managing three parks. The Forest Service and the Bureau of Sport Fisheries and Wildlife, with their ample facilities, staff, and budget, are not, so far as I can determine, beyond the thinking stage in meeting the management requirements of the Wilderness Act. Though much of their research would apply, the Forest Service has apparently not yet laid plans for biological management programs in wilderness areas. "Let us not assume that the wagon cannot be stuck because there are so many horses pulling on it!"

The three agencies are not unfamiliar with the use of fire as a management tool. While in the last few decades the Forest Service has done a great deal of research on this, to date it has been carried out chiefly in cutover and slash and has not yet been applied to management of wilderness.

The Fish and Wildlife Service actively manages refuges by the use of fire, but only on those refuges or portions that are outside the wilderness system. According to the Albuquerque office of the bureau, as soon as a unit is incorporated into the wilderness system, active management ceases because they have not yet developed methods for management that would be appropriate under the restrictions of the Wilderness Act. In the valleys, natural fires are permitted to run, but lightning hits in lowland habitats are extremely rare; lightning fires that start in the highlands and that could run into the basins where the refuges are situated are put out by Forest Service or fish-and-wildlife personnel. Lack of fire in lowland marsh habitats serves to diminish the diversity and abundance of the very game species these wilderness refuges are supposed to encourage. It may well be that the reason the Fish and Wildlife Service is reluctant to include managed habitats or habitats of endangered species in the wilderness system is because it feels that active management involving permanent structures is required. But the problem of protecting species is not answered only by keeping the habitat out of the wilderness system; it can also be answered by putting it into the system and developing habitat manipulation techniques that are permitted under the Wilderness Act.

The National Park Service initiated its first burning program in 1958 in Everglades National Park. Two years ago it started a second experimental burning plot in Sequoia National Park. To my knowledge this is the sum total of experimentation with fire in that service. It is now considering plans for habitat control on Isle Royale in Lake Superior where growing populations of moose are running out of natural food browse that is mainly initiated after burning. Let's hope this program gets under way before the moose ruin that wilderness area.

As conservationists, I think we must realize that the old protectionist philosophy is outmoded because it is not broad enough; and if this philosophy continues without modification for the next twenty years, we have everything to lose and little to gain. In this connection, the National Academy of Sciences, at the request of the Secretary of the Interior, appointed a study committee to examine the question of biological research and management of the national parks and their component wilderness areas. In their report published in 1963, this committee said, "Each park should be regarded as a system of interrelated plants, animals, and habitat (an ecosystem) in which evolutionary processes will occur under such human control and guidance as seems necessary to preserve its unique features." In calling attention to the meager support given to ecological research in the parks, they said: "In fact, unless drastic steps are immediately taken there is a good possibility that within this generation several, if not all, the national parks will be degraded to a state totally different from that for which they were preserved and in which they were to be enjoyed."

The academy points to many specific examples in which ecological degradation has occurred in national parks because (1) research was never done at all, (2) research on which management should have been based was not done in time, (3) proper research was done but management did not implement it, (4) proper research was planned but not funded.

In summary, the nation's long-range interests in the welfare of the public wilderness will be best served if well-rounded ecological research programs are carried out by the administering agencies. If they plan and carry out the research themselves, implementation of the results would be at least likely. While Congress must become convinced that such research is needed in order to fund it, the agencies should direct their efforts toward action in meeting the ecological requirements of the Wilderness Act.

Michael Frome

THE QUALITY OF PEOPLE
IN WILDERNESS

Appearing on the program at this late stage has both its advantages and its disadvantages. One of the advantages is that the Secretary of Agriculture and the Director of the National Park Service have departed the scene and I may speak as sharply about them as Anthony Wayne Smith did, and I may very well do so. The Chief of the United States Forest Service is no longer at the head table, but sitting in the audience, relaxed, with his favorite pipe, and unable to rebut. As for disadvantages, the old saying goes in show biz, if you can't top it, don't follow it. Some of the best quotations from Walt Whitman, Mark Twain, and Ralph Waldo Emerson have already been pre-empted. Some of the best speeches on wilderness have been given.

I must say that attending this conference has been an inspiration and an education. I have been impressed not only by the quality of the remarks that have preceded mine, but by the array of scholarship. I have heard from professors who have been to Dartmouth, Yale, Harvard, Berkeley, Oxford, and Cambridge, and, in a few cases, to all of them. This has been most impressive to one like myself who has been to three colleges and is still a lower sophomore.

I listened keenly to Sig Olson yesterday when he talked about hitting that 98 per cent of the population and I want to tell Sig that the 98 per cent are looking for you to hit them. My experience shows that my fellow man is essentially a moral and intellectual creature. He rises above other life forms. But he feels himself as part of a universal design woven of infinite natural features. Therefore, he instinctively comprehends and seeks wilderness as the qualitative essence that he must have for sustenance and survival.

For twenty years I have observed and written about the travel patterns of the American people, where they go, and why, what they do en route and when they arrived at their destinations. For ten years my writing was aimed directly at the great mass called the motoring public. Somewhere along the line I learned the wisdom of placing one's faith in the intellectual capacity of the American people, of never looking down, writing down, thinking down, or planning down to our constituents.

Therefore, I find myself in sharp disagreement with a recent statement I have here from Dr. Stanley Cain, the distinguished Assistant Secretary of the Interior. "Ingenuity and practicality," he said, "are being demonstrated by the federal government in developing compromise and cooperative proposals that allow accomplishments that would otherwise risk failure. The art of the possible is being employed instead of the shibboleths of the impossible. Half a loaf is still better than none."

If we accept this premise, we find ourselves accepting a very attractive parkway in the Great Smoky Mountains wilderness—because it is possible, though unprincipled. If we accept this premise, we find ourselves endorsing the weak-kneed compromise program of the Fish and Wildlife Service, which professes to save endangered species while promoting the use of deadly poisons to destroy some of the finest and the most endangered of all species—the predators. If we accept this premise, we accept Hooker Dam flooding into the Gila Wilderness, the first wilderness of the national forest system, as the price for saving the Grand Canyon. This sort of political "ingenuity and practicality" is simply not based on faith in the competence of the people to understand the issues.

I was distressed to learn from the Chief of the Forest Service that Sylvania, a magnificent new addition to the national forest system in Upper Michigan, may be managed for logging, roads, and mass recreation, rather than for capitalization on the rare opportunities for ecological study and quality recreation. I would much prefer to have them pursue the art of the highest principle than the art of the possible and the easy way.

The American people, in their hunger for quality, hunger also for wilderness. They want all the wilderness they can get. It was in 1923 that Estella Leopold's father talked of wilderness in terms of recreation; he warned of the imminent "wilderness recreation famine." He understood the people's needs and aspirations. The situation has not gotten any better since Aldo Leopold's day; the famine is more critical. Thus, if the secretaries of Agriculture and the Interior, and the chiefs and directors under them, are wholehearted in their commitment to wilderness, they must determine to preserve all the land that qualifies under the wilderness law.

Of all forms of travel and recreational experiences, wilderness represents the highest quality. During the past year I have been to many places all over North America, but those I remember best—and I am sure the same would be true of almost any traveler who had been with me—are not the Hilton hotels, Kon Tikis, Trader Vic's, the topless joints, or the Haight–Ashbury, congested and infested highways, or even congested campgrounds. These are all cut from a mold; only the geographic location is different.

But in the whole world there can be only one Aleutians, a bridge between two continents; only one Mt. McKinley, with its life complex of caribou, wolves, and Dall sheep; only one Everglades, with its complex linked in a chain from the microscopic aquatic life to the huge pink birds, white birds, and alligators; only one range called the High Uintas, epitomizing the natural marvels of the pioneer West, with high broad basins, green meadows, and rocky canyon walls of many colors; and only one range called the Great Smokies, the fertile masterwork of plant life among the coves, valleys, and lonely high ridges of Appalachia. It is probably also true there could be only one Las Vegas, for which moralists would say, "Thank God!" I think all of us here would enjoy Las Vegas as a synthetic spectacle, but hardly anyone would want it remembered as the hallmark of our era. Protecting the natural wilderness is a much better testament of a civilized age.

Looking back on experiences of the past ten years, three qualities of wilderness stand out in my mind.

First, wilderness represents a wonderful document of history and the finest possible education in American culture and art, art of the land and of the people. This I learned on my first real wilderness trip, which I made at the invitation of the Forest Service. We rode for ten days in the Bridger Wilderness of Wyoming, following the trails of Jim Bridger and the fur trappers, of John C. Fremont and his guide, Kit Carson, where Fremont was drawn by shiny ice caps to scale what he believed to be the highest peak in the Rockies. We came upon the very scenes painted by Alfred Jacob Miller in 1837, the wild river places he found "as fresh and beautiful as if just from the hands of the Creator," and the setting of Albert Bierstadt's massive painting, *Rocky Mountains*, which hangs in the Metropolitan Museum in New York. Their work is part of the national cultural heritage. So too is the source of their inspiration: the artistry of earth in carving glacial forms, in painting the dark forest and the contrasting brightness of flowers and waterfalls.

Second, the American wilderness has a truly international quality. While in Europe three years ago, I visited the first national park of France, in the Vanoise Alps. The mission of that park is to secure wilderness and with it the future of a vanishing species of mountain goat. This is a new concept for the French, born of the American idea. The park is a regional plan in itself with four zones. The heart is preserved as wilderness. Around it, the park encompasses whole villages and a really complete system of zoning. People asked me, "Tell us about the unroaded mountains in America. Tell us about the great parks, and animals that roam free." Two years ago in Germany it was the same thing. Those I met were not deeply concerned with the sights of Manhattan, Chicago, and Hollywood. The director of the Frankfurt zoo told me of his proposal to develop six thousand acres of the Taunus Mountains as a wild land zone for the reintroduction of native animal species nearing extinction. This is a considerable tract for a tightly populated country, and his plan has had some opposition. However, he is able to reply, "But America allocates much larger areas for wilderness."

Before the world, wilderness demonstrates that ours is an enlightened, idealist nation not wholly consumed by materialism. It strikes me that our international posture is much better served in such ways than in a wasteful war in Vietnam. In the latter, we are committed to the defoliation of forests and the destruction of people, an incredible means of advocating democratic principles; we are committed to the expenditure of immense resources, in youthful blood and muscle, in soaring portions of the national budget, funds that are now denied to establishment of the promised Great Society. Yes, we must press the cause of liberty throughout the world, but we should do so by example: with demonstrable action in rebuilding our cities, control of pollution of air and water, control of population size and rate of growth, protection of the soils, management of forests, enhancement of wilderness through fulfillment of the wilderness law—all are related to assure a fuller life and enjoyment of democracy's fruit.

Third, the quality of wilderness embodies an affirmation of America's faith in its destiny, and of man's belief in himself. This I learned in the Great Smoky Mountains of North Carolina and Tennessee. When I began to write my book about the Smokies I did not know what kind of book it would be. But as I lived and worked in that area I found that here were 500,000 acres of wild land set aside in the midst of a sea of cities, and that only an enlightened people could take such action to protect this land for themselves and for the future. Consequently, I am one of those devoted to the Smokies' cause and to defense of our magnificent Appalachian wilderness from desecration, which is now imminent as a result of political dealing and inadequate thinking.

I wish that federal officials would exercise themselves to develop a better grasp of the true meaning of the Smoky Mountains and of their own responsibilities in fulfilling the President's directives in the area of natural beauty and conservation.

On one side of the mountains, we have the Tennessee Valley Authority embarked on a ruthless adventure to destroy the beautiful valley of the Little Tennessee River by construction of an unneeded, unwanted dam that would flood an archaeological and anthropological treasure, the ancient capital of the Cherokee Nation.

Across the mountains, in North Carolina, the Bureau of Indian Affairs has been engaged in suppression of the culture of the true children of wilderness, the last surviving vestige of the Cherokee Nation in the eastern mountains.

I must tell you a little more about Appalachia and the problems we face. Now we have a new agency called the Appalachian Regional Commission, which is planning to bestow the blessing of highways and smokestacks upon the free-spirited people of the mountains and thus solve all their problems. Recently this agency released a report on "Recreation as an Industry," prepared by not one but two consulting firms. I am sure they meant well, but they lacked a long-range, balanced focus, and produced a study in superficiality. The governor of Kentucky said he was so appalled when he first read it that he nearly dropped his teeth.

In my book on the Smokies, *Strangers in High Places,* I wrote at length about conditions in the community of Cherokee. I referred to an awful place in this community of North Carolina called Cherokee Frontier Land in these words: "Despite the state publicity that Frontier Land represents 'an authentic re-creation of the old West,' however, the only authenticity is that it stands as a classic form of tourist blight—a tawdry amusement park, abusing and misusing history. It may employ a few Indians, but certainly not as descendants in the line of Junaluska, Sequoyah, and Drowning Bear—while the high profits in serving low fare to the traveling public go out of the hills."

The experts of the Appalachian Commission did not agree. They characterized Frontier Land as "a re-enactment of the 'wild-west' complete with gunfire, forts and an authentic 1860 train." I do not know what in the world the wild West has to do with the cultural history of Appalachia, but we read on: "While many have criticized the 'tourist-trap' appearance of local establishments, the field reports have noted that most of the motel clients during the summer were industrial workers (Midwest and South) with young families, and an income of $6,500 to $7,000." In short, since these travelers are factory hands of modest earning, they are considered by the Appalachian consultants as fit for the plucking, and let it proceed.

The same experts are so anxious to turn a dollar in the hills that they endorse the proposed dilution of the Great Smoky Mountains National Park through construction of a transmountain road, which all those who love the Smokies for what they are, and indeed, conservationists and nature lovers throughout America, oppose. "This wide all-weather road," we learn in the report, would make tourist travel more pleasant, allow more people into the area, and could be a stimulus to each one of the communities it enters as well as the region as a whole. In addition, multilane roads are needed in this area to meet the demands of today's mobile population."

We have every reason to expect a different approach from our friends of the Interior Department, led by Secretary Udall, who has been heard from repeatedly about the conservation ethic. That is, we should expect more from them unless they are playing the game of the art of the possible.

The distinguished Director of the National Park Service, a good friend of mine, has reported here about the wilderness plans of his agency. On other occasions, however, Mr. Hartzog has told us the transmountain road is justified because of a commitment made by the federal government to the North Carolina communities in 1943; that it now represents a moral and legal obligation. I do not agree that this commitment is valid, and furthermore the transmountain road between Bryson City in North Carolina and Townsend, Tennessee, is only one of a sequence of major desecrations projected for the Smokies—which I fear would now be well under way were it not for the strength of the wilderness law and with it the voice of shocked public protest.

The master plan for the Great Smokies is inadequate at best, a design of roads and more roads gutting the wilderness, of six small wilderness pieces covering no more than half the park, and of massive campgrounds of two hundred, three hundred, five hundred, and six hundred units that rob the camper of a true park experience and take up priceless national real estate for sheer bedroom space.

The present park superintendent has been promoting this plan. He does not talk only about "the legal and moral commitment." To quote his statement from the Knoxville *News-Sentinel* of November 2, 1966: "None of us is getting younger. In fact, we're all getting older. So we can't all hike, visit the waterfalls, or camp out. We must open new roads for visitors who are growing older. Many can't hike anymore." This is from a national park superintendent in a time when people of all ages—not to forget future generations—crave and need the stimulation of foot trails, and the guidance to pursue them.

Then we have the effort made by the chief park naturalist. On page 22 of the *Student Conservation Program Newsletter* for Spring–Summer, 1966, a periodical issued for a group of young people who had visited the park the preceding summer, we find a letter from the naturalist. He endeavors to promote the transmountain road on grounds that: "It will not invade the wilderness nor destroy any because the proposed route will be through lands that were clear-cut by railroad logging about twenty-five years ago. About two-thirds of this land was farmed and logged-over before the park was established and with the protection it now receives, eventually it will be a delightful playground for the American people."

Let us go on with this statement to the young conservationist from the chief park naturalist of the Smokies:

> Since the National Park Service is a people-serving agency, we must consider all aspects of preservation and visitor use. If the people did not visit the parks and use them, the Service would not be here. We must carefully weigh each decision between use and preservation before it is made.
>
> A cross-mountain route such as proposed is needed to divert the heavy traffic we now experience. Nearly six million people visited the park in 1965 and if some of these visitors could be diverted to other areas of the park this congestion could be relieved for several years if not forever. Secondly, the proposed route would provide several loop trips, using existing state roads of considerable distance, which we believe visitors would take. Visitors would then be in their cars several hours longer driving and as long as they are in cars, no damage to the natural features can be done.

As I mentioned earlier, one is wise when he learns never to look down or to think down to his constituents, especially not to the young. As if in response to this pseudonaturalist, a lad named Andy Maloney, who was sponsored on the Student Conservation Program by the Westmoreland Sanctuary of New York, wrote this brief report:

> While I was in the Smokies and even now a great battle is being fought to save the park from a second trans-mountain highway. The National Park Service and business people favor it. Groups such as the Wilderness Society, Appalachian Trail Conference, Sierra Club, and other conservation groups are fighting to preserve the area as a wilderness. From what I have seen, I certainly hope the latter are successful and that I myself have helped in a small way during this summer as a part of the Student Conservation Program.

The Student Conservation Program is a cooperative venture of the Garden Clubs and the National Park Service, ironically enough.

I would like to add some words of my own to those of Andy Maloney. The last chapter of my book on the Smokies, entitled "The Sanctuary," includes the following paragraphs:

> The primeval portions [of the Smokies] have endured as a sanctuary of nature, a composition of endless themes and variations in the life cycle, a grand theater of universality. In these forests, death needs no apology, but has a beauty of its own in advancing through history as the nourishing helpmate of birth in the folds of earth.
>
> . . .
>
> The genius of the Smokies, however, is inherent not only in the untouched primeval portions. This sanctuary of nature is also a place of restoration, or "comeback." Those areas once disturbed, or even destroyed by man have rejoined their own.
>
> When a mountaineer's cabin was abandoned, the paper wasps arrived; then came the phoebe birds, the white-footed mice, the wood rats, the insects and spiders. The wood rotted, the roof fell down, the floor caved in. Each stage of life prepared the way for the next in the tedious cycle of successive growths. . . . Given seventy-five years, a first-class forest, teeming with life, will have claimed its place where the cabin was abandoned.
>
> . . .
>
> The immediate issue is whether to go ahead with construction of a proposed road. . . . In a broader sense, we shall write the record of our age in the pages of history; we shall demonstrate the degree of our respect for the ancientness of these mountains, and for the right of generations hence to see them in their natural state. . . . It is our chance to prove worthy of a heritage and to establish a mark for the future.*

I feel stunned from time to time, in the Smokies and throughout the country, by the attitude of some of the public officials toward people in wilderness. Some of the leading federal foresters have said, "It is disproportionate to have 8 per cent of National Forest land visited by only 2 or 3 per cent of those who come for recreation. This is a minority use." But every motorist driving the Beartooth Highway in Montana is a wilderness user and appreciator. When he reaches Beartooth Pass he sees sweeping vistas encompassing an area as large as all the New England states combined; the wilderness of purple canyons and snowy peaks is the great unscarred, unroaded scenic backdrop of his experi-

* The proposed transmountain road through Great Smoky Mountains National Park was disapproved by Secretary of the Interior Udall in early 1968.—*The Editors.*

ence. And every motorist on the Blue Ridge Parkway in North Carolina uses the wilderness of the Great Smokies; when he comes to the open crest of Waterrock Knob, straight ahead rise the Smokies, a mountain wall seventy miles wide, the greatest height and mass in eastern America.

Friends in the Park Service have said to me, "We can't encourage *everybody* to hike on wilderness trails. They would hurt the wilderness. Therefore, we have to keep them in the visitor centers and build more roads."

I do not agree with this line of thinking. I object to the continued reduction by the Park Service in the number of guided overnight walking trips and to the reduction of day-long trips from seven hours to four or two hours. There should be more, and better, guided walks and hikes. There should be no apology for wilderness, no reluctance to introduce people to it. For wilderness adventure breeds enthusiasm, idealism, love of life, and the wilderness adventurer champions enlightened use and appreciation of quality.

I recognize that there would be no wilderness in the Smokies at all had it not been for the continuing efforts of National Park Service people from the early twenties to this day; there would be little quality to enjoy in the Everglades, the high Uintas, or the Bridger Wilderness without the concern and devotion of exceptional people in both the Park Service and Forest Service. In the Bridger, horses already are restricted from some drainages because of erosion from overuse and a corps of wilderness patrol rangers is responsible for encouraging back country travelers to respect their surroundings. Such measures, by protecting the land, serve to expand, rather than to restrict, recreation in the back country.

Perhaps what is needed is a basic guide to the theory and practice of wilderness use, published by the agencies, with cooperation of public groups—or vice versa. It should spell out the need for planning and rerouting of foot and horse trails so that they are located on gradients that minimize erosion hazards, and for maintaining them under primitive standards compatible with the setting. It should set a standard for outfitters, to leave their power saws at home and to pack in feed where pasturage is scant. It should set a pattern for more spot-packing, with the outfitter carrying groups to a single base camp, from which they travel by foot, and for parties of smaller size than on some trips. The emphasis should be on back country skills, particularly foot travel, the most elemental and least damaging kind of back country mobility. In fragile parts of the Sierras, the horse will have to go. It should set forth the precise methods of packing out all debris that campers cannot dispose of by burning, and underscore the opportunity visitors have to direct the destiny of wilderness by taking care of it and adhering to simple rules that make complicated rules less necessary.

I think it was heartening to hear the Director of the National Park Service announce yesterday that he was going to call a meeting to discuss precisely this sort of thing. There should be more discussion, more cooperation. We should support the Park Service in coping with its problem of inholdings. I think there should be more "show-me" trips both by the Park Service and the Forest Service for conservation groups—not after the wilderness plans are all made up, but when the plans are first being devised.

The discussion here today on deserts demonstrated that our administrators do not know all there is to know about the land in their charge. If I were an administrator, I would want to tap the rich storehouse of scholarship and knowledge in this hall.

There is repeated conversation about rationing wilderness use in order to protect the environment. That time may come. Certainly there is need for some form of check-in and check-out, or comparable traffic control system, at extremely popular areas like the Boundary Waters of Minnesota and the John Muir Wilderness in California. But I feel that more important than figuring how to keep people out is how to get more people into wilderness so they may share the exultation that we have known and the sense of devotion that has brought us here in a common cause.

The decisive factor is the carrying capacity of the land. Land managers apply this expression "carrying capacity of the land" in dealing with livestock grazing. Precisely the same principle applies in terms of human recreational activities. We need clear definitions of appropriate uses and optimum, not maximum, numbers, based on leaving the land unimpaired for future generations to enjoy. When people understand the needs, they will accept the discipline of limited use.

The quality of wilderness and the quality of people are indivisible. One nurtures the other. Thus, I think of myself not as one of the chosen few who enjoys wilderness, but as one of the multitude of users who need and endorse it for the quality of our lives.

FROM THE SATURDAY AFTERNOON DISCUSSION

R. H. Hultman: Any time I am asked to talk on wilderness, it kind of reminds me of a story. Up in Montana we still have circuit-riding ministers, especially in small towns up north. In the wintertime they have a pretty tough proposition. Sometimes they don't get too many customers. This fellow one time rode into a little town and he got the saloon opened up and all ready for church services that morning. He waited around and it was blizzarding outside pretty badly. One old rancher came in, shucked off his coat, wiped all the frost off and sat down. Finally the reverend said, "Well, seeing there is just one of you this morning, I think we had probably better dispense with the services."

The old rancher looked at him. "Reverend," he said, "when I load my hay rack with hay and I go out to feed my cows, if I run into just one cow I feed her."

So the reverend took the hint. He started out with a couple of hymns, a great big long prayer, a long sermon, more hymns, another prayer, and closed it with a benediction. He ran out to say goodby to the rancher. The rancher got back into his coat, shook hands with the reverend and he said, "Reverend, one thing I forgot to tell you. If I run into just one cow, I don't give her the whole durned load."

I can't give you the whole load on wilderness, or quality of wilderness in ten minutes, or in ten hours, or ten days. This is something that is so important and so dear to me that it would take me weeks to discuss it with you. One thing that surprised me on my speaking tour through the East was that all the service clubs and outdoor organizations I talked with had little knowledge about wilderness and wilderness areas. One of our biggest problems if we are ever to have and to hold quality wilderness is education.

208

I'll bet 90 per cent of the people had no idea what I was talking about. They think they reach wilderness when they drive out in the forest some place, get out of their car and walk a little way until the car is out of sight. They look down and see a deer track, or an elk track, and they think they are in wilderness. Or they are driving down a highway and look up at a beautiful mountain that is full of timber and they think that is primeval wilderness. They think that is *it*. They do not realize that we have reserved in Montana and Idaho, and other areas in the West, such places as the Bob Marshall Wilderness Area and the Bitterroot–Selway Wilderness Area that contain several millions of acres.

One gentleman in an engineer's club in Baltimore, after I was through talking, said, "Mr. Hultman, I would like to use that area. It sounds great. Tell me, how are the motel accommodations in there?"

They cannot understand that we are trying to leave a heritage for them. And unless we can get out and tell these people that this is theirs, they must use it before they lose it, and how it gets protection, we are going to lose the wilderness because we will not have the support of the people we need.

Another thing that is not realized is the Forest Service's special program of multiple use. The multiple use program is a good program— the most use to the most people in these various areas. Many people back there who know anything at all about wilderness have no confidence in conservationists. They have heard that we are nothing but land-grabbers who want to take and lock up all these lands, who want to put them under lock and key so that only the millionaires can enjoy them. This is their thinking. They think that we want to stop all natural resource development, we want to lock out the loggers, the mining industry, and all other commercial development. When it is explained to them that we have less than 4 per cent of the commercial timber in our wilderness and primitive system; that we have less than 8 per cent of the Forest Service lands in our primitive and wilderness system, it is a little bit different. When it is explained that under multiple use management the Forest Service surveys these wilderness areas and holds classification hearings, and that all kinds of people from hunters to bird watchers and miners and the timber industry have a say, it is also a little bit different.

This is the educational program that we need, that we must give to the people. I think the agencies should advertise their management purposes more in order that the general public may realize what is going on.

As a user of the Bob Marshall Wilderness Area, probably the major outfitter in that area, I want to say one thing that I think we should do to help in wilderness preservation. I am sure that what I mention to you folks today on the Bob Marshall is just as true in other wilderness areas. Now there are certain areas in these wildernesses that should be only for hikers. I am thinking particularly of one very nice place in the Bob Marshall and it is a very common and very popular place, the Big Salmon Lake area. You can go down to the Big Salmon Lake in a two-day hike, or one day with a horse train, but for a hiker it is a nice two-day trip. There is a beautiful little campground, but it is small. There is a small meadow at the head of the lake, about three acres. I could go in there with a party of six or seven, stay there overnight or maybe two days and all the grass from the meadow for the entire year will be eaten by my stock. There would be nothing to do but to tie up the stock in these campgrounds, yet this too would overuse these areas.

Instead, why don't the agencies take areas such as this and say, "Now look, you horse people, stay out of there." Not only the commercial outfitter, but also the individual horserider and ranchers who go in with a bunch of horses. Save this for the hiker, or save this for the hiker who has got one packhorse. If he comes in there he can use that campground all year and have plenty of grass in the meadow for one packhorse. There would be no reason at all for him to have to tie up around camp and overuse the camp.

Another thing about how to maintain high-quality wilderness: I believe that our wilderness areas are getting overdeveloped. A wilderness area is supposed to be a wilderness. I think the agencies governing these are going a little overboard. For instance, there are a couple places where they are building horse corrals. There is a reason for building corrals. You build a corral so you don't tie your horses to trees and kill the trees. That is fine. But these corrals do not have to be beside the trail. When you are riding down the trail you see these peeled pole things that look like a backyard of a ranch someplace. These should be placed out of the way, off the trails. They do not have to be accessible to run your stock into because if you are going to tie up your stock every night you have to catch them anyway. You might as well catch them and lead them into a corral as catch them to tie them up to a tree.

And the same goes for these outdoor privies. These might be all right in the middle of campgrounds, but I think these things should be hidden away in a wilderness. I think a wilderness should be what we want it to be, a wilderness. As Mike Frome says, let's get rid of all these chain saws and everything that is mechanical. The wilderness bill says we are to do that. If we want wilderness, let's have wilderness.

I think there are too many signs, although after twenty-five years of wilderness travel, I am still awful tickled to see a sign once in a while; don't get me wrong. But on the other hand, I think this practice is overdone. In some of these areas that have these big signs, where-you-are deals, they keep putting on all kinds of stuff for the next eight or ten miles to show you exactly where you are.

There is another program, that was started about six years ago; it seems the Forest Service has stopped it now. At least, it is static at present, and I would like to see them go ahead with it. This is the program of placing recreation guards in wilderness areas. I don't know how many of you folks have heard about it. We have one in the Bob Marshall, and they have been telling us for years we are going to have six. I think six will be fine. You ride down to where this guard is, to an area called Salmon Fork, and he can tell you where other camps are in the area. He knows, he should know—it's his job—where all the other camps are within a radius of ten or twelve miles. He can tell you where there is horse feed. He can tell you where there is a good place to go fishing. He knows the size of your outfit, he knows exactly what you need. This will give the folks more of a wilderness experience because they won't be running into so many people. They won't be going around looking for a camp spot because they will know where to go. This is a program that can level off the overgrazing and the overuse in certain camp areas. I would like to see the Forest Service continue this and push it a little bit farther. I think this is very important.

Another matter is the trail system in wildernesses. A few years back the Forest Service's practice was to keep trails to an 8 to 10 per cent grade. As a matter of fact, they redid some of the main trails to conform to this easier grade. Now I will agree that it does make for easier maintenance, and probably not so much maintenance, but that is all I will agree to. They will tell the hiking people they have to do this for the horseman. They will tell the horse people, "Oh, no, we have to do this for the hiker."

The Sierra Club has assured me that 12 to 15 per cent grade is swell for hikers; it is easy for horses, though 18 per cent would be their limit. The thing is, I am not rough with my stock and I do not want to be. But for an example, there is a trail that is going to be eight miles when it gets to the top—let's say the old trail up to the top of Gordon Pass at Holland Lake. They have a new trail built for two miles of this and the rest is all surveyed, and so far, for these two miles, there is a difference of seventeen minutes. Now to take that up to the top, there is going to be a difference of sixty-eight minutes. That is over an hour, and it is over three miles. When one goes down the other side it will be the same way. We have ordinarily a fifteen-mile trip into our camp the first night. The new trail makes it twenty-one miles. Dinner would be later. Guests would be more tired, and the stock would be tired. We don't need this.

There is another point about building easy trails. We have the wilderness bill, and it says no motorized equipment. I hate to say this because a forest ranger told it to me—he said, "Man put the wilderness bill in and man can knock it out." More people want to get into the back country with motor scooters and jeeps on good trails that they can use without danger. If all this money is going to be spent to build these trails, we are going to have the scooter people right down our necks because they outnumber the horsemen, believe me. And they are going to be in there and if they have fancy trails, we are not going to be able to keep them out.

So, if we are going to be wilderness users, let's make it a little bit tougher. After all, we are going into some place that is a little bit better than any place else in the world. So if we do not have a little more heart and a little more desire, we do not deserve to use it. If we want a wilderness experience, we are not like the fellow who drives up to a campground and is tickled to death if he can find a picnic table. That is the one thing we do not want to find—just to get twenty feet away from somebody else.

I would like to comment a little on Dr. Leopold's controlled burning. I think it is very important. One phase of this that she missed is that without controlled burning we will not have any winter range for our wildlife. When you have a big stand of heavy timber that has come up and nothing has been done with it, you cannot get a fire into the area, and there is no brush or browse. It is gone because it is all shaded out by the trees. We have to have burning. We have to let the brush and the browse come back up. The Forest Service people, I believe, are beginning to realize this, and so are many others. There is only one thing that is wrong: they have done too good a job in fire protection. As Dr. Leopold says about Smokey the Bear, they have oversold him. They light a match and somebody blows it out because Smokey says no. You can overdo a good thing. We do have to have controlled burning.

I will say again, we need better understanding of wilderness, and the local outfitters have a job to do too. On my trip back East there was a fellow in the audience I had met while hunting in the Bob Marshall Wilderness. I missed the boat with him because when I got through talking he said, "Buff, I didn't know all this about that wilderness area." And I had lived ten days with him on that Western trip! But we all have to tell people what wilderness is. We have to tell them that we need it. This is a heritage that we are saving. This is the only chance we have of leaving a place where our children and our grandchildren are going to see a deer, an elk, or an animal in its natural state. This is the only place, believe me ladies and gentlemen, where you are going to catch a fish that the good Lord planted and that was not raised on horsemeat. So let's spread the good word, and thank you.

John A. Zivnuska: Whenever we speak about quality, whether of wilderness or of anything else, we are implicitly invoking some normative scale and the question of a relationship to man. The quality of wilderness is essentially a matter of man's perception of the wilderness. Since each of us approaches wilderness with his own highly personal pattern of knowledge, of ignorance, of sensibilities, and of value scales, each of us will perceive the quality of a wilderness in his own special way.

Few, if any, will perceive the quality of wilderness in terms of the change in the chemical composition of the atmosphere that has surely occurred in every wilderness area in the United States in the last fifty years. Perhaps only a few more will note the presence of a non-native species of grass blended into the cover of a mountain meadow. Our sense of the quality of wilderness is not affected by this exotic plant because few of us are actively aware of the species of grass and sedges in the meadow. In view of the widespread introduction of exotic grasses that has in fact occurred in wilderness areas, we are perhaps fortunate in our ignorance in this case.

More of us will notice the presence of a non-native species of tree. And almost all wilderness users will have a strong sense of clash and quality reduction when confronted with a road or structure made by man. Yet, oddly enough, for many of us the winding trail leading peacefully into the wilderness is not a conflict with wilderness but an invitation to wilderness. The trail is perceived as a symbol of man's relationship to wilderness. Thus it introduces the human element, which gives wilderness a meaning to us. Certain forms of the introduction of the human element and human impact in wilderness can actually enhance our sense of the quality of wilderness.

Each of us sees wilderness differently because each of us perceives it through his own pattern of knowledge and ignorance. My sense of the quality of wilderness differs from the perceptions of each of you, just as each of you perceives quality differently from all the others at this meeting. However, as a forester, I face a special problem and responsibility in looking at the quality of wilderness. I am a member of the profession that has the primary administrative responsibility for the wilderness areas of the nation—the profession that also has the responsibility for administration and management of the other wild lands of the nation for the full range of social purposes. Thus, in looking at wilderness quality, I must seek an interpretation that is not simply my own unique interpretation. Instead, I must seek a standard that can provide a meaningful guide for the administration and management of such areas.

Certainly one such standard of wilderness quality is provided by the National Park Service report to which Dr. Estella Leopold referred (a report commonly known as the Leopold Report, in recognition of the service of her brother, Starker Leopold, as chairman of the study committee). This is a standard based on conditions as they existed when first seen by European man.

I would like to suggest another approach to such a standard. From the standpoint of wilderness administration, I would argue that the quality of wilderness is enhanced by any change that reduces the appearance of human impact on the wilderness landscape. The operative concept in this definition or goal is the reduction of the appearance of human impact, not the reduction of the human impact itself. Human impact on wilderness is inevitable and sure to increase, both because of increasing peripheral change and because of increasing direct human use by an expanding population that is increasingly aware of the special values offered by wilderness experience. In addition, of course, we have impacts on wilderness through policies established for one set of purposes, such as fire control, which have effects of other kinds as well. Thus we face the problem of reacting to accidental human impact with intentional human impact. We must try to counteract what we do to the wilderness unintentionally by making use of human intelligence. This is wilderness management—using our knowledge, using our abilities, to reduce the appearance of human activity on the wilderness landscape.

From this viewpoint of wilderness management, it is somewhat encouraging to sense the growing acceptance of the prescribed use of fire as an approach to maintaining wilderness ecosystems at some particularly desired developmental stage. The encouraging aspect of this support for prescribed burning is that this is an approach that involves a positive response to the obvious fact that wilderness quality cannot be maintained by doing nothing intentionally while doing a great many things accidentally.

My sense of encouragement is limited, however, by the common tendency to link this recognition of the role of prescribed burning with the reaction that this is the only manipulative technique that should be introduced. There seems to be some sense that, since accidental fires occurred naturally before man was present, fire is a natural force even when deliberately introduced by man with the hope of burning under controlled conditions, whereas other management inputs are "unnatural."

I think we need to free our thinking from this kind of orientation to a single management technique, based on some nebulous concept that it is "natural." We are dealing in each instance with a particular ecosystem; we want to produce certain changes in the development of that ecosystem, or at least to reduce or counteract some other changes we have introduced unintentionally, and our approach should be to use the best techniques or tools available for that particular situation. Fire must be recognized as perhaps the most ecologically complex of the management tools with which we have to work. In addition, it is a tool that we can control less fully than a great many other management techniques.

If we are to manage wild lands successfully, we must base our approach on working with ecological processes, not on working with particular tools. For example, in many situations the need is to expose mineral soil at a particular time to favor one group of plant species over other groups of plant species. This may involve the prescribed use of fire in a mountain meadow to favor the maintenance of the grasses against a tendency for invasion by brush or tree species. Alternatively, it may involve the clear-cutting of a stand of coastal redwood to establish conditions of exposed mineral soil favorable to the re-establishment of desired species of trees. Because of the very different social purposes to be served and the differences in scale of visual impact, the same people who are learning to accept the first practice and who view it as natural may continue to reject the second as unnatural. This reflects a failure to understand that in both cases man has deliberately acted to develop a set of environmental conditions favoring a particular kind of regeneration that is wanted for some social purpose.

In the case of the *Sequoia gigantea*—big tree or Sierra redwood— some groups interested in parks may just be learning that fire can have an important role in favoring the redwood over the associated species. Foresters have known for at least thirty years that we can suppress the white fir and encourage and foster the Sierra redwood by the prescribed use of fire. We have also known and demonstrated that we can do this equally well or better through heavy logging of the associated species. Both practices, I think, involve substantial aesthetic conflicts with park purposes and the danger of undesirable related effects. I would hope that we can develop additional techniques without these conflicts that would enable us to control white fir and favor the Sierra redwood through an understanding of the ecological requirements involved and the use of whatever tool is best for meeting these requirements. We must free ourselves of the pseudonaturalism that there is something inherently and even morally different about using a match than using a knife or an ax or a saw. If man introduces the agent, then any agent is unnatural to the extent that man is unnatural.

To turn to another aspect of wilderness management, I think we must be realistic about the alternatives actually available to us. When we are confronted with an overgrazed mountain meadow, with channel cutting in the stream and a dropping water table, plus a related invasion by lodgepole pine and other species, we have the choice of letting this deterioration continue or of doing something about it with small check dams and other man-made channel improvements, along with possibly some direct control of the invading species. We do not have the choice of the unmodified meadow of 1850, but we can begin to move toward something approximating this through management practices.

As a third point, I would like to stress that our practices must be responsive to the nature and traditions of the wilderness areas with which we deal. Thus the pack string of horses and mules may be judged wholly alien to the natural quality of some Sierra wilderness areas, while at the same time a competently handled pack string may enhance our sense of wilderness quality in some of the Idaho or Montana wilderness country.

Fourth, we must respond to the fact that remoteness and difficulty of access serve to enhance wilderness quality. Trail improvement is urgently needed in many areas to reduce the accelerating damage to the wilderness, but improvements to reduce damage to the environment should never be confused with the kind of trail engineering that simply increases the problems of policing against mechanized access and nonconforming use. This point has been made much more eloquently by Mr. Hultman.

There is another perhaps minor point about which I feel strongly, which may serve only to illustrate the half-serious contention that wilderness quality is the way things were when we were youngsters. To me, the small white and green enamel signs that I encountered in the Sierra wilderness areas in the 1930's conflicted far less with the quality of wilderness than do the large routed wood signs now used by the administrative agencies under the fetish of natural materials. Sometimes a small enamel sign can be more natural, I think, than a large wooden sign, particularly when the species of wood involved is commonly one I recognize as not being indigenous to the wilderness area.

In closing, I would simply like to stress that the Wilderness Act and the vigorous efforts to classify areas under it have assured us of the continuing existence of a substantial area of classified wilderness. Legal classification, however, cannot insure the quality of wilderness. The maintenance of wilderness quality in the face of mounting human impact is one of the many fascinating challenges to our ability to apply intelligence and sensitivity to the management of our wild land areas. It is just such challenges that make forestry a particularly satisfying profession.

Moderator Raymond J. Sherwin: * Dr. Zivnuska's and Buff Hultman's comments about trails remind me of something that struck my sense of humor. Once I was tramping through the area between the Devil's Post Pile and the north fork of the San Joaquin River on a very conspicuous and fairly well rutted trail and there were wood signs after wood signs along the trail whose only legend was "Trail."

We do have time for a few questions and the first is a double-barrelled one addressed to Dr. Leopold: How can you speak of returning to primeval conditions an entity such as a forest that is not static? How do you reconcile management by burning practices with the problem of air pollution?

Estella B. Leopold: On the first question on rolling back plant succession, I would like to point out that in individual natural fires this is exactly what does occur. For example, in the pine stands of the Gila Wilderness, the aggressive thick brush can be cleared out by use of fire. In the Everglades, the hardwood species normally replace pine stands unless the hardwoods and brush are controlled by natural fires. So what I have been advocating is to allow natural fires to run without control in certain situations, or set them by prescribed burning— preferably the latter; it is safer. Yes, in the particular kind of fire climax of which we were speaking, roll back succession initially, and then keep rolling it back with fires where feasible every two or three years.

On the second question, concerning air pollution, we should consider the recent wildfire damage. In the southwestern semiarid country, about 80,000 acres of timber were burned in four different fires between 1951 and 1956. That is considerable acreage and timber burned, as well as a lot of smoke. Let's compare that with little ground fires occurring here and there in that area under natural conditions under the program I have suggested. This includes controlled burning techniques where only the understory and ground vegetation is burned. I do not believe air pollution resulting from controlled burning in most forest areas of the West would be a serious problem.

* The Wilderness Conference Committee wishes to express its appreciation to Judge Sherwin for serving as moderator of this session in the absence of David Brower, who was suddenly taken ill.

Moderator Sherwin: The next question is addressed to Mr. Frome, and it reads: How can the Forest Service and the National Park Service assume leadership in wilderness preservation to overcome some of their present foot-dragging attitudes as confronted in the Great Smokies Park, the Selway-Magruder corridor wilderness declassification, and the traditional "too much wilderness" arguments?

Michael Frome: I think that the Director of the Park Service gave part of the answer to that: he invites our comments, our criticisms, and public participation. It requires—as Senator Moss put it—"resourceful and articulate leadership," and rational leadership by the citizen groups, the Sierra Club, the Wilderness Society, and other groups, plus a recognition of the place of public participation by the agencies.

Last summer I had great pleasure in participating in a trip in the High Uintas of Utah at the invitation of the Forest Service, together with Stewart Brandborg and Cliff Merritt of the Wilderness Society. We spent a week exploring the high country; we examined the boundaries, discussed the plans; we listened to them and they listened to us. It was an extremely healthy exchange and a true recognition by both sides, the citizen groups and the agencies, of each other's place in the fulfillment of wilderness plans. The agencies must have more of that sense of commitment on the ground that they express in words before us in a pleasant hotel room in California.

If I could make one more point, there is much courtesy in the room here. Afterwards some public official will say, "Well, the Sierra Club really is a minority group," or one of us will treat with his kind as "Those damn agency people." I think we ought to recognize that most of the agency people—I am sorry Ed Cliff left the room; I was going to say a kind word about him—are great guys. Through the years they have given me cooperation and inspiration to be a better conservationist and lover of wilderness. They are men who need help and support, and when they are smart, they ask for it.

I think they should welcome the activity of people who care. The Fish and Wildlife Service, in the Great Swamp, wanted to have a small hearing on wilderness. The superintendent and naturalist of the Great Smoky Mountains National Park did not want to have people who were interested in the park coming to the hearings, and they deprecated those who did come. There has to be a great confidence and trust. We have to start with the feeling that the other fellow wants to do the right thing. I would rather not use the term "foot-dragging" but instead would ask how we can help each other exercise proper leadership. The answer, in connection with the wilderness hearings or any problem, should be consultation and cooperation from the outset—and continuing thereafter.

Moderator Sherwin: Now we have a question for Dr. Burke. How would you propose to influence industry to accept responsibilities in the area of environmental problems? The attitude of "not rocking the boat" has been so ingrained in people from top to bottom in order to preserve their organizational lives that they carry this attitude along with them wherever the corporation interferes with the outside world. How do we get around this?

Albert E. Burke: I do not mean to be facetious when I say this, but one of the answers to dealing with this problem is anti–Dale Carnegie-ism. If it is necessary to be obnoxious while influencing people, then, by all means, be obnoxious. If standing for principle means you are not going to make friends, then it is for you to decide which is more impor-tant. I do not know any way to deal with a man who has great power and influence other than to hit him as hard as you can. But, in the same sense, do not emulate a corporate employee who insists on harmony in his dealings. The only way you can get anywhere is by making it clear you do have principles to stand for.

There is something else. When I said during my talk that it is impor-tant to go back to your roots to be refreshed periodically, I had in mind what is expected of a man with great power in our society. There is a great difference between a Roger Blough, or a Krupp, or an Ivanovich, at least in terms of what the founders intended. There is no difference between a Blough, a Krupp, or an Ivanovich in the privileges they have enjoyed, their power, or the knowledge they use to do their job. But there is in the basic papers of the land a clear understanding that other great men with great power decided they would sacrifice every-thing—their lives, fortune, and sacred honor—to, among other things, promote the general welfare. It is expected that a man with power in this society will exercise it responsibly, and if they forget it, for heaven's sake, don't you forget it.

Moderator Sherwin: This next question is addressed to Dr. Ziv-nuska and reads: Are you suggesting that since fire is acceptable, to expose mineral soil by clear-cutting in the redwoods is the same thing?

John A. Zivnuska: My point is that both practices do represent the same management philosophy, and that there are some strong parallels in the ecological processes involved. I will confess to having selected examples that might strike some of you as extreme in an effort to stress this point.

In an ecological sense, many of the types associated with our wilderness areas are subclimax types. Such a subclimax may be a fire subclimax, a land-clearing subclimax, a logging subclimax, and so on. In all of these cases some external force has been introduced into the ecosystem, disrupting the normal successional pattern toward a climax that represents a state of equilibrium between the biota and the climate. If we wish to maintain subclimax vegetation, we must periodically interrupt the successional sequence by some means.

For example, many people have now become concerned because of the normal successional development of a dense white fir understory in our Sierra redwood stands. Prescribed burning has been proposed as a means of interrupting this development and favoring the Sierra redwood. I am confident that these same people would be unhappy if tanoak and Douglas fir took over our groves of coastal redwood that occur on alluvial flats. In the coastal redwood, this successional development has been periodically interrupted by fire and by normal flooding and siltation. With intensive fire control and successful flood control through dams, some deliberate action by man will be required to prevent the heavy invasion of these cathedral groves of redwood by a dense understory of other species.

In both these instances of management for wilderness or park purposes, exposure of fresh mineral soil appears to be one of the elements involved. If the social purpose in land management is to grow new crops of redwood timber so that the people of California can continue to live in redwood homes and enjoy all the other uses of wood that make us the highest per capita consumers of forest products in the world, then in some circumstances the exposure of fresh mineral soil may also be necessary. Clear-cutting is one means of achieving this.

Broadly, my point is that so long as we are faced with increasing population and an essentially fixed land area, man must try to use his intelligence to get from the land what he wants, whether this is wilderness quality or timber crops. To do this, he must take actions to foster ecological conditions appropriate to the particular environment and the particular human purpose. We must concentrate on this, and not on the question as to whether the tool used is prescribed burning, logging, or the harrow.

Robert Rienow

POLITICAL THICKETS
SURROUNDING WILDERNESS:
A SUMMARY OF THE CONFERENCE

It would be presumptuous for me to confirm, select, or contend with the observations of your eminent experts whom you have heard over the last few days. I can, however, identify the kernel of thought that has permeated these deliberations. So pronounced are my reactions that I am not satisfied with terming them a summary, but have given them a new title.

Every seven and one-half seconds a new American is born. He is a disarming little thing, but he begins to scream loudly in a voice that will be heard for seventy years. He is screaming for 26 million tons of water, 21,000 gallons of gasoline, 10,150 pounds of meat, 28,000 pounds of milk and cream, 9,000 pounds of wheat, and great storehouses of all other foods, drinks, and tobaccos. These are his lifetime demands from his country and its economy.

He is requisitioning a private endowment of $5,000 to $8,000 for school building materials, $6,300 worth of clothing, $7,000 worth of furniture, and 210 pounds of peanuts to pass through his hot, grasping little hand. He is yelping for a Paul Bunyan chunk, in his own right, of the nation's pulpwood, paper, steel, zinc, magnesium, aluminum, and tin.

He is heralded as a prodigious consumer in a nation that accounts for one-fifteenth of the earth's people but consumes half of its total product. In one year we use up enough big trees to build a ten-foot boardwalk thirty times around the world at the equator, says Mr. Weyerhaeuser with pride.

Up to the time he has requisitioned his last foot of lumber for his coffin and his three-by-six plot of land (probably arable), he will have been internationally respected for the voraciousness and extensiveness of his appetite, for the zestful way he fulfills his consumptive role in an opulent society. An awe-inspiring amount of the soil's resources (for all things come from the soil) will have passed through him like earth through an earthworm and will have ended in the watercourses and in the evermounting junkpiles of the nation.

Most important of all, this new American is a consumer of land. He is a consumer of wilderness. He is a destroyer. This is the stage setting for *Moment in the Sun*, a new book I wrote with my wife Leona. It must be the stage setting for any realistic appraisal of wilderness.

With every one of these demands of our growing and expectant population our wild heritage is beaten back. It is further stripped, grazed, gouged, decimated, and diminished. There is an underlying terror at this conference—the heart-rending realization that we are faced with a dwindling resource of wilderness. We must come to grips with the fact that this is a new era, an era in which we can no longer revel in abundance, an era, in fact, in which there is no longer an abundance of wild anything.

The pressures of consumption are relentless. The issue is now joined. It is wilderness *vs.* meat, estuaries *vs.* development, canyons *vs.* waterpower. These are not drawing room decisions, teacup determinations. They are of necessity the gladiatorial contests of the political arena. And they, like the ancient gladiatorial contests, are to the death—they are for keeps.

There is much gloating in conservation circles over the new and marked awareness, the growing political acceptability, of the conservationist's viewpoint. Some have even dubbed this new phenomenon a "conservation conscience." I submit that this so-called conservation conscience is an illusion.

My wife and I were walking down Broadway last summer when we saw in the next block a neon sign that read "HOT MARTINI."

"What in the world is a hot martini?" she asked.

I am always ready to find out about such things, so I said, "Let's drop in and see."

We kept on walking nearer. When we were within a short distance of the place, we saw that some of the neon letters had blacked out. The sign actually read "HOTEL MARTINIQUE." We were victims of an illusion.

Unfortunately, we are not witnessing a great reformation of the American soul. A foreigner once commented: "You Americans are strange people. You devote one day of the year to your mothers and an entire week to pickles." Likewise the dominant American gives lip service to wilderness preservation and a whole summer to golf.

We are merely living through a crisis of wilderness menaces so imminent and acute as to thrust itself irresistibly into the maelstrom of politics. The odds, indeed, are not with us; they are against us. True, the conservation movement now has allies in high places, but the political opposition is also savagely intensified. With only scattered remnants of our wild heritage left, the miners slaver to prospect, the lumbermen press to apply their chain-saw husbandry, the graziers with a hungry market clamor at the boundaries with an avidity in inverse proportion to the wilderness we have left.

In a day of commercial development, in an age of a degrading population explosion, in a time of utmost faith in scientific manipulation, the defense of wilderness becomes a thousand times more critical and demanding. In an easier era, the predatory band of land barons could placate the lovers of wilderness and avoid a political showdown because there was still ample room to satisfy their personal avarice. Magnanimously they could cluck their consent to a magnificent sop here and another there. But now, like prodigal sons, they come home to the last rich wilderness for a final feast.

Our American values have not changed. The utilization doctrine is still foremost, the appetite still rules the spirit. Because the inbred dominance of mercenary values over other considerations intensifies in our society, the lovers of wilderness will have to increase their own efforts in like degree. An old Hindu saying is "God doesn't mind your faults—he minds your indifference."

Today we cannot save the land unless we are ready to stir the political mud. A political candidate in 1966 boasted: "I know every cranny and crook in town." The political statesmen and men of vision in government support the cause of conservation now. But it is the "crannies and crooks" that give us pause.

Look over the proceedings of this tenth biennial Wilderness Conference and what strikes you: the initial session focused on the political framework where wilderness decisions are made. It was an account of the battle between wilderness goals and a variety of utilitarian interests. We are still hung up on a basic problem, the shibboleth of multiple use. I heard clearly from this rostrum that we must compare wilderness with the need for other resources. It should have no clearer priority because wilderness cannot afford to lose more than once.

A second session was given to justifying wilderness against the claims of commercial exploitation and mass consumption. Here is a proposition that can be made to prevail only in the political forum.

The session this morning was pointed toward the problem of salvaging the natural value of desert, cave, shoreline, wild river, and underwater areas from the pressures of people—all under the aegis of political authority.

And the final gathering this afternoon has frankly concentrated on the preservation of the wilderness environment under the regulating power of the government. It has concentrated on political power, the political sponsorship of research as well as political responsibility.

The evidence is overwhelming. The pace of economic change places wilderness values at the mercy of lawmakers, administrators, and an assortment of political decision-makers. If you protect the wild lands at all you protect them by social choice, legally, over alternative claimants. This is politics.

Just as wilderness itself is no longer a morsel inadvertently pushed to one side of the plate while society gorged on the main dishes, so wilderness protection is no longer possible with a leftover portion of energy and money. The commercial challenge is now too fierce and multisided to be met on a part-time basis of whimsical philanthropy. The attack is on every front at once: the Everglades, the California redwoods (and may I inject here the fact that the conservation movement without a major redwood national park is like a country without a flag), the Grand Canyon, the Great Smokies, the Adirondack Forest Preserve, the Yukon Flats, the Olympic Forest, and the North Cascades.

The defense against these assaults requires full-scale mobilization of political power. How do you keep snowmobiles from destroying the peace of the wilderness and decapitating all the young trees? How do we go about salvaging Article XIV—New York State's famous "forever wild" clause—from the orgy of greed and pressures on the "all-up-for-grabs" constitutional convention? * We in New York are this spring and summer facing a crisis in the preservation of our wilderness.

At this hour we cannot save these things with raised eyebrows or polite conversations. For over a year we have been applying organized pressure on the Constitutional Convention delegates. We are employing the political devices.

Because, then, wilderness is making its final stand amid an assort-

* Substantially the same protection for New York's Forest Preserve was included in the proposed new state constitution, but the entire constitution was defeated at the polls in the fall of 1967.—*The Editors.*

ment of pressures—a continued worship of the icon of production graphs, an ever spiraling population, a deprived world clamoring for all the material things we have—because these forces are crashing and crushing upon us, we may be faced not only with a desperate condition but a disaster. With all the suddenness of an avalanche the doom may be upon us.

Combine these two factors, the political character of the problem and the powers of sudden destruction inherent in the situation, and wilderness preservation takes on a new, a challenging, and an urgent complexion. As the late Congressman Magnus Johnson once said: "What we have to do is take the bull by the tail and look the situation in the face."

Two Martians land on earth. One walks up to a fire hydrant and says, "Take me to your leader."

The other Martian says: "What are talking to him for? He's only a kid."

Like the Martians, we can no longer talk to fire hydrants or tilt with windmills. We have to go directly to the leaders. If we are living through a revolution in which wilderness is being hacked to death, and if the sword of defense has shifted to the corridors of governmental power, then we must be there to wield it. We cannot wish the oak back into the acorn. In the course of modern events we are now committed to something more than exchanging descriptions of the sunset—even over the mountains.

Secretary of Labor Willard Wirtz quotes a colleague as saying, "I tell you, we've got to do something to get a toehold in the public eye." We are called upon to do something equally drastic.

The conservation group that shies from the mobilization of public support for the particular area of crisis because it prefers the comfort of generalization, is astride a dead horse. It has sold out. If the wilderness is saved from the deadly forces that beset it, it will have been because there are implacable activists in our number, unrelenting in zeal, unafraid under harassment. They will fight as Muir fought, resist as Thoreau resisted. But they will also organize and mobilize as effectively as the science of social and political engineering permits. And they will aim with deliberate and devastating effect.

Next in importance to having a great aim is to know when to pull the trigger. This reminds me of the cowboy who sauntered into the bar with one foot heavily swathed in bandages. "What happened to Joe?" inquired one fellow at the bar. "Oh," said the second fellow, "Joe's fast on the trigger—but slow on the draw."

The wilderness is the business of this generation. Unless we are successful, it will not be here for the next generation to worry about. And if it is to be saved, it will be saved only by a level-headed but determined militancy, employing all advantages of modern communications, and by groups such as the host of this conference: the indomitable Sierra Club.

I think that this conference, by its programming, underlines that the quality of life we aspire to is a matter of social and therefore political choices. The meetings were superb, and on behalf of the participants may I extend our gratitude to Professor Gilligan and his cohorts and to the Sierra Club because it senses where we are, knows what we must do, and has the courage to pursue its ends. Thank you.

Appendices

APPENDIX A

The Wilderness Act of 1964

COMPLETE TEXT OF THE WILDERNESS ACT

Be it enacted by the Senate and House of Representatives of the United States of America in Congress assembled,

SHORT TITLE

SECTION 1. This Act may be cited as the "Wilderness Act."

WILDERNESS SYSTEM ESTABLISHED STATEMENT OF POLICY

SEC. 2. (a) In order to assure that an increasing population, accompanied by expanding settlement and growing mechanization, does not occupy and modify all areas within the United States and its possessions, leaving no lands designated for preservation and protection in their natural condition, it is hereby declared to be the policy of the Congress to secure for the American people of present and future generations the benefits of an enduring resource of wilderness. For this purpose there is hereby established a National Wilderness Preservation System to be composed of federally owned areas designated by Congress as "wilderness areas," and these shall be administered for the use and enjoyment of the American people in such manner as will leave them unimpaired for future use and enjoyment as wilderness, and so as to provide for the protection of these areas, the preservation of their wilderness character, and for the gathering and dissemination of information regarding their use and enjoyment as wilderness; and no Federal lands shall be designated as "wilderness areas" except as provided for in this Act or by a subsequent Act.

(b) The inclusion of an area in the National Wilderness Preservation System notwithstanding, the area shall continue to be managed by the Department and agency having jurisdiction thereover immediately before its inclusion in the National Wilderness Preservation System unless otherwise provided by Act of Congress. No appropriation shall be available for the payment of expenses or salaries for the administration of the National Wilderness Preservation System as a separate unit nor shall any appropriations be available for additional personnel stated as being required solely for the purpose of managing or administering areas solely because they are included within the National Wilderness Preservation System.

DEFINITION OF WILDERNESS

(c) A wilderness in contrast with those areas where man and his own works dominate the landscape, is hereby recognized as an area where the earth and its community of life are untrammeled by man, where man himself is a visitor who does not remain. An area of wilderness is further defined to mean in this Act an area of undeveloped Federal land retaining its primeval character and influence, without permanent improvements or human habitation, which is protected and managed so as to preserve its natural conditions and which (1) generally appears to have been affected primarily by the forces of nature, with the imprint of man's work substantially unnoticeable; (2) has outstanding opportunities for solitude or a primitive and unconfined type of recreation; (3) has at least five thousand acres of land or is of sufficient size as to make practicable its preservation and use in an unimpaired condition; and (4) may also contain ecological, geological, or other features of scientific, educational, scenic, or historical value.

NATIONAL WILDERNESS PRESERVATION SYSTEM—EXTENT OF SYSTEM

SEC. 3. (a) All areas within the national forests classified at least 30 days before the effective date of this Act by the Secretary of Agriculture or the Chief of the Forest Service as "wilderness," "wild," or "canoe" are hereby designated as wilderness areas. The Secretary of Agriculture shall—

(1) Within one year after the effective date of this Act, file a map and legal description of each wilderness area with the Interior and Insular Affairs Committees of the United States Senate and the House of Representatives, and such descriptions shall have the same force and effect as if included in this Act: *Provided, however,* That correction of clerical and typographical errors in such legal descriptions and maps may be made.

(2) Maintain, available to the public, records pertaining to said wilderness areas, including maps and legal descriptions, copies of regulations governing them, copies of public notices of, and reports submitted to Congress regarding pending additions, eliminations, or modifications. Maps, legal descriptions, and regulations pertaining to wilderness areas within their respective jurisdictions also shall be available to the public in the offices of regional foresters, national forest supervisors, and forest rangers.

Classification. (b) The Secretary of Agriculture shall, within ten years after the enactment of this Act, review, as to its suitability or nonsuitability for preservation as wilderness, each area in the national forests classified on the effective date of this Act by the Secretary of Agriculture or the Chief of the Forest Service as "primitive" and report his findings to the President.

Presidential recommendation to Congress. The President shall advise the United States Senate and House of Representatives of his recommendations with respect to the designation as "wilderness" or other reclassification of each area on which review has been completed, together with maps and a definition of boundaries. Such advice shall be given with respect to not less than one-third of all the areas now classified as "primitive" within three years after the enactment of this Act, not less than two-thirds within seven years after the enactment of this Act, and the remaining areas within ten years after the enactment of this Act.

Congressional approval. Each recommendation of the President for designation as "wilderness" shall become effective only if so provided by an Act of Congress. Areas classified as "primitive" on the effective date of this Act shall continue to be administered under the rules and regulations affecting such areas on the effective date of this Act until Congress has determined otherwise. Any such area may be increased in size by the President at the time he submits his recommendations to the Congress by not more than five thousand acres with no more than one thousand two hundred and eighty acres of such increase in any one compact unit; if it is proposed to increase the size of any such area by more than five thousand acres or by more than one thousand two hundred and eighty acres in any one compact unit the increase in size shall not become effective until acted upon by Congress. Nothing herein contained shall limit the President in proposing, as part of his recommendations to Congress, the alteration of existing boundaries of primitive areas or recommending the addition of any contiguous area of national forest lands predominantly of wilderness value. Notwithstanding any other provisions of this Act, the Secretary of Agriculture may complete his review and delete such area as may be necessary, but not to exceed seven thousand acres, from the southern tip of the Gore Range–Eagles Nest Primitive Area, Colorado, if the Secretary determines that such action is in the public interest.

Report to President. (c) Within ten years after the effective date of this Act the Secretary of the Interior shall review every roadless area of five thousand contiguous acres or more in the national parks, monuments and other units of the national park system and every such area of, and every roadless island within, the national wildlife refuges and game ranges, under his jurisdiction on the effective date of this Act and shall report to the President his recommendation as to the suitability or nonsuitability of each area or island for preservation as wilderness.

Presidential recommendation to Congress. The President shall advise the President of the Senate and the Speaker of the House of Representatives of his recommendation with respect to the designation as wilderness of each such area or island on which review has been completed, together with a map thereof and a definition of its boundaries. Such advice shall be given with respect to not less than one-third of the areas and islands to be reviewed under this subsection within three years after enactment of this Act, not less than two-thirds within seven years of enactment of this Act, and the remainder within ten years of enactment of this Act.

Congressional approval. A recommendation of the President for designation as wilderness shall become effective only if so provided by an Act of Congress. Nothing contained herein shall, by implication or otherwise, be construed to lessen the present statutory authority of the Secretary of the Interior with respect to the maintenance of roadless areas within units of the national park system.

Suitability. (d) (1) The Secretary of Agriculture and the Secretary of the Interior shall, prior to submitting any recommendations to the President with respect to the suitability of any area for preservation as wilderness—

Publication in Federal Register. (A) give such public notice of the proposed action as they deem appropriate, including publication in the Federal Register and in a newspaper having general circulation in the area or areas in the vicinity of the affected land;

Hearings. (B) hold a public hearing or hearings at a location or locations convenient to the area affected. The hearings shall be announced through such means as the respective Secretaries involved deem appropriate, including notices in the *Federal Register* and in newspapers of general circulation in the area: *Provided.* That if the lands involved are located in more than one State, at least one hearing shall be held in each State in which a portion of the land lies;

(C) at least thirty days before the date of a hearing advise the Governor of each State and the governing board of each county, or in Alaska the borough, in which the lands are located, and Federal departments and agencies concerned, and invite such officials and Federal agencies to submit their views on the proposed action at the hearing or by no later than thirty days following the date of the hearing.

(2) Any views submitted to the appropriate Secretary under the provisions of (1) of this subsection with respect to any area shall be included with any recommendations to the President and to Congress with respect to such areas.

Proposed modification. (e) Any modification or adjustment of boundaries of any wilderness area shall be recommended by the appropriate Secretary after public notice of such proposal and public hearing or hearings as provided in subsection (d) of this section. The proposed modification or adjustment shall then be recommended with map and description thereof to the President. The President shall advise the United States Senate and the House of Representatives of his recommendations with respect to such modification or adjustment and such recommendations shall become effective only in the same manner as provided for in subsection (b) and (c) of this section.

USE OF WILDERNESS AREAS

SEC. 4. (a) The purposes of this Act are hereby declared to be within and supplemental to the purposes for which national forests and units of the national park and wildlife refuge systems are established and administered and—

(1) Nothing in this Act shall be deemed to be in interference with the purpose for which national forests are established as set forth in the Act of June 4, 1897 (30 Stat. 11), and the Multiple-Use Sustained-Yield Act of June 12, 1960 (74 Stat. 215).

(2) Nothing in this Act shall modify the restrictions and provisions of the Shipstead-Nolan Act (Public Law 539, Seventy-first Congress, July 10, 1930; 46 Stat. 1020), the Thye-Blatnik Act (Public Law 733, Eightieth Congress, June 22, 1948; 62 Stat. 568), and the Humphrey-Thye-Blatnik-Andresen Act (Public Law 607, Eighty-fourth Congress, June 22, 1956; 70 Stat. 326), as applying to the Superior National Forest or the regulations of the Secretary of Agriculture.

(3) Nothing in this Act shall modify the statutory authority under which units of the national park system are created. Further, the designation of any area of any park, monument, or other unit of the national park system as a wilderness area pursuant to this Act shall in no manner lower the standards evolved for the use and preservation of such park, monument, or other unit of the national park system in accordance with

the Act of August 25, 1916, the statutory authority under which the area was created, or any other Act of Congress which might pertain to or affect such area, including, but not limited to, the Act of June 8, 1906 (34 Stat. 225; 16 U.S.C. 432 et seq.); section 3(2) of the Federal Power Act (16 U.S.C. 796(2); and the Act of August 21, 1935 (49 Stat. 666; U.S.C. 461 et seq.).

(b) Except as otherwise provided in this Act, each agency administering any area designated as wilderness shall be responsible for preserving the wilderness character of the area and shall so administer such area for such other purposes for which it may have been established as also to preserve its wilderness character. Except as otherwise provided in this Act, wilderness areas shall be devoted to the public purposes of recreational, scenic, scientific, educational, conservation, and historical use.

PROHIBITION OF CERTAIN USES

(c) Except as specifically provided for in this Act, and subject to existing private rights, there shall be no commercial enterprise and no permanent road within any wilderness area designated by this Act and, except as necessary to meet minimum requirements for the administration of the area for the purpose of this Act (including measures required in emergencies involving the health and safety of persons within the area), there shall be no temporary road, no use of motor vehicles, motorized equipment or motorboats, no landing of aircraft, no other form of mechanical transport, and no structure or installation within any such area.

SPECIAL PROVISIONS

(d) The following special provisions are hereby made:

(1) Within wilderness areas designated by this Act the use of aircraft or motorboats, where these uses have already become established, may be permitted to continue subject to such restrictions as the Secretary of Agriculture deems desirable. In addition, such measures may be taken as may be necessary in the control of fire, insects, and diseases, subject to such conditions as the Secretary deems desirable.

(2) Nothing in this Act shall prevent within national forest wilderness areas any activity, including prospecting, for the purpose of gathering information about mineral or other resources, if such activity is carried on in a manner compatible with the preservation of the wilderness environment. Furthermore, in accordance with such program as the Secretary of the Interior shall develop and conduct in consultation with the Secretary of Agriculture, such areas shall be surveyed on a planned, recurring basis consistent with the concept of wilderness preservation by the Geological Survey and the Bureau of Mines to determine the mineral values, if any, that may be present; and the results of such surveys shall be made available to the public and submitted to the President and Congress.

Mineral leases, claims, etc. (3) Notwithstanding any other provisions of this Act, until midnight December 31, 1983, the United States mining laws and all laws pertaining to mineral leasing shall, to the same extent as applicable prior to the effective date of this Act, extend to those national forest lands designated by this Act as "wilderness areas"; subject, however, to such reasonable regulations governing ingress and egress as may be prescribed by the Secretary of Agriculture consistent with the use of the land for mineral location and development and exploration, drilling, and production, and use of land for transmission lines, waterlines, telephone lines, or facilities necessary in exploring, drilling, producing, mining, and processing operations, including where essential the use of mechanized ground or air equipment and restoration as near as practicable of the surface of the land disturbed in performing prospecting, location, and, in oil and gas leasing, discovery work, exploration, drilling, and production, as soon as they have served their purpose. Mining locations lying within the boundaries of said wilderness areas shall be held and used solely for mining or processing operations and uses reasonably incident thereto; and hereafter, subject to valid existing rights, all patents issued under the mining laws of the United States affecting national forest lands designated by this Act as wilderness areas shall convey title to the mineral deposits within the claim, together with the right to cut and use so much of the mature timber therefrom as may be needed in the extraction, removal, and beneficiation of the mineral deposits, and if the timber is cut under sound principles of forest management as defined by the national forest rules and regulations, but each such patent shall reserve to the United States all title in or to the surface of the lands and products thereof, and no use of the surface of the claim or the resources therefrom not reasonably required for carrying on mining or prospecting shall be allowed except as otherwise expressly provided in this Act: *Provided*, That, unless hereafter specifically authorized, no patent within wilderness areas designated by this Act shall issue after December 31, 1983, except for the valid claims existing on or before December 31, 1983. Mining claims located after the effective date of this Act within the boundaries of wilderness areas designated by this Act shall create no rights in excess of those rights which may be patented under the provisions of this subsection. Mineral leases, permits, and licenses covering lands within national forest wilderness areas designated by this Act shall contain such reasonable stipulations as may be prescribed by the Secretary of Agriculture for the protection of the wilderness character of the land consistent with the use of the land for the purposes for which they are leased, permitted, or licensed. Subject to valid rights then existing, effective January 1, 1984, the minerals in lands designated by this Act as wilderness areas are withdrawn from all forms of appropriation under the mining laws and from disposition under all laws pertaining to mineral leasing and all amendments thereto.

Water resources. (4) Within wilderness areas in the national forests designated by this act, (1) the President may, within a specific area and in accordance with such regulations as he may deem desirable, authorize prospecting for water resources, the establishment and maintenance of reservoirs, water-conservation works, power projects, transmission lines, and other facilities needed in the public interest, including the road construction and maintenance essential to development and use thereof, upon his determination that such use or uses in the specific area will better serve the interests of the United States and the people thereof than will its denial; and (2) the grazing of livestock, where established prior to the effective date of this Act, shall be permitted to continue subject to such reasonable regulations as are deemed by the Secretary of Agriculture.

(5) Other provisions of this Act to the contrary notwithstanding, the management of the Boundary Waters Canoe Area, formerly designated as the Superior, Little Indian Sioux, and Caribou Roadless Areas, in the Superior National Forest, Minnesota, shall be in accordance with regulations established by the Secretary of Agriculture in accordance with the general purpose of maintaining, without unnecessary restrictions on other uses, including that of timber, the primitive character of the area, particularly in the vicinity of lakes, streams, and portages: *Provided,* That nothing in this Act shall preclude the continuance within the area of any already established use of motorboats.

(6) Commerical services may be performed within the wilderness areas designated by this Act to the extent necessary for activities which are proper for realizing the recreational or other wilderness purposes of the areas.

(7) Nothing in this Act shall constitute an express or implied claim or denial on the part of the Federal Government as to exemption from State water laws.

(8) Nothing in this Act shall be construed as affecting the jurisdiction or responsibilities of the several States with respect to wildlife and fish in the national forests.

STATE AND PRIVATE LANDS WITHIN WILDERNESS AREAS

SEC. 5. (a) In any case where State-owned or privately owned land is completely surrounded by national forest lands within areas designated by this Act as wilderness, such State or private owner shall be given such rights as may be necessary to assure adequate access to such State-owned or privately owned land by such State or private owner and their successors in interest, or the State-owned land or privately owned land shall be exchanged for federally owned land in the same State of approximately equal value under authorities available to the Secretary of Agriculture:

Transfers, restriction. Provided, however, That the United States shall not transfer to a State or private owner any mineral interests unless the State or private owner relinquishes or causes to be relinquished to the United States the mineral interest in the surrounded land.

(b) In any case where valid mining claims or other valid occupancies are wholly within a designated national forest wilderness area, the Secretary of Agriculture shall, by reasonable regulations consistent with the preservation of the area as wilderness, permit ingress and egress to such surrounded areas by means which have been or are being customarily enjoyed with respect to other such areas similarly situated.

Acquisition. (c) Subject to the appropriation of funds by Congress, the Secretary of Agriculture is authorized to acquire privately owned land within the perimeter of any area designated by this Act as wilderness if (1) the owner concurs in such acquisition or (2) the acquisition is specifically authorized by Congress.

GIFTS, BEQUESTS, AND CONTRIBUTIONS

SEC. 6. (a) The Secretary of Agriculture may accept gifts or bequests of land within wilderness areas designated by this Act for preservation as wilderness. The Secretary of Agriculture may also accept gifts or bequests of land adjacent to wilderness areas designated by this Act for preservation as wilderness if he has given sixty days advance notice thereof to the President of the Senate and the Speaker of the House of Representatives. Land accepted by the Secretary of Agriculture under this section shall become part of the wilderness area involved. Regulations with regard to any such land may be in accordance with such agreements, consistent with the policy of this Act, as are made at the time of such gift, or such conditions, consistent with such policy, as may be included in, and accepted with, such bequest.

(b) The Secretary of Agriculture or the Secretary of the Interior is authorized to accept private contributions and gifts to be used to further the purposes of this Act.

ANNUAL REPORTS

SEC. 7. At the opening of each session of Congress, the Secretaries of Agriculture and Interior shall jointly report to the President for transmission to Congress on the status of the wilderness system, including a list and descriptions of the areas in the system, regulations in effect, and other pertinent information, together with any recommendations they may care to make.

APPENDIX B

Administration and Use of National Forest Wilderness and National Forest Primitive Areas *

In Part 251 of Title 36, Code of Federal Regulations, Sections 251.20, 251.21, and 251.21a are hereby revoked; and Sections 251.70 to 251.84 and Section 251.86 are added, under the heading "Administration and Use of National Forest Wilderness and National Forest Primitive Areas," as follows:

Section 251.70—*Definition*

National Forest Wilderness shall consist of those units of the National Wilderness Preservation System which at least 30 days before the Wilderness Act of September 3, 1964, were designated as Wilderness and Wild under Secretary of Agriculture's Regulations U-1 and U-2 (36 C.F.R. 251.20, 251.21), the Boundary Waters Canoe Area as designated under Regulation U-3 (36 C.F.R. 251.22), and such other areas of the National Forests as may later be added to the System by act of Congress. Sections 251.70 to 251.84 apply to all National Forest units now or hereafter in the National Wilderness Preservation System, including the Boundary Waters Canoe Area, Superior National Forest, except as that area is subject to Section 251.85.

Section 251.71—*Objectives*

Except as otherwise provided in these regulations, National Forest Wilderness shall be so administered as to meet the public purposes of recreational, scenic, scientific, educational, conservation, and historical uses; and it shall also be administered for such other purposes for which it may have been established in such a manner as to preserve and protect its wilderness character. In carrying out such purposes, National Forest Wilderness resources shall be managed to promote, perpetuate, and, where necessary, restore the wilderness character of the land and its specific values of solitude, physical and mental challenge, scientific study, inspiration, and primitive recreation. To that end:

a. Natural ecological succession will be allowed to operate freely to the extent feasible.

b. Wilderness will be made available for human use to the optimum extent consistent with the maintenance of primitive conditions.

c. In resolving conflicts in resource use, wilderness values will be dominant to the extent not limited by the Wilderness Act, subsequent establishing legislation, or these regulations.

Section 251.72—*Control of Uses*

To the extent not limited by the Wilderness Act, subsequent legislation establishing a particular unit, or these regulations, the Chief, Forest Service,

---

* Approved by Secretary of Agriculture Orville L. Freeman, June 3, 1966.
    Title 36—Parks, Forests, and Memorials, Chapter II—Forest Service, Department of Agriculture, Part 251—Land Uses.

may prescribe measures necessary to control fire, insects, and disease and measures which may be used in emergencies involving the health and safety of persons or damage to property and may require permits for, or otherwise limit or regulate, any use of National Forest land, including, but not limited to, camping, campfires, and grazing of recreation livestock.

Section 251.73—*Maintenance of Records*

The Chief, Forest Service, in accordance with Section 3(a)(2) of the Wilderness Act, shall establish uniform procedures and standards for the maintenance and availability to the public of records pertaining to National Forest Wilderness, including maps and legal descriptions; copies of regulations governing Wilderness; and copies of public notices and reports submitted to Congress regarding pending additions, eliminations, or modifications. Copies of such information pertaining to National Forest Wilderness within their respective jurisdictions shall be available to the public in the appropriate offices of the Regional Foresters, Forest Supervisors, and Forest Rangers.

Section 251.74—*Establishment, Modification, or Elimination*

National Forest Wilderness will be established, modified, or eliminated in accordance with the provisions of Sections 3(b), (d), and (e) of the Wilderness Act. The Chief, Forest Service, shall arrange for issuing public notices, appointing hearing officers, holding public hearings, and notifying the Governors of the States concerned and the governing board of each county in which the lands involved are located.

a. At least 30 days' public notice shall be given of the proposed action and intent to hold a public hearing. Public notice shall include publication in the *Federal Register* and in a newspaper of general circulation in the vicinity of the land involved.

b. Public hearings shall be held at locations convenient to the area affected. If the land involved is in more than one State, at least one hearing shall be held in each State in which a portion of the land lies.

c. A record of the public hearing and the views submitted subsequent to public notice and prior to the close of the public hearing shall be included with any recommendations to the President and to the Congress with respect to any such action.

d. At least 30 days before the date of the public hearing, suitable advice shall be furnished to the Governor of each State and the governing board of each county or, in Alaska, the borough in which the lands are located, and Federal Departments and agencies concerned; and such officers or Federal agencies shall be invited to submit their views on the proposed action at the hearing or in writing by not later than 30 days following the date of the hearing. Any views submitted in response to such advice with respect to any proposed Wilderness action shall be included with any recommendations to the President and to the Congress with respect to any such action.

Section 251.75—*Commerical Enterprises, Roads, Motor Vehicles, Motorized Equipment, Motorboats, Aircraft, Aircraft Landing Facilities, Airdrops, Structures, and Cutting of Trees*

Except as provided in the Wilderness Act, subsequent legislation establishing a particular Wilderness unit, or Sections 251.27, 251.28, 251.30, 251.75(c) and (d), 251.76, 251.77, and 251.81 through 251.85, inclusive, of these regulations, and subject to existing rights, there shall be in National Forest Wilderness no commercial enterprises; no temporary or permanent roads, no aircraft landing strips, no heliports or helispots; no use of motor vehicles, motorized equipment, motorboats, or other forms of mechanical transport; no landing of aircraft; no dropping of materials, supplies, or persons from aircraft; no structures or installations; and no cutting of trees for non-wilderness purposes.

a. "Mechanical transport," as herein used, shall include any contrivance which travels over ground, snow, or water on wheels, tracks, skids, or by flotation and is propelled by a nonliving power source contained or carried on or within the device.

b. "Motorized equipment," as herein used, shall include any machine activated by a nonliving power source, except that small battery-powered, hand-carried devices such as flashlights, shavers, and Geiger counters are not classed as motorized equipment.

c. The Chief, Forest Service, may authorize occupancy and use of National Forest land by officers, employees, agencies, or agents of the Federal, State, and county governments to carry out the purposes of the Wilderness Act and will prescribe conditions under which motorized equipment, mechanical transport, aircraft, aircraft landing strips, heliports, helispots, installations, or structures may be used, transported, or installed by the Forest Service and its agents and by other Federal, State, or county agencies or their agents, to meet the minimum requirements for authorized activities to protect and administer the Wilderness and its resources. The Chief may also prescribe the conditions under which such equipment, transport, aircraft, installations, or structures may be used in emergencies involving the health and safety of persons, damage to property, or other purposes.

d. The Chief, Forest Service, may permit, subject to such restrictions as he deems desirable, the landing of aircraft and the use of motorboats at places within any Wilderness where these uses were established prior to the date the Wilderness was designated by Congress as a unit of the National Wilderness Preservation System. The Chief may also permit the maintenance of aircraft landing strips, heliports, or helispots which existed when the Wilderness was designated by Congress as a unit of the National Wilderness Preservation System.

Section 251.76—*Grazing of Livestock*

The grazing of livestock, where such use was established before the date of legislation which includes an area in the National Wilderness Preservation System, shall be permitted to continue under the general regulations covering grazing of livestock on the National Forests and in accordance with special provisions covering grazing use in units of National Forest Wilderness which the Chief of the Forest Service may prescribe for general application in such units or may arrange to have prescribed for individual units.

The Chief, Forest Service, may permit, subject to such conditions as he deems necessary, the maintenance, reconstruction, or relocation of those livestock management improvements and structures which existed within a Wilderness when it was incorporated into the National Wilderness Preservation System. Additional improvements or structures may be built when necessary to protect wilderness values.

Section 251.77—*Permanent Structures and Commercial Services*
Motels, summer homes, stores, resorts, organization camps, hunting and fishing lodges, electronic installations, and similar structures and uses are prohibited in National Forest Wilderness. The Chief, Forest Service, may permit temporary structures and commercial services within National Forest Wilderness to the extent necessary for realizing the recreational or other wilderness purposes, which may include, but are not limited to, the public services generally offered by packers, outfitters, and guides.

Section 251.78—*Poisons and Herbicides*
Poisons and herbicides will not be used to control wildlife, fish, insects, or plants within any Wilderness except by or under the direct supervision of the Forest Service or other agency designated by the Chief, Forest Service; however, the personal use of household-type insecticides by visitors to provide for health and sanitation is specifically excepted from this prohibition.

Section 251.79—*Jurisdiction over Wildlife and Fish*
Nothing in these regulations shall be construed as affecting the jurisdiction or responsibility of the several States with respect to wildlife and fish in the National Forests.

Section 251.80—*Water Rights*
Nothing in these regulations constitutes an expressed or implied claim or denial on the part of the Department of Agriculture as to exemption from State water laws.

Section 251.81—*Access to Surrounded State and Private Lands*
States or persons, and their successors in interest, who own land completely surrounded by National Forest Wilderness shall be given such rights as may be necessary to assure adequate access to that land. "Adequate access" is defined as the combination of routes and modes of travel which will, as determined by the Forest Service, cause the least lasting impact on the primitive character of the land and at the same time will serve the reasonable purposes for which the State and private land is held or used. Access by routes or modes of travel not available to the general public under these regulations shall be given by written authorization issued by the Forest Service. The authorization will prescribe the means and the routes of travel to and from the privately owned or State-owned land which constitute adequate access and the conditions reasonably necessary to preserve the National Forest Wilderness.

Section 251.82—*Access to Valid Mining Claims or Valid Occupancies*
Persons with valid mining claims or other valid occupancies wholly within National Forest Wilderness shall be permitted access to such surrounded claims or occupancies by means consistent with the preservation of National Forest Wilderness which have been or are being customarily used with re-

spect to other such claims or occupancies surrounded by National Forest Wilderness. The Forest Service will, when appropriate, issue permits which shall prescribe the routes of travel to and from the surrounded claims or occupancies, the mode of travel, and other conditions reasonably necessary to preserve the National Forest Wilderness.

Section 251.83—*Mining, Mineral Leases, and Mineral Permits*

Notwithstanding any other provisions of these regulations, the United States mining laws and all laws pertaining to mineral leasing shall extend to each National Forest Wilderness for the period specified in the Wilderness Act or subsequent establishing legislation to the same extent they were applicable prior to the date the Wilderness was designated by Congress as a part of the National Wilderness Preservation System.

a. Whoever hereafter locates a mining claim in National Forest Wilderness shall within 30 days thereafter file a written notice of his Post Office address and the location of that mining claim in the office of the Forest Supervisor or District Ranger having jurisdiction over the National Forest land on which the claim is located.

b. Holders of unpatented mining claims validly established on any National Forest Wilderness prior to inclusion of such unit in the National Wilderness Preservation System shall be accorded the rights provided by the United States mining laws as then applicable to the National Forest land involved. Persons locating mining claims in any unit of National Forest Wilderness on or after the date on which the said unit was included in the National Wilderness Preservation System shall be accorded the rights provided by the United States mining laws as applicable to the National Forest land involved and subject to provisions specified in the establishing legislation. All claimants shall comply with reasonable conditions prescribed by the Chief, Forest Service, for the protection of National Forest resources in accordance with the general purposes of maintaining the National Wilderness Preservation System unimpaired for future use and enjoyment as wilderness and so as to provide for the preservation of its wilderness character; and a performance bond may be required.

(1) Prior to commencing operation or development of any mining claim, or to cutting timber thereon, mining claimants shall file written notice in the office of the Forest Supervisor or District Ranger having jurisdiction over the land involved. Unless within 20 days after such notice is given the Forest Service requires the claimant to furnish operating plans or to accept a permit governing such operations, he may commence operation, development, or timber cutting.

(2) No claimant shall construct roads across National Forest Wilderness unless authorized by the Forest Service. Application to construct a road to a mining claim shall be filed with the Forest Service and shall be accompanied by a plat showing the location of the proposed road and by a description of the type and standard of the road. The Chief, Forest Service, shall, when appropriate, authorize construction of the road as proposed or shall require such changes in loca-

tion and type and standard of construction as are necessary to safeguard the National Forest resources, including wilderness values, consistent with the use of the land for mineral location, exploration, development, drilling, and production and for transmission lines, waterlines, telephone lines, and processing operations, including, where essential, the use of mechanical transport, aircraft or motorized equipment.

(3) Claimants shall cut timber on mining claims within National Forest Wilderness only for the actual development of the claim or uses reasonably incident thereto. Any severance or removal of timber, other than severance or removal to provide clearance, shall be in accordance with sound principles of forest management and in such a manner as to minimize the adverse effect on the wilderness character of the land.

(4) All claimants shall, in developing and operating their mining claims, take those reasonable measures, including settling ponds, necessary for the disposal of tailings, dumpage, and other deleterious materials or substances to prevent obstruction, pollution, excessive siltation, or deterioration of the land, streams, ponds, lakes, or springs, as may be directed by the Forest Service.

(5) On mining claims validly established prior to inclusion of the land within the National Wilderness Preservation System, claimants shall, as directed by the Forest Service and if application for patent is not pending, take all reasonable measures to remove any improvements no longer needed for mining purposes and which were installed after the land was designated by Congress as Wilderness and, by appropriate treatment, restore, as nearly as practicable, the original contour of the surface of the land which was disturbed subsequent to the date this regulation is adopted and which is no longer needed in performing location, exploration, drilling, and production and promote its revegetation by natural means. On such part of the claim where restoration to approximately the original contour is not feasible, restoration for such part shall provide a combination of bank slopes and contour gradient conducive to soil stabilization and revegetation by natural means.

(6) On claims validly established after the date the land was included within the National Wilderness Preservation System, claimants shall, as directed by the Forest Service, take all reasonable measures to remove improvements no longer needed for mining purposes and, by appropriate treatment, restore, as near as practicable, the original contour of the surface of the land which was disturbed and which is no longer needed in performing location and exploration, drilling and production, and to revegetate and to otherwise prevent or control accelerated soil erosion.

c. The title to timber on patented claims validly established after the land was included within the National Wilderness Preservation System remains in the United States, subject to a right to cut and use timber for mining purposes. So much of the mature timber may be cut and used as is needed in the extraction, removal, and the beneficiation of the mineral deposits, if needed timber is not otherwise reasonably available. The cutting shall comply with the requirements for sound principles of forest management as defined by the National Forest rules and regulations and set forth in stipulations issued by the Chief, Forest Service, which as a minimum incorporate the following basic principles of forest management:

(1) harvesting operations shall be so conducted as to minimize soil movement and damage from water runoff; and

(2) slash shall be disposed of and other precautions shall be taken to minimize damage from forest insects, disease, and fire.

d. Mineral leases, permits, and licenses covering lands within National Forest Wilderness will contain reasonable stipulations for the protection of the wilderness character of the land consistent with the use of the land for purposes for which they are leased, permitted, or licensed. The Chief, Forest Service, shall specify the conditions to be included in such stipulations.

e. Permits shall not be issued for the removal of mineral materials commonly known as "common varieties" under the Materials Act of July 31, 1947, as amended and supplemented (30 U.S.C. 601–604).

Section 251.84—*Prospecting for Minerals and Other Resources*

The Chief, Forest Service, shall allow any activity, including prospecting, for the purpose of gathering information about minerals or other resources in National Forest Wilderness except that any such activity for gathering information shall be carried on in a manner compatible with the preservation of the wilderness environment, and except, further, that:

a. No person shall have any right or interest in or to any mineral deposits which may be discovered through prospecting or other information-gathering activity after the legal date on which the United States mining laws and laws pertaining to mineral leasing cease to apply to the specific Wilderness, nor shall any person after such date have any preference in applying for a mineral lease, license, or permit.

b. No overland motor vehicle or other form of mechanical overland transport may be used in connection with prospecting for minerals or any activity for the purpose of gathering information about minerals or other resources except as authorized by the Chief, Forest Service.

c. Any person desiring to use motorized equipment, to land aircraft, or to make substantial excavations for mineral prospecting or for other purposes shall apply in writing to the office of the Forest Supervisor or District Ranger having jurisdiction over the land involved. Excavations shall be considered "substantial" which singularly or collectively exceed 200 cubic feet within any area which can be bounded by a rectangle containing 20 surface acres. Such use or excavation may be authorized by a permit issued by the Forest Service. Such permits may provide for the protection of National Forest resources, including wilderness values, protection of the public, and restoration of disturbed areas, including the posting of performance bonds.

d. Prospecting for water resources and the establishment of new reservoirs, water-conservation works, power projects, transmission lines, and other facilities needed in the public interest and the subsequent maintenance of such facilities, all pursuant to Section 4(d)(4)(1) of the Wilderness Act, will be permitted when and as authorized by the President.

Section 251.86—*National Forest Primitive Areas*

Within those areas of National Forests classified as "Primitive" on the effective date of the Wilderness Act, September 3, 1964, there shall be no roads or other provision for motorized transportation, no commercial timber cutting, and no occupancy under special-use permit for hotels, stores, resorts, summer homes, organization camps, hunting and fishing lodges, or similar uses: *Provided,* That existing roads over National Forest lands reserved from the public domain and roads necessary for the exercise of a statutory right of ingress and egress may be allowed under appropriate conditions determined by the Chief, Forest Service.

Grazing of domestic livestock, development of water storage projects which do not involve road construction, and improvements necessary for the protection of the National Forests may be permitted, subject to such restrictions as the Chief, Forest Service, deems desirable. Within Primitive Areas, when the use is for other than administrative needs of the Forest Service, use by other Federal agencies when authorized by the Chief, and in emergencies, the landing of aircraft and the use of motorboats are prohibited on National Forest land or water unless such use by aircraft or motorboats has already become well established, the use of motor vehicles is prohibited, and the use of other motorized equipment is prohibited except as authorized by the Chief. These restrictions are not intended as limitations on statutory rights of ingress and egress or of prospecting, locating, and developing mineral resources.

(78 Stat. 890, 16 U.S.C. 1131–1136; 30 Stat. 35, as amended 16 U.S.C. 551; 74 Stat. 215, 16 U.S.C. 528–531)

Done at Washington, D.C., this 31st day of May, 1966

/s/ Orville L. Freeman
Secretary of Agriculture

National Park Service Wilderness Management Criteria

Revised August 1966

OBJECTIVES

Park wilderness areas will be administered for the use and enjoyment of the American people in such manner as will leave them unimpaired for future use and enjoyment as wilderness, and so as to provide for the protection of these areas, the preservation of their wilderness character, and for the gathering and dissemination of information regarding their use and enjoyment as wilderness. Further, designation of Park Wilderness shall not lower the standards evolved for the use and preservation of the parks, monuments or other units of the National Park System in which such wilderness is located.

MANAGEMENT PRACTICES AND FACILITIES

Management Facilities, Practices, and Uses—Only those structures, management practices and uses necessary for management and preservation of the wilderness qualities of an area will be permitted. These would include, but need not be limited to, patrol cabins and limited facilities associated with saddle and pack stock control.

Fire Control—Wildfire will be controlled as necessary to prevent unacceptable loss of wilderness values, loss of life, damage to property, and the spread of wildfire to lands outside the wilderness. Use of fire lookout towers, fire roads, tool caches, aircraft, motorboats, and motorized fire-fighting equipment would be permitted for such control.

Insect and Disease Control—Such control may be undertaken only with the approval of the Director. The measure of control would depend on a determination of whether the insects or diseases are causing the complete alteration of an environment which is expected to be preserved, but controls will generally be limited to disaster conditions which threaten whole ecosystems. Any controls instituted would be those which would be most direct for the target insect or disease and which would have minimal effects upon other components of the ecosystems of which the wilderness is composed.

Rescue and Other Emergency Operations—In emergency situations involving the health and safety of persons and to meet recognized management needs, use of aircraft, motorboats, or other motorized or mechanical equipment will be permitted.

Regulation of Excess Wildlife Population—Population control through natural predation would be encouraged. Trapping and transplanting of excess animals would be practiced by park personnel as necessary. If these prove insufficient, direct reduction by park personnel would be instituted.

Non-native Plants and Animals—Non-native species of plants and animals will be eliminated where it is possible to do so by approved methods which will preserve wilderness qualities.

COMPATIBLE USES BY OR DEVELOPMENTS FOR THE PUBLIC

Research—The Service recognizing the scientific value of wilderness areas as natural outdoor laboratories, would encourage those kinds of research and data gathering which require such areas for their accomplishment. The Service would establish reasonable limitations to control the size of the areas which may be used for varying types of research projects within national park wilderness and projects exceeding those limitations would be subject to approval by the Director.

Fishing—Fishing is an appropriate use and will be permitted under applicable rules and regulations.

Visitor Use Structures and Facilities—Primitive trails for foot and horse travel are acceptable. Narrow trails which blend into the landscape will be allowed in wilderness with footbridges and horsebridges where they are essential to visitor safety. Stock holding corrals or discreetly placed drift fences will be permissible if needed in the interest of protection of wilderness values. No improvements will be permitted that are primarily for the comfort and convenience of visitors such as developed campgrounds and picnic facilities. However, trailside shelters may be permitted where they are needed for the protection of wilderness values.

Boating—Boating except with motorboats and airboats is an acceptable use of park wilderness. Where the use of motor powered craft has become established by custom or usage on lakes, streams or other bodies of water prior to their inclusion in wilderness, such use may be permitted to continue subject to established rules and regulations and any special restrictions that may be imposed for the protection of wilderness.

Commercial Services—Saddle and pack stock and guided boat trips in water areas are acceptable uses, but the number, nature and extent of these services will be carefully controlled through regulations and permits so as to protect the wilderness values.

NON-CONFORMING USES OR DEVELOPMENTS

Mining and Prospecting—These uses will not be permitted in national park wilderness. Where these activities are expressly authorized by statute, the area in question will be recommended for wilderness only with the provisos that such activities be discontinued and the authorization be revoked. Actively operated claims, based on valid existing rights, will be excluded from the proposed wilderness. It will be the policy to phase out existing active mining claims and acquire the lands involved. When this is accomplished such lands will be proposed for designation as wilderness if they otherwise meet the criteria for such areas.

Inholdings—Unless acquisition by the United States is assured, they will be excluded from the area designated as wilderness. It will be the policy to acquire such inholdings as rapidly as possible, and as they are acquired, the lands will be proposed for designation as wilderness if they otherwise meet the criteria for such areas.

Water Development Projects—Such projects, whether for improvement of navigation, flood control, irrigation, power, or other multiple purposes, are not acceptible in wilderness. Where these activities are authorized by statute, the area in question will be recommended for wilderness only with the proviso that such authorization be discontinued.

Grazing—Grazing is not an acceptable use in national park wilderness. Except where grazing is conducted under permits which may be expected to expire at a fixed or determinable date in advance of legislative action on the wilderness proposal, lands utilized for that purpose will not be proposed for wilderness designation. It will be the policy to phase out such operations as rapidly as possible, and as this is done, the lands will be proposed for designation as wilderness if they otherwise meet the criteria for such areas.

Timber Harvesting—This will not be permitted in national park wilderness.

Hunting—Public hunting will not be permitted in national park wilderness.

Motorized Equipment—The use of aircraft for airdrops or otherwise and the use of motorized trail vehicles, generators, and similar devices will not be permitted in national park wilderness, except as otherwise provided herein to meet the needs of management.

Roads and Utilities—Public use roads and utility line rights of way are not permitted.

APPENDIX D

Regulations on Public Use of Federal Wildlife Refuge and Range Areas *

Authority: The provisions of this Part 28 issued under R.S. 161, as amended, sec. 2, 33 Stat. 614, as amended, sec. 5, 43 Stat. 651, secs. 5, 10, 45 Stat. 449, 1224, secs. 4, 2, 48 Stat. 402, as amended, 1270, sec. 401, 49 Stat. 383, as amended, sec. 4, 76 Stat. 653; 5 U.S.C. 22, 16 U.S.C. 685, 725, 690d, 715i, 664, 43 U.S.C. 315a, 16 U.S.C. 715s, 460k; 80 Stat. 926.

Source: The provisions of this Part 28 appear at 31 F.R. 16024, Dec. 15, 1966, unless otherwise noted.

* Code of Federal Regulations.

§ *28.1   Access to areas.*

(a) Any person entering or using any wildlife refuge area will comply with the regulations in this subchapter, the provisions of any special regulations, and all official notices posted in the area.

(b) A permit may be required for any person to enter a wildlife refuge area, unless otherwise provided in this subchapter. The permittee will abide by all the terms and conditions set forth in the permit.

§ *28.2   Access to headquarters.* The headquarters office of any wildlife refuge area will be open to public access and admission during regularly established business hours.

§ *28.3   Access when escorted.* A permit is not required for access to any part of a wildlife refuge area by a person when accompanied by the officer in charge.

§ *28.4   Access for economic use privileges.* Access to and travel upon wildlife refuge areas by a person granted economic use privileges on a wildlife refuge area are to be in strict accordance with the provisions of his agreement, lease, or permit.

§ *28.5   Emergency shelter.* A permit is not required for access to any wildlife refuge area for temporary shelter or temporary protection in the event of emergency conditions.

§ *28.6   Use of roads and trails.* Entrance to, travel on, and exit from any wildlife refuge area are permitted only on such roads, trails, footpaths, walkways, or other routes which may be designated for public use under the provisions of this subchapter. (See also §§ 26.3 and 26.14 of this subchapter.)

§ *28.7   Operation of vehicles.* When the operation of vehicles is permitted within a wildlife refuge area, under § 26.14 of this subchapter, the vehicles will be subject to the following operating requirements:

(a) The vehicles are to be mechanically safe and are to be operated in a safe and proper manner so as not to endanger life and property.

(b) The operation of vehicles will conform to the laws of the State in which the area is located governing the operation of such vehicles, except where further restricted under the provisions of this subchapter.

(c) No person is to operate any vehicle while under the influence of intoxicating liquor, narcotics, or tranquilizing drugs.

(d) Drivers of all vehicles are to comply with the directions of all official traffic signs posted on the area and with the directions of authorized Federal or State personnel.

(e) The speed of any vehicle must be reasonable and proper for the existing road conditions and at all times be within the established speed limits. Vehicle speed limits are 35 miles an hour except where otherwise posted.

(f) Load and weight limitations, as may be necessary, are those prescribed and posted from time to time. Such limitations are to be complied with by the operators of all vehicles. Schedules showing load and weight limitations are available at the wildlife refuge area headquarters.

(g) The parking or leaving unattended of any vehicle on any wildlife refuge area, or upon public roads where title to the land is vested in the

United States, is permitted only in those places which are designated for that purpose under the provisions of this subchapter.

(h) Such other requirements which are established under the provisions of this subchapter. (See also § 27.6 of this subchapter.)

§ 28.8 *Firearms.* Only the following persons may possess, use, or transport firearms on wildlife refuge areas, in accordance with applicable Federal and State law:

(a) Persons authorized to take specimens of wildlife for scientific purposes when the use of firearms is necessary for such purposes.

(b) Persons authorized by special permit to possess or use firearms for the protection of property, for field trials, and for other special purposes.

(c) Persons carrying unloaded firearms that are dismantled or cased over regularly established routes of travel.

(d) Persons commercially transporting weapons and explosives in accordance with applicable State or Federal laws and regulations.

(e) Persons using firearms for public hunting under the provisions of Part 32 of this subchapter.

(f) Such other persons as may be permitted under this subchapter. (See also § 26.12 of this subchapter.)

§ 28.9 *Fires.* When the use of fires on wildlife refuge areas is permitted, under § 26.17 of this subchapter, such use must be in accordance with State or local law, and approved recreational and management rules established under the provisions of this subchapter. (See also § 27.8 of this subchapter.)

§ 28.10 *Scientific study.* The use of wildlife refuge areas for scientific study is encouraged. Permits are required and may be obtained without charge for entry on such areas for scientific study and for similar purposes.

§ 28.11 *Scientific specimens.* The collection of specimens of plant and animal life by recognized scientific institutions and Government agencies may be authorized under special permit. (See also § 26.8 of this subchapter.)

§ 28.12 *Archeological and paleontological studies; search and removal of valued objects.*

(a) Permits are required for archeological studies on wildlife refuge areas in accordance with the provisions of 43 CFR, Part 3.

(b) Permits are required for paleontological studies on wildlife refuge areas in accordance with the provisions of this subchapter.

(c) Persons may not search for or remove semiprecious rocks or mineral specimens, except as provided in § 26.28 of this subchapter.

§ 28.13 *Public safety.* Persons using wildlife refuge areas are to comply with the safety requirements which are established under the provisions of this subchapter for each individual area, and with any safety provisions which may be included in leases, agreements, or use permits.

§ 28.14 *Public sanitation.* Persons using a wildlife refuge area are to comply with the sanitary requirements which are established under the provisions of this subchapter for each individual area, and with the sanitation provisions which may be included in leases, agreements, or use permits. (See also § 26.19 of this subchapter.)

§ *28.15 Reporting of accidents.*

(a) Accidents of whatever nature occurring within the boundaries of any wildlife refuge area are to be reported as soon as possible by the persons involved, to the officer in charge or other Federal personnel on duty at the wildlife refuge area headquarters.

(b) A motor vehicle involved in an accident is not to be moved until an investigating officer arrives at the scene of the accident, unless such vehicle constitutes a traffic or safety hazard.

§ *28.16 Lost and found articles.* Lost articles or money found on a wildlife refuge area are to be immediately turned in to the nearest refuge office.

§ *28.17 Public recreation.*

(a) Wildlife refuge areas offer unusual opportunities for outdoor recreation that constitute a beneficial and proper use of national significance. Wildlife refuge areas vary greatly in their physical adaptability and accessibility for public recreational use.

(b) Public recreation of the types set forth in §§ 28.18 and 28.20 (a) and (b), will be permitted on wildlife refuge areas as an appropriate incidental or secondary use, only after it has been determined that such recreational use is practicable and not inconsistent with the primary objectives for which each particular area was established or with other previously authorized Federal operations.

(c) After consideration of all authorized uses, purposes, and other pertinent factors relating to individual areas, all public recreational use or certain types of public recreational uses within individual areas or in portions thereof may be curtailed whenever it is considered that such action is necessary. The public will be notified of such curtailment under the provisions of this subchapter.

§ *28.18 Sightseeing, nature observations, and photography.* Priority is given to the development of facilities and services which will enhance those recreational uses directly associated with wildlife in its habitat, and which give the public enjoyment from observation, appropriate utilization, interpretation, and a better understanding of wildlife populations, habitat, and conservation values. These recreational uses include sightseeing, nature observation and photography, interpretive centers and exhibits, fishing and hunting, and other similar activities. Tour routes may be closed when these activities may disturb wildlife during the breeding, concentration, or hunting seasons and when roads are damaged or susceptible to damage, or fire hazards are high. When these recreational uses and activities are permitted, the public will be notified under the provisions of this subchapter. The recreational uses and activities will be limited to designated portions of the wildlife refuge area, to specific times, and to those periods of the year which will result in the least disturbance to wildlife and its habitat.

§ *28.19 Hunting and fishing.* Hunting and fishing are permitted only in accordance with Parts 32 and 33, respectively, of this subchapter. (See also §§ 26.5, 26.6, 26.7, and 26.8 of this subchapter.)

§ *28.20 Limitation on certain recreational uses.*

(a) When recreational uses, which are not directly related to the primary function of wildlife refuge areas, such as bathing, boating, camping, ice skating, picnicking, swimming, water skiing, and other similar activities are permitted, the public will be notified under the provisions of this subchapter. These recreational uses will be limited to designated portions of the wilderness refuge area, to specific times, and to those periods of the year which will result in the least disturbance to wildlife and its habitat.

(b) If golf, baseball, target shooting, and other similar activities which are foreign to the concept of conservation areas are permitted, the public will be notified under the provisions of this subchapter.

§ 28.21 *Operation of boats.* When the use of boats is permitted on any wildlife refuge area, the public will be notified under the provisions of this sub-chapter, and the following operational requirements and limitations will apply:

(a) A permit may be required before any boat is placed in or allowed to operate upon the waters of any wildlife refuge area. (See also § 26.15 of this subchapter.)

(b) All boats operated on wildlife refuge area waters are to conform with the provisions of applicable Federal, State, and local laws, and regulations, and the provisions of this subchapter. (See also § 27.7 of this subchapter.)

(c) All boats are to conform with the terms and conditions of boat and motor specifications which are posted or otherwise established under the provisions of this subchapter.

(d) No person will operate any boat in a manner which unreasonably interferes with other boats or with the free and proper navigation of the waterways of the areas.

(e) Government-owned docks, piers, and floats are not to be used for loading and unloading of boats, except in emergencies or unless specifically authorized by the provisions of this subchapter.

(f) Boats will be operated in a safe and reasonable manner, at speeds which are reasonable and proper for existing conditions.

(g) No boats, except sailboats, are to be operated with any person riding or sitting on the gunwales or on the decking over the bow.

(h) No person is to operate any boat while under the influence of intoxicating liquor, narcotics, or tranquilizing drugs.

(i) Such other requirements or limitations which are established under the provisions of this subchapter.

§28.22 *Water skiing.* When water skiing is permitted upon wildlife refuge area waters, the public will be notified under the provisions of this subchapter and the following requirements and limitations will apply:

(a) Water skiing is permitted only in large deep water areas during periods of low waterfowl use, in daylight hours and on those waters of the area which are posted or otherwise designated under the provisions of this subchapter.

(b) There must be two persons in the boat at all times when a skier is in "tow," with one person acting as an observer of the skier in tow.

(c) The direction of a tow boat when circling will be counter clockwise.

(d) Skiers must wear ski belts, or U.S. Coast Guard approved life jackets or buoyant vests.

(e) Water skiing is prohibited within 300 feet of harbors, swimming beaches, and mooring areas, and within 100 feet of any person swimming outside a designated swimming area.

(f) Such other requirements and limitations which are established under the provisions of this subchapter.

§ 28.23 *Facilitating services.*

(a) Recreational facilities may be operated by concessionaires under appropriate contract on wildlife refuge areas where there is a demonstrated justified need for large scale recreational activities such as boat rentals, swimming facilities, conducted tours of special natural attractions, shelters, tables, trailer lots, food, lodging, and related services.

(b) Facilities and services directly supporting interpretation, fishing, or hunting activity will be provided and managed either by the Bureau, by State conservation agencies, or by nonprofit organizations under appropriate arrangements.

§ 28.24 *Fees, charges, and permits.*

(a) Reasonable charges and fees may be established and permits issued for public recreational use of national wildlife refuges.

(b) The Bureau encourages private capital or local sponsoring groups to provide and maintain recreational services or facilities whenever it is feasible. This is normally done through contracting authority of the Department of the Interior, and when so done, may allow for the charging of fees and charges commensurate with the cost of furnishing the services, providing a fair profit to the concessionaire and an equitable return to the Government.

§ 28.25 *Special regulations.*

(a) Special regulations may be issued for public use, access, and recreation within certain individual wildlife refuge areas where special control problems exist or where the posting of official signs would be inadequate to afford the public notice. The issued special regulations will supplement the provisions in this Part 28.

(b) Special recreational use regulations may contain the following items:

(1) Recreational uses authorized.

(2) Seasons, periods, or specific time of use.

(3) Description of areas open to recreation.

(4) Specific conditions or requirements.

(5) Other provisions.

(c) Special regulations for public use, access, and recreation are published in the daily issue of the FEDERAL REGISTER but are not codified in the Code of Federal Regulations. They are limited to one season, issued annually, and are effective upon publication in the FEDERAL REGISTER or in as many days thereafter as it is practical to allow under the circumstances. Such special regulations will be available at the headquarters of the wildlife refuge to which they relate.

§ 28.26 *Penalties; visitor control and protection.*

(a) Any person who violates any of the provisions, rules, regulations, posted signs, or special regulations of this subchapter, or any items, conditions or restrictions in a permit, license, grant, privilege, or any other limitation established under this subchapter shall be subject to the penalty provisions of § 27.10 of this subchapter.

(b) Refuge managers are authorized pursuant to authority delegated from the Secretary and which has been published in the *Federal Register* (Administrative Manual 4 AM 4.9), to protect fish and wildlife and their habitat and prevent their disturbance, to protect Bureau property and facilities, and to insure the safety of the using public to the fullest degree possible. The control of recreational use will be enforced to meet these purposes pursuant to Federal, State and local laws and regulations; the provisions of this subchapter and any special regulation issued pursuant thereto; and the prohibitions and restrictions as posted.

§ 28.27   *Public notice and posting.*

(a) Whenever a particular public access, use, or recreational activity of any type whatsoever, not otherwise expressly permitted under this subchapter, is permitted on a wildlife refuge area, or where public access, use, or recreational activities previously permitted are curtailed, the public will be notified by one of the following methods, all of which supplement this subchapter:

(1) Official signs posted conspicuously at appropriate intervals and locations;

(2) Special regulations issued under the provisions of this subchapter;

(3) Maps available in the office of the refuge manager; and

(4) Other appropriate methods which will give the public actual or constructive notice of the permitted public access, use, or recreational activity.

(b) All public access, use, or recreational activity is prohibited in a wildlife refuge area unless the public is notified that such activity is permitted by the provisions of this subchapter. At no time will the public be notified when public access, use, or recreational activity is prohibited, unless such activity is being curtailed.

§ 28.28   *Special regulations, public access, use, and recreation; for individual wildlife refuge areas.* Note: for *Federal Register* citations to regulations affecting temporary and special regulations of wildlife refuge areas, see List of Sections Affected.

APPENDIX E

The First Period Wilderness Reviews Required by the
Wilderness Act of 1964

Proposals for wilderness units by the administering agencies and conservationists
during the first three-year review period that ended September 3, 1967. Acreage
figures are approximate. Data compiled by the Wilderness Society.

Name and Location	Field Hearing Date	Agency's Proposal (Acres)	Conservationists' Proposal (Acres)	Difference (Acres)
FOREST SERVICE				
San Rafael Wilderness (Calif.) (was San Rafael Primitive Area, enlarged)	Nov. 8, 1965	142,722	145,000	2,278
San Gabriel Wilderness (Calif.) (name change from Devil Canyon–Bear Canyon Primitive Area)	July 27, 1966	36,137	36,137	–0–
Spanish Peaks Wilderness (Mont.) (Spanish Peaks Primitive Area)	Sept. 9, 1966	63,300	78,000	14,700
Mt. Baldy Wilderness (Ariz.) (Mt. Baldy Primitive Area)	Sept. 15, 1966	6,975	8,500	1,525
Flat Tops Wilderness (Colo.) (Flat Tops Primitive Area)	Oct. 10, 1966	142,230	250,000	107,770
High Uintas Wilderness (Utah) (High Uintas Primitive Area, enlarged)	Oct. 12, 1966	322,998	374,000	51,002
Mt. Jefferson Wilderness (Ore.) (Mt. Jefferson Primitive Area)	Oct. 26, 1966	96,462	125,000	28,538
Pine Mountain Wilderness (Ariz.) (Pine Mountain Primitive Area)	Nov. 15, 1966	19,569	19,569	–0–
Washakie Wilderness (Wyo.) (to include Stratified Primitive Area and Absaroka Wilderness)	Dec. 8, 1966	679,520	725,333	45,813
Sycamore Canyon Wilderness (Ariz.) (Sycamore Canyon Primitive Area)	Mar. 15, 1967	46,542	50,500	3,958
Desolation Wilderness (Calif.) (Desolation Valley Primitive Area, enlarged)	April 26, 1967	63,469	64,097	628
Ventana Wilderness (Calif.) (Ventana Primitive Area, enlarged)	June 7, 1967	94,728	101,142	6,414

	Field Hearing Date	Agency's Proposal (Acres)	Conserva- tionists' Proposal (Acres)	Difference (Acres)
BUREAU OF SPORT FISH- ERIES AND WILDLIFE				
Monomoy National Wildlife Refuge (Mass.)	Jan. 11, 1967	2,600	2,600	–0–
Wisconsin Island Refuges: Green Bay N.W.R. Gravel Island N.W.R.	Feb. 15, 1967	29 2 27	29 2 27	–0–
Great Swamp National Wild- life Refuge (N.J.)	Feb. 17, 1967	3,650	3,650	–0–
Bear River Migratory Bird Refuge (Utah)	Feb. 21, 1967	none	none	–0–
Washington Island Refuges: Copalis N.W.R. Quillayute Needles N.W.R. Flattery Rocks N.W.R.	Mar. 28, 1967	250 5 117 125	250 5 117 125	–0–
Michigan Islands National Wildlife Refuge	Mar. 29, 1967	12	12	–0–
Bosque del Apache National Wildlife Refuge (N. Mex.)	Mar. 29, 1967	25,000	28,000	3,000
Southeastern Alaska Island Refuges: Forrester Island N.W.R. Hazy Islands N.W.R. St. Lazaria N.W.R.	April 4, 1967	2,939 2,832 42 65	2,939 2,832 42 65	–0–
Oregon Islands National Wildlife Refuge (formerly called Goat Island Reservation)	April 4, 1967	21	21	–0–
Three Arch Rocks National Wildlife Refuge (Ore.)	April 4, 1967	17	17	–0–
Pelican Island National Wildlife Refuge (Fla.)	April 5, 1967	403	403	–0–
Bitter Lake National Wild- life Refuge (N. Mex.)	April 5, 1967	8,500	11,500	3,000
Florida Island Refuges: Cedar Keys N.W.R. Island Bay N.W.R. Passage Key N.W.R.	April 7, 1967	418 378 20 20	418 378 20 20	–0–
Moosehorn National Wildlife Refuge (Me.)	April 12, 1967	2,782	6,300	3,518
Hart Mountain National Antelope Refuge (Ore.)	April 12, 1967	48,000	45,500	(2,500)
Wichita Mountains Wildlife Refuge (Okla.)	April 18, 1967	8,900	10,000	1,100
Okefenokee National Wildlife Refuge (Ga.)	April 21, 1967	319,000	319,000	–0–

	Field Hearing Date	Agency's Proposal (Acres)	Conserva- tionists' Proposal (Acres)	Difference (Acres)
Alaska Island Refuges:	April 25, 1967	47,663	47,922	259
Bogoslof N.W.R.		41,113	41,113	
Bering Sea N.W.R.		160	390	
Tuxedni N.W.R.		6,390	6,419	
Malheur National Wildlife Refuge (Ore.)	May 2, 1967	30,000	48,000	18,000
Huron Islands National Wild- life Refuge (Mich.)	May 10, 1967	147	147	–0–
Seney National Wildlife Refuge (Mich.)	May 10, 1967	25,150	25,150	–0–
NATIONAL PARK SYSTEM				
Great Smoky Mountains Na- tional Park (N.C. and Tenn.)	June 13, 1966; June 15, 1966	247,000	350,000	103,000
Craters of the Moon National Monument (Ida.)	Sept. 19, 1966	40,785	40,800	15
Lassen Volcanic National Park (Calif.)	Sept. 27, 1966	73,333	101,000	27,667
Sequoia–Kings Canyon National Park (Calif.)	Nov. 21–22, 1966	740,000	828,000	88,000
Isle Royale National Park (Mich.)	Jan. 31, 1967	119,618	130,000	10,382
Pinnacles National Monu- ment (Calif.)	Feb. 10, 1967	5,330	13,000	7,670
Lava Beds National Monu- ment (Calif.)	Feb. 17, 1967	9,197	37,900	28,703
Petrified Forest National Park (Ariz.)	May 23, 1967	50,260	60,400	10,140
Cumberland Gap National Historical Park (Ky., Tenn., and Va.)	June 8, 1967; June 9, 1967	8,980	15,250	6,270
Shenandoah National Park (Va.)	June 14, 1967	61,940	91,000	29,060

The National Park Service was unable to complete all its required reviews. Remaining at the end of the first review period were the following units:

Cedar Breaks National Mon- ument (Utah)	Dec. 11, 1967	4,600	5,300	700
Bryce Canyon National Park (Utah)	Dec. 11, 1967	17,900	23,800	5,900
Capitol Reef National Monu- ment (Utah)	Dec. 12, 1967	23,074	30,150	7,076
Arches National Monument (Utah)	Dec. 14, 1967	12,742	28,417	15,675

	Field Hearing Date	Agency's Proposal (Acres)	Conservationists' Proposal (Acres)	Difference (Acres)
Theodore Roosevelt National Memorial Park (N. Dak.)	——			
Great Sand Dunes National Monument (Colo.)	——			
Chaco Canyon National Monument (N. Mex.)	——			
Crater Lake National Park (Ore.)	——			
Zion National Park (Utah)	——			

APPENDIX F

The Tenth Biennial Wilderness Conference

April 7 and 8, 1967

PROGRAM PLANNING COMMITTEE
Dr. James P. Gilligan, *Chairman*
Maxine E. McCloskey, *Executive Assistant*

Phillip S. Berry — Dr. Edgar Wayburn
Dr. Daniel B. Luten — Peggy Wayburn
J. Michael McCloskey — Caspar W. Weinberger

The committee acknowledges advisory assistance from:

Dr. and Mrs. Harold C. Bradley — Mr. and Mrs. James McCracken
Lewis F. Clark — Judge Raymond J. Sherwin
Randal F. Dickey, Jr. — Dr. and Mrs. Martin Tarcher

Dr. John A. Zivnuska

ARRANGEMENTS CHAIRMEN

Art Work, Allen E. Powell, Shi Pratini, John Shelton
Audio-Visual, Robert Partanen
Exhibits, John Olmsted, Sonya Thompson
Field Trip, Robert W. Rausch, Claude A. Look
General Assistance, David Gordon
Hostesses, Suzanne Soulé
Hotel Arrangements, Charlotte Mailliard
Poster Distribution, Sonya Thompson, Stephen Zwerling
Publicity, Gordon Sears, Jean Rand
Registration, Kenneth and Dona Goodden
Seating, Kent Watson
Speakers' Booth, Dr. Lucille Mlodnosky
Special Assignments, Helen Willard
Timekeepers, James and Betty McCracken

These chairmen were assisted by nearly fifty additional volunteers whose contributions of time and talent made the Wilderness Conference possible.

APPENDIX G

Biographical Sketches

PHILLIP S. BERRY is an attorney with offices in Oakland, California. A member of the Sierra Club since 1950, he first served the club as pot-scrubber on high trips. He has continually increased his involvement in club affairs, serving as counsel in numerous legal matters including Bodega Head litigation, forest practices litigation and legislative campaigns, freeway controversies, and litigation involving Bay fill projects. He is also a past member of the San Franciso Bay Chapter Executive Committee, and for two years has been chairman of the Sierra Club Legal Committee. His memberships include the American Alpine Club and the Section on Mineral and Natural Resources Law of the American Bar Association. He earned the LL.B. degree at Stanford University.

STEWART M. BRANDBORG is executive director of the Wilderness Society, Washington, D.C. Previously employed by the Forest Service and by state fish and game agencies in Idaho and Montana, he has published the results of intensive ecological and life history studies of the mountain goat under the auspices of the Idaho Cooperative Wildlife Research Unit, University of Idaho. In 1954 he was appointed assistant conservation director of the National Wildlife Federation. Becoming a member of the governing council of the Wilderness Society in 1956, he joined its staff in 1960. He received his M.S. degree in Forestry (wildlife management) at the University of Idaho.

NOBLE E. BUELL is assistant director of operations, Bureau of Sport Fisheries and Wildlife. He has served as biologist in the Bureau and its predecessor agencies since 1935, except during World War II. He is a graduate of the University of Nebraska.

ALBERT E. BURKE is a news and political analyst in television and radio and a lecturer whose home is in Connecticut. From 1951 to 1957 he was director of Graduate Studies in Conservation and Resource Use at Yale University. He has traveled extensively in Europe, the Soviet Union, and the Far East, and is a persuasive analyst in the fields of conservation, geography, geopolitics, and world affairs. During his travels in the United States he spent considerable time working and living with Southwestern Indians. His book *Enough Good Men—A Way of Thinking*, was published in 1962 and he is currently writing, producing, and distributing his television series, "The Cutting Edge," and a five-minute daily radio broadcast. His Ph.D. degree in international relations was earned at the University of Pennsylvania.

EDWARD P. CLIFF is chief of the United States Forest Service. He advanced to this office in 1962, culminating a thirty-five-year career that began in 1931 with his first assignment as an assistant ranger in the Wenatchee

National Forest in Washington. He continued to serve in various posts in Washington and Oregon until he was transferred to Washington, D.C., in 1944. After promotion to assistant regional forester for the Intermountain Region with headquarters at Ogden, Utah, in 1946, he transferred to Denver, Colorado, in 1950 as regional forester for the Rocky Mountain Region. He has played a key personal role in the designation of national forest wilderness areas. Past chairman of the U.S. Board on Geographic Names and of the North American Forestry Commission of the United Nations' Food and Agriculture Organization, he received the Department of Agriculture's Distinguished Service Award in 1962. He was honored by the Utah State University with a degree of Doctor of Science in 1965.

ROBERT H. FINCH is California's thirty-eighth Lieutenant Governor. His election in 1966 marked the largest vote total and largest plurality of any Republican in the state's history in a contested election. Before entering politics, he organized and became senior partner of his own law firm, and served as officer or board member of five financial institutions. A Marine Corps veteran, he earned his law degree at the University of Southern California.

ORVILLE L. FREEMAN is Secretary of Agriculture, the youngest man ever named to that post. Before this, he served three successive terms as Governor of his home state, Minnesota. He built a successful law practice in the early fifties while participating in Democratic party politics. He earned the LL.B. degree at the University of Minnesota.

MICHAEL FROME is one of the country's foremost authors on travel and conservation. His books include Strangers in High Places and Whose Woods These Are. He is contributing editor of Changing Times, featured columnist of American Forests, and a frequent contributor to Holiday and other leading magazines. He is vice-president of Defenders of Wildlife and past president of the Society of American Travel Writers. He lives in Alexandria, Virginia.

RUDOLPH GILBERT has been the minister of the Unitarian Church of Spokane, Washington, since 1956. Other settlements have included the Unitarian Churches of Bloomington, Illinois and Denver, Colorado, and the Chicago Ethical Society. He and his wife are enthusiastic campers with wilderness experience ranging from the high country of Colorado to the swamps of Alabama to the mountain peaks of the Pacific Northwest. A native of Iowa, his graduate work was done at Meadville Theological School, Chicago, and the University of Chicago.

JAMES P. GILLIGAN, chairman of the conference, is extension forester at the University of California, Berkeley. Previously he was professor of forestry at Oklahoma State University, and before that was instructor of zoology at Boise Junior College, Idaho. Because of his special background in land use and wilderness allocation, he was director of the President's Outdoor Recreation Resources Review Commission study Wilderness and Rec-

reation, ORRRC Report No. 3 (1961). He is past chairman of the recreation division and forest wildlife division of the Society of American Foresters, and he is the author of many articles on wilderness, outdoor recreation, forest and wild land use. He received the Ph.D. degree from the School of Natural Resources, University of Michigan.

CADET HAND is professor of zoology and director of the University of California Bodega Marine Laboratory at Bodega Bay. In addition to teaching at Mills College and the Scripps Institution of Oceanography (1948–53), he has conducted research in Australia, New Zealand, and the Caroline Islands. Since 1963 he has served as consultant to the National Institutes of Health and the National Science Foundation. He has published fifty articles on systematic and natural history studies of invertebrates, particularly hydroids and sea anemones, and he has memberships in the Society of Systematic Zoology, the Society of Limnology and Oceanography, and the Ecological Society. He took his Ph.D. degree in zoology from the University of California, Berkeley.

GEORGE B. HARTZOG, JR. is director of the National Park Service. A native of South Carolina, he served in the U.S. Army during World War II, then started his career with the Department of the Interior in 1946 as attorney and administrator with the Bureau of Land Management and the National Park Service. After assignments at Rocky Mountain National Park, Colorado, Great Smoky Mountains National Park, North Carolina–Tennessee, Jefferson National Expansion Memorial, Missouri, he was privately employed as executive director of Downtown St. Louis, Inc. (1962–63). In February, 1963, he was appointed associate director of the Service, advancing to his present position the following year. He has written three volumes of National Park Service Administrative Manual Series, and he has received the Distinguished Service Award of the Department of the Interior, 1962, and the Alumni Recognition Award from The American University, Washington, D.C., 1966.

LAWRENCE G. HINES is professor of economics and former chairman of the economics department at Dartmouth College. From 1957 to 1962 he was consultant to the Water Pollution Control Division, U.S. Public Health Service. Recipient of the Ford Foundation essay prize award in 1958, he also received a National Science Foundation Research Grant 1965–66. He pioneered the application of economic analysis to the question of wilderness preservation in his article, "Wilderness: A Problem in Extra Market Allocation." With B. W. Knight, he was co-author of the text *Economics: An Introductory Analysis of the Level, Composition, and Distribution of Economic Income* published in 1952. His Ph.D. degree is from the University of Minnesota.

R. H. (BUFF) HULTMAN operates the 33–Bar Ranch at Seeley Lake, Montana, a combination guest and stock ranch. He has been a commercial outfitter and guide in the Bob Marshall Wilderness Area and Mission Mountain Wild Area for twenty-five years. Vice president of the Montana Wilderness Association, he is also past president of the Montana Outfitters and Guides Association, and immediate past president of the Montana Wilderness Guides Association.

CHARLES B. HUNT, a geologist, has been professor in the Isaiah Bowman Department of Geography since 1961 at the Johns Hopkins University in Baltimore, Maryland. His vast field experience in the Southwest started in 1927 with the U.S. Geological Survey; his latest work for the USGS is a geologic history of the Colorado River. He served as chief of the General Geology Branch of USGS from 1948–53, and from 1961–65 he served on advisory panels of the National Science Foundation. The results of his geological research have been published in scholarly journals and his *Physiography of the United States* was published in 1967. One of his many distinctions is the Distinguished Service Award given in 1962 by the Department of the Interior. His graduate studies were done at Yale University.

ESTELLA B. LEOPOLD is professor adjoint, Department of Biology, University of Colorado, Boulder. Her special research interest is in the late Tertiary and Pleistocene floras of the Rocky Mountain Region and Alaska. Her interest in conservation was stimulated at an early age by her father, Aldo Leopold, and she became actively involved in the long legislative struggle for enactment of the wilderness bill. A board and conservation committee member of the Colorado Mountain Club and a founder and board member of the Colorado Open Space Coordinating Council, she has been active in state and national conservation issues such as removal of bounties on big game species and opposition to Grand Canyon dams. Her Ph.D. degree in botany was taken at Yale University.

GEORGE E. LINDSAY is director of the California Academy of Sciences at Golden Gate Park, San Francisco, California. Before that he was director of the San Diego Natural History Museum (1956–63). His botanical interests have taken him from Arizona to Point Barrow, Alaska, to Baja California. From 1940–50 he was a self-employed citrus-grower except for three years spent as a photographic expert with the Army Air Force. His Ph.D. degree in taxonomic botany was earned at Stanford University.

NORMAN B. LIVERMORE, JR., is the Resources Administrator for California. He is also Secretary for Resources and Development, coordinating the activities of many agencies directly under the governor. His long association with the Sierra Club began as a summer guide in the High Sierra. He has written numerous articles on wilderness and conservation subjects. Until his present appointment, he served as treasurer of the Pacific Lumber Company. A native Californian, he is a graduate of Stanford University and he did graduate work at the Harvard School of Business.

DANIEL B. LUTEN has been lecturer in the Department of Geography, University of California, Berkeley, since 1962. Before this he had a distinguished career in chemistry with the Shell Oil and Shell Development

Companies (1935–61) and produced many patents and publications. He was technical adviser, National Resources Section, Civil Administration of Occupied Japan from 1948 to 1950, and he did the technical revision of Ackerman's *Japanese Natural Resources*. His more recently published papers deal with population dynamics and conservation. He holds office in several conservation organizations. His Ph.D. degree in chemistry was earned at the University of California, Berkeley.

J. MICHAEL McCLOSKEY is conservation director of the Sierra Club, San Francisco, California. Before transferring to the national office in 1965, he represented the Sierra Club and the Federation of Western Outdoor Clubs in the Pacific Northwest. He has published numerous articles in conservation and law journals, including "The Wilderness Act of 1964: Its Background and Meaning" in the *Oregon Law Review* (1966). He earned the B.A. degree in American government from Harvard University, served in the U.S. Army 1956–58, then he took his LL.B. degree from the University of Oregon.

DEAN E. McHENRY is chancellor and professor of comparative government, University of California at Santa Cruz. After teaching at Williams College and Pennsylvania State University, he returned to his native California to rise from assistant professor of political science at the University of California at Los Angeles to his present position. Not only is he a writer of numerous articles and nine books, but he is also a world traveler. He took his Ph.D. degree from the University of California, Berkeley.

GEORGE MARSHALL, president of the Sierra Club 1966–67, has been a member of its Board of Directors since 1959. For more than three decades he has devoted his skills as an economist and editor to conservation. As a charter member of the Wilderness Society, a member of its Executive Committee, and managing editor of *The Living Wilderness* 1957–61, he has been deeply concerned in preserving wilderness. He edited a book by Robert Marshall (his late brother), *Arctic Wilderness*, published in 1956. A charter member of the Adirondack Mountain Club, a member of its Board of Governors, and assistant editor of *The Adirondack*, he is a director of Trustees for Conservation, the Sierra Club Foundation, and the California Conservation Council. A member of Phi Beta Kappa, he earned the Ph.D. degree from the Robert Brookings Graduate School of Economics and Government. He resides in Los Angeles, California.

FRANK E. MOSS is United States Senator from Utah, serving his second term. He is a member of the Senate Interior and Insular Affairs Committee. He started his career on the legal staff of the Securities and Exchange Commission, was a law clerk to the Utah Supreme Court, and was in private practice in Utah. Born and reared in Utah, he earned the Juris Doctor degree at George Washington University Law School, Washington, D.C.

RODERICK NASH is assistant professor of history at the University of California, Santa Barbara. With the publication of *Wilderness and the Amer-*

ican Mind by Yale University Press in 1967, and after more than a dozen articles on wilderness and conservation, he is recognized as the authority on the history of wilderness. His *The American Environment: Readings in the History of Conservation* is in press. He is currently working on a comparative history of conservation in Canada and the United States. His Ph.D. degree was earned at the University of Wisconsin.

KENNETH S. NORRIS is associate professor of zoology at the University of California at Los Angeles. As curator of Marineland of the Pacific (1953–59), he developed methods of capture, handling, and training of many cetacean species. Since 1961 he has been a consultant in cetacean biology to the U.S. Naval Ordnance Test Station at China Lake, and since 1963 he has served as consulting member of the Brain Research Institute at UCLA. A recognized authority on whales, he has published fifty papers on cetaceans as well as on fishes, birds, and desert reptiles. Among his honors are the Mercer Award given by the Ecological Society of America, 1964, and the Brain Research Institute Award, 1966. He received his Ph.D. degree in zoology from the Scripps Institution of Oceanography and UCLA.

SIGURD F. OLSON, veteran writer and conservationist, is no stranger to lovers of wilderness who have read his innumerable magazine articles. He has traveled through most of the wilderness regions on the North American continent plus Hawaii by foot and over the major northern waterways by canoe. His five interpretative books based on these travels have increased public awareness of and appreciation for wilderness. They are: *The Singing Wilderness, Listening Point, The Lonely Land, Runes of the North,* and *Open Horizons* (in press). His unique contribution to the wilderness cause has been recognized in many awards and honorary doctorate degrees. He is past president of the National Parks Association, and is vice-president of the Wilderness Society. For forty-five years his home has been Ely, Minnesota. He earned the M.S. degree at the University of Illinois.

DENNIS A. RAPP is chief of the Evaluation and Editorial Group, Public Land Law Review Commission. Although he served most recently in the Bureau of the Budget, his diverse public service career has been in the agencies concerned with forest land management and forest economics research; land tenure and mineral development; evaluation of national outdoor recreation policies and programs; and review of federal water resources. He was awarded a Ford Foundation (Resources for the Future) Fellowship in conservation in 1957. He received the Master of Public Administration degree at Harvard University.

BOYD L. RASMUSSEN is director of the Bureau of Land Management. Before this appointment in 1966, he spent thirty years in the Forest Service, chiefly in the West, advancing to the position of deputy chief. During his last assignment, being in charge of Cooperative Forestry Programs throughout the fifty states, Puerto Rico, and the Virgin Islands, he was responsible for the Forest Service's operations involving state and private forestry. He is the sixth director of the Bureau since its formation in 1946. Born in Idaho and reared in Oregon, he received the B.S. degree in forestry from Oregon State College.

ROBERT RIENOW is professor of political science, Graduate School of Public Affairs, State University of New York, Albany. He is the author of many widely used college and high school texts on American government, including *The Skinned Land; Of Snuff, Sin, and the Senate; The Lonely Quest;* and his latest book (coauthored with his wife, Leona) *Moment in the Sun—a Report on the Deteriorating Quality of the American Environment.* He has contributed many articles to leading professional journals and encyclopedias. He is chairman of the Eastern New York Chapter and member of the National Board of Governors of Nature Conservancy, and member of the Board of Trustees of Defenders of Wildlife. His Ph.D. degree was earned at Columbia University.

RAYMOND J. SHERWIN is judge, Superior Court, Solano County, California. Long active in Sierra Club affairs, he is chairman of the Minaret Summit Road Task Force, which in each session of the Assembly since 1960 has successfully opposed construction of that road. He is also a member of the National Audubon Society, Conservation Law Society, Planning and Conservation League, and the California Roadside Council. He earned his LL.B. degree at Boalt Hall, University of California, Berkeley.

ANTHONY WAYNE SMITH is president and general counsel of the National Parks Association, Washington, D.C. In earlier years he was secretary to Governor Gifford Pinchot of Pennsylvania, and practiced law in New York. For twenty years he served in executive capacities with the Congress of Industrial Organizations. A commercial dairyman in Pennsylvania since 1954, he is member of and executive in various farm and conservation organizations. His LL.B. degree was earned at Yale School of Law.

WALTER PENN TAYLOR is professor emeritus of conservation education at Claremont Graduate School and University Center in Claremont, California. For twenty years he did research on wildlife with the Departments of Agriculture and Interior, and since 1932 he has held several professorships in the biological sciences in Texas, the Midwest, and California. In addition to traveling widely through Europe and the Pacific, he has published more than three hundred articles on ecology and conservation. He is a member and officer of many civic and scientific organizations, including being president of the Desert Protective Council in 1960. Among his honors are the Aldo Leopold Award for Distinguished Service to Wildlife Conservation, 1961, and the Gold Medal of the Department of the Interior, 1951. His Ph.D. degree was obtained at the University of California, Berkeley.

ADAN E. TREGANZA is professor of anthropology and chairman of the department at San Francisco State College. He is a former consultant to the National Park Service. In addition to archaeological studies in Sicily and Europe, his specialization is archaeological and ethnological research in western North America from Alaska to southern Mexico. He has published more than forty articles and monographs based on this research. Born in Utah, he received the Ph.D. degree from the University of California at Berkeley.

PEGGY WAYBURN, wife of Sierra Club Director Edgar Wayburn, has created her own special place in the field of conservation through her ability as a writer, researcher, and speaker. The Wayburns are working as a team in the historic struggle for a redwood national park in northwestern California. Her participation in the wilderness conferences is unmatched: she was chairman of the ninth, secretary of the seventh and eighth, and served on the committee of the sixth. Residing in San Francisco, she is a member and director of the Citizen's Committee for Regional Recreation and Parks and the Point Reyes Foundation. Born in New York City, she earned the B.A. degree (Phi Beta Kappa) in philosophy at Barnard College.

CASPAR W. WEINBERGER, a San Francisco attorney, is chairman of the Commission on California State Government Organization and Economy. Long active in Republican Party affairs, he served six years in the California Legislative Assembly where he was voted the most able member in 1955. Moderator of a regular weekly local public affairs television program, he is also active in numerous civic organizations. His LL.B. degree was earned at Harvard Law School.

JOHN A. ZIVNUSKA is dean of the School of Forestry and Conservation and director of the Wildland Research Center of the University of California, Berkeley. He has served as consultant in forest economics to the Forest Industries Council, Stanford Research Institute, the Economic Commission for Asia and the Far East, the Navajo Tribal Council, and forest products corporations. He was Fulbright lecturer at the Agricultural College of Norway (1954–55), and in 1965 he completed a world tour to analyze problems of world timber developments. Author of more than sixty publications, he is a member of the Sierra Club, the Wilderness Society, and the Society of American Foresters, among others. His Ph.D. degree in agricultural economics was earned at the University of Minnesota.

DATE DUE

NO 1 6 64			
MR 7 94			
GAYLORD			PRINTED IN U.S.A.